KENNETH G. PRYKE is a member of the Department of History at the University of Windsor, Windsor, Ontario.

In the early 1860s Nova Scotia was a confident and prosperous colony; by 1867 it was a reluctant junior partner in a newly established federal system. Colonial union was a realistic recognition of the existing balance between the North American colonies, but the open declaration of Nova Scotia's subordination to the upper colonies caused bitterness which the promise of new political and economic frontiers did little to ease.

The political cross-currents in Nova Scotia after 1867 reflect its uneasy yet inevitable position in the new union. Even as the anti-confederate party was congratulating itself on an overwhelming victory in the federal and provincial elections of 1867, it was beginning to disintegrate. The various factions – confederates, anti-confederates, Howe compromisers, and local compromisers – ultimately were forced to work within a framework imposed on the province from the outside. By 1874 the differing groups were absorbed into the two major political parties of the dominion, yet the consolidation failed to reflect any clear political pattern. Local issues – schools, railways, distribution of patronage – continued to splinter provincial politics and to weaken its efforts to establish a basis of political authority in the federal system.

Kenneth Pryke's study of the period reveals the complex interplay of personalities, economic interests, social attitudes, and political ideas which shaped Nova Scotia's hesitant course before 1867 and its reluctant acceptance of the new federal system.

CANADIAN STUDIES IN HISTORY
AND GOVERNMENT

A series of studies edited by Goldwin French, sponsored by the Social Science Federation of Canada, and published with financial assistance from the Social Sciences and Humanities Research Council of Canada. The series is now complete.

1 *Church and State in Canada West, 1841–1867.* By John S. Moir
2 *The French Shore Problem in Newfoundland: An Imperial Study.* By Frederic F. Thompson
3 *The Alignment of Political Groups in Canada, 1841–1867.* By Paul G. Cornell
4 *The Private Member of Parliament and the Formation of Public Policy: A New Zealand Case Study.* By Robert N. Kelson (out of print)
5 *The San Juan Water Boundary Question.* By James O. McCabe
6 *The Mark of Honour.* By Hazel C. Mathews
7 *The Political History of Newfoundland, 1832–1864.* By Gertrude E. Gunn
8 *The Clergy Reserves of Upper Canada: A Canadian Mortmain.* By Alan Wilson
9 *Land Policies of Upper Canada.* By Lillian F. Gates (out of print)
10 *Soldier of the International: A History of the Communist Party of Canada, 1919–1929.* By William Rodney
11 *The Jesuits' Estates Question, 1760–1888: A Study of the Background for the Agitation of 1889.* By Roy C. Dalton
12 *The Politics of the Yukon Territory, 1898–1909.* By David R. Morrison
13 *The Franchise and Politics in British North America, 1755–1867.* By John Garner
14 *The Emergence of the Federal Concept in Canada, 1839–1845.* By William Ormsby
15 *Nova Scotia and Confederation, 1864–1874.* By Kenneth G. Pryke

KENNETH G. PRYKE

Nova Scotia and Confederation 1864-74

University of Toronto Press
TORONTO   BUFFALO   LONDON

© University of Toronto Press 1979
Toronto Buffalo London
Printed in Canada

Canadian Cataloguing in Publication Data

Pryke, Kenneth G., 1932–
  Nova Scotia and Confederation

(Canadian studies in history and government; 15)

Includes index.
ISBN 0-8020-5389-0

1. Nova Scotia – Politics and government – 1763–1867. 2. Canada – Politics and government – 1841–1867. 3. Canada – History – Confederation, 1867.*
I. Title. II Series.

FC2322.4.P79   971.6   C79-094235-6
E1038.P79

Contents

ACKNOWLEDGMENTS vii
INTRODUCTION ix

1 The introduction of Confederation 3

2 Approval of union in principle 19

3 Passage of the Act of Union 33

4 The federal and provincial elections of 1867 46

5 The repeal movement 60

6 Howe and the federal government 80

7 A time for reassessment 98

8 The Treaty of Washington, Confederation, and Nova Scotia 119

9 Maintaining the status quo 137

10 The failure of the coalition 148

11 The winter election 163

12 New ways and old conflicts 173

CONCLUSION 189
NOTES 195
NOTE ON SOURCES 227
INDEX 231

Acknowledgments

During the course of my work on this book I have incurred many debts to individuals and institutions. Appreciation must be expressed for the continuous service provided by the Public Archives of Canada. Similar recognition should be paid to the Public Archives of Nova Scotia and in particular to Dr Phyllis R. Blakeley for her unfailing courtesy and unflagging interest. Research for this book was supported in part by funds provided by the Social Sciences and Humanities Research Council of Canada. Lastly I wish to pay tribute to my wife, Kathleen, whose criticisms and good humour both contributed so much.

This book has been published with the help of grants from the Social Science Federation of Canada, using funds provided by the Social Sciences and Humanities Research Council of Canada, and the University of Toronto Press Publication Fund.

Introduction

In 1851 Nova Scotia was a confident and prosperous colony of 325,000 people, loyal to Great Britain, and enjoying a dynamic economy marked by the growth of banks, a development of exports, and diversification of industry. For the next twenty years its shipyards produced ever more and larger ships and its towns were gradually linked by rail. It is not surprising, then, that Nova Scotian politicians and merchants failed to anticipate the crises and tensions of the 1860s. They ignored the shifts in power within British North America, as also the changes in British policy towards its colonies. Suddenly in the mid-1860s Nova Scotia had to respond to an entirely new set of challenges and priorities in which other groups had claimed the initiative, had formulated policies, and Nova Scotia, unprepared and apathetic, had no alternative but to enter the Canadian confederation.

Any complacency in Nova Scotia towards its relations abroad might have been justified by the military garrison in Halifax and British ships in the harbour. Yet England was gradually drawing a clearer line between colonial and imperial interests, and Nova Scotia, sooner or later, would be affected as much as any of the other colonies. Already the British government had refused to restore military strength throughout British North America to the levels which had existed prior to the Crimean War. With the outbreak of the American Civil War British troops were hurriedly despatched to the colonies. This sudden, costly adventure involving unspecified commitments forced the British government into a review of its responsibilities in British North America. The eventual decision to limit its role had the support of the Foreign Office and the War Office but above all the endorsement of Treasury. While colonial politicians were aware of the severe political consequences this British withdrawal would bring, their influence was limited as the colonial secretary still commanded an authority in British North America both directly through the governors and through the more intangible element of loyalty. Given a sense of urgency a colonial secretary could make it difficult for a colony to oppose for long the British government.

Any shift in British policy would have particularly serious repercussions in Nova Scotia since that colony had tried to use British political and military power to balance the economic power of the United States. Yet the balance had been less than perfect for some years because in the early 1850s, during the negotiations for the Reciprocity Treaty with the United States, the British government had left many of the details to the Canadians and the latter had only reluctantly and imperfectly consulted the Maritimers. Resentment at the procedures used in negotiating the treaty were obscured by the growth in trade with the United States during the late 1850s, and again during the Civil War. By the mid sixties trade relations were threatening to take another erratic swing as opponents of the treaty were gathering strength in Congress to have it revoked.

Apart from economic relations, Nova Scotian attitudes to the United States tended to flow with events. During the 1850s some Tories, in protest against the cabinet system of government, developed a sudden warmth for the American constitutional separation of powers. From this perspective it was reasonable for these same Tories in the early 1860s to sympathize with the Confederacy. The presence of a number of prominent Halifax residents prepared to aid the South contributed to the sometimes shrill cry that a victorious North would pose a military threat to the British colonies. And, indeed, the possibility of a military threat did exist, as was later revealed by the Fenian raids.

The sense of impending change in the policies of both Great Britain and the United States probably influenced politicians in Nova Scotia, as well as in Prince Edward Island and New Brunswick, to consider the possibility of maritime union. The passage of resolutions for union in the legislatures of all three colonies in March 1864 reflected some recognition that the existing colonies provided a limited scope for political activities and economic development. Yet the proposal never became identified with any broad objective and the actual resolutions authorizing a conference on maritime union were largely in response to pressure from both the Colonial Office and the respective lieutenant-governors.

While the Maritimers were giving halting consideration to a limited colonial union the Canadians were being driven to a more substantial scheme which would eventually federate all of British North America.

The immediate pressure for change was based on the sound conclusion that the existing legislative union of Canada West and Canada East was no longer operative and had to be altered to allow greater freedom for the differing ambitions of the constituent parts. The search for a new political formula became a blueprint for the future. Some, but by no means all Canadians, saw a way whereby a solution to the political impasse could assist in meeting their defence problems, as well as absorb the colonies to the east and territories to the west. Unlike the suggestion for maritime union, the scheme in the Canadas became identified with broad political and economic goals which embraced a vision of a new nation.

Once this plan was presented by the Canadians the Nova Scotians had little alternative but to acquiesce, particularly since the Colonial Office had concluded that it was a workable solution to colonial ills. The scheme did have an internal logic in its solution to the growing resentment by the Nova Scotians to the increasing control over Nova Scotian affairs by the Canadians. While Nova Scotia objected to Canadian influence, the balance of power had unalterably tipped to the advantage of the Canadians. The solution, ironical and bitter as it was, was for Nova Scotia to enter into a political union with the Canadas.

Colonial union was a realistic recognition of the existing balance but it nonetheless caused bitterness in Nova Scotia during the debate over union and a sullen reception to union after 1867. The necessity of accepting an unwelcome subordination, no matter how it might be presented by the advocates of union, contributed to the many cross-currents in Nova Scotia after 1867. Each faction, whether confederates, anti-confederates, Howe compromisers, or local compromisers, ultimately was forced to work within a framework being imposed on the province. By 1874 these differing groups were absorbed into the two major parties, the Liberals and the Conservatives, of the dominion. Yet this division itself did not reflect any clear pattern in the province. There was friction over local issues, such as schools, railways, Roman Catholics, and patronage, but no overriding issue to act as a catalyst or to give focus to the political debates. Nor after 1867 did any political leader manage to extricate himself from the morass. This factionalism not only precluded a clear and consistent Nova Scotian role in dominion politics but prevented the strong pursuit of repeal with anything like a consensus of opinion. By default, then, Nova Scotia entered into and remained in confederation.

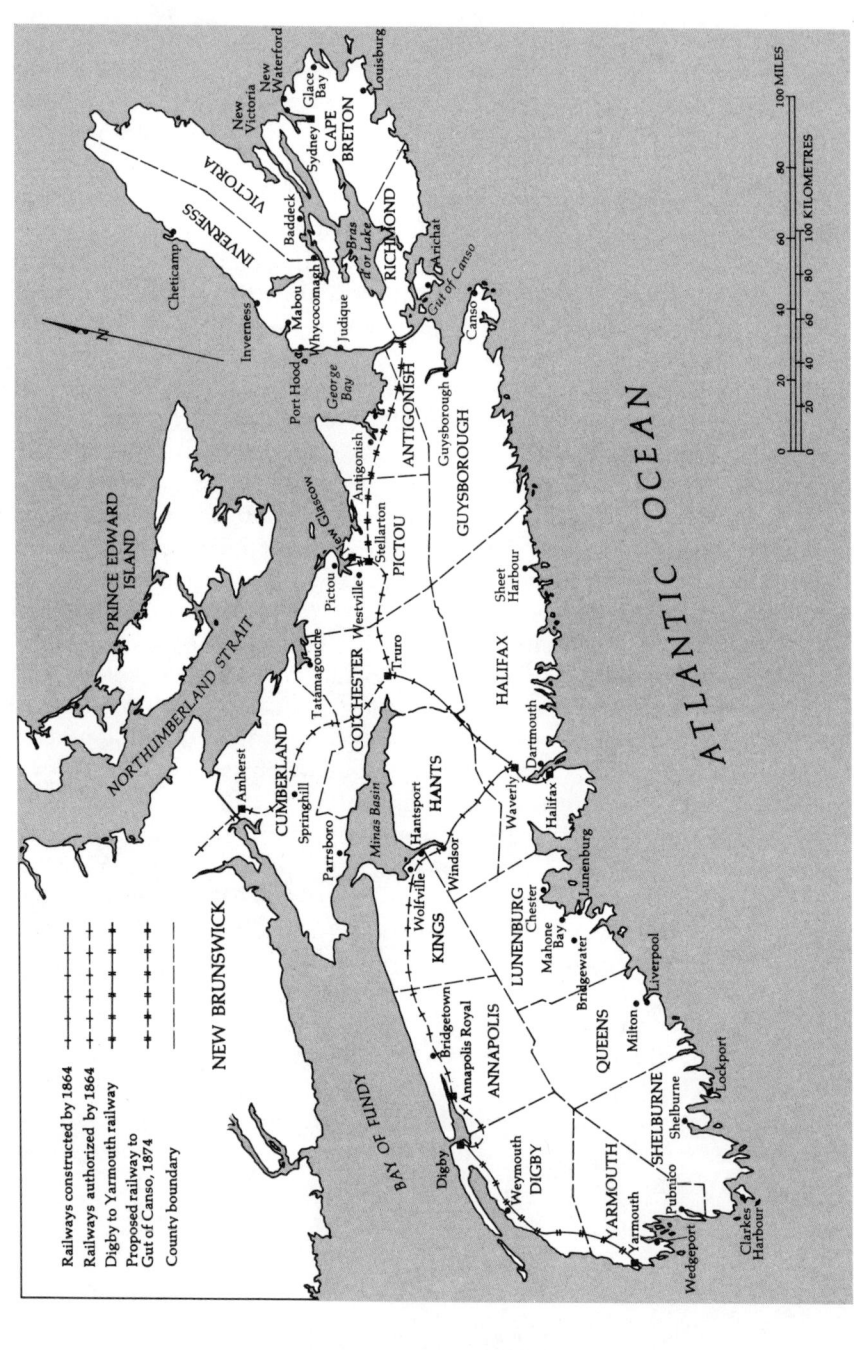

NOVA SCOTIA AND CONFEDERATION

1

The introduction of Confederation

MARITIME UNION PROPOSED

On the 28th of March 1864 Dr Charles Tupper, the provincial secretary, rose in the Nova Scotia House of Assembly to move a resolution in favour of maritime union. The essential idea behind colonial union had been raised before and seemed to require little explanation. In 1854, and again in 1861, the legislature had discussed proposals for the union of British North America, and in both 1857 and 1862 the government had appointed delegates who were authorized to consider the scheme. Familiarity with the concept did not imply consent, but at least some members had shown that they were prepared to consider it.

Union of the Maritime provinces could be regarded by the Nova Scotians as the restoration of a unity which had existed prior to the separation of Prince Edward Island in 1771 and of New Brunswick in 1784. For Tupper and other members of the assembly the desire for colonial union went beyond mere gratification of some sense of Nova Scotian supremacy in the Maritimes. They felt, rather, that union would erase the artificial political barriers which obstructed co-operation among the colonies. With union the Maritime colonies could better develop their means of communication, expand their economies, and satisfy their ambitions.

As member after member of the Nova Scotian assembly rose to speak, it became clear that maritime union was not to be a return to the past. The urge for union emerged as a manifestation of the movement which would turn British North America into a Canadian nation. Although the subject of the debate was maritime union, several members seemed to be thinking of a general colonial union. While perhaps inevitable, the larger scheme, declared Tupper, was impracticable for the time being if only because the

Canadian government was paralyzed by internal feuds. Some day, he continued, a larger colonial union would be formed and 'no wiser step could take place than the union of the Maritime Provinces in the first instance ...' One or two members indicated that, because of the growing threat from the United States, the colonies could not afford to delay union. The premier, J.W. Johnston, insisted that the colonies could not evade the responsibility for their own security, particularly with Great Britain growing more and more restive under the burden of colonial defence.[1] Thus, if political and economic ambitions did not lead to union, necessity could well drive the provinces together.

Not all the members were convinced by the arguments in favour of union, but the assembly, without division, passed a motion authorizing the government to appoint delegates to discuss the question with New Brunswick and Prince Edward Island. Similar resolutions were passed by the assemblies of the other two provinces. No one, however, took the initiative to set a time or place for the proposed conference. Public interest in the project was revived in June when the governor general of Canada, Viscount Monck, asked if Canadian delegates could attend the meeting of the maritime colonies in order to discuss a union of all the colonies. In Nova Scotia the request was received by the newly arrived lieutenant-governor, Sir Richard Graves MacDonnell,[2] who had come to Nova Scotia under instructions from the Colonial Office to do all he could to further maritime union. MacDonnell resented the Canadian initiative, but he could scarcely ignore the request.[3] He therefore made arrangements to hold the conference in Charlottetown on 1 September 1864.

MacDonnell was a lawyer by profession who had served in the colonies since 1843. He had no understanding of the cabinet system as it operated in British North America and had little regard for colonial politicians. Shortly after his arrival in Nova Scotia he began to insist on playing a very active role in cabinet decisions. He particularly wished to abolish the practice of political patronage and seriously considered dismissing his government if it did not change its procedures.[4] Tupper, who had become premier following the appointment of Johnston as judge-in-equity, was forced to compromise with MacDonnell. A governor could still wield considerable influence in the colony and in England, and it was better for a premier to pacify a governor than to insist that all the forms of cabinet government be observed.

MacDonnell felt that maritime union would help purify colonial politics by presenting a greater political challenge and thereby attracting more capable people into politics. From the instant he arrived in Nova Scotia he had an unshakable conviction that the province could not provide proper political leadership to look after its own affairs. For MacDonnell and many Conservatives in Nova Scotia, support for colonial union was essentially a reflection of their lack of confidence in the province and its political institutions. Johnston too had advocated colonial union as one means of compensating for the system of cabinet government introduced in 1848. It was a sense of pessimism which moved MacDonnell and not any vision of a new empire, as sketched by D'Arcy McGee.[5] Indeed, MacDonnell viewed the Canadian proposals as the result of political frustrations and as a possible obstacle to the more plausible scheme of maritime union.[6] Despite his misgivings, arrangements for the conference went ahead. After some manœuvring Tupper managed to select five delegates, including two from the Liberal party, to represent the province at Charlottetown.[7]

The Charlottetown Conference convened as scheduled on 1 September. After a brief discussion of maritime union,[8] the Maritime delegates resolved to adopt the far more ambitious and captivating proposal advanced by the Canadians. Before disbanding, however, the participants agreed to make a tour of the other Maritime provinces and then reassemble at Quebec City on 1 October. This tour was useful, but more than public dinners was needed to erase the poor image of the Canadians which had been appearing for years in the Maritime press.[9] This image had grown worse with an improvement in communications between the upper and lower provinces and an increase in contacts. Past quarrels might be briefly put to one side[10] but they could not be ignored since they reflected differing interests and priorities.

Tupper, accompanied by the same delegates as before, went to Quebec City for the opening of the new conference on 10 October. At Charlottetown the delegates had agreed upon a federal system of union, a decision which was confirmed at Quebec. For some delegates, the essence of this federal system was to be found in the relations between the upper and lower houses of the federal legislature rather than in those between the federal and provincial governments.[11] The provincial governments were to remain, but John A. Macdonald, attorney-general for Canada West, was insistent that they must be made dependent upon the federal government.[12] Hence the delegates decided that the lieutenant-governors, who had the power to reserve and to veto provincial legislation, would become federal officers.[13] In many ways this would not represent a major departure from existing practice in the Maritimes since many governors, such as MacDonnell, took an active role in local affairs.

These men, however, had behind them their authority as representatives of the British crown, a prestige which would not be available to the agents of Ottawa.

Under the proposed system the powers of the provinces were to be sharply curtailed. The pre-eminent federal power would be exercised directly through the executive or through the federal members from the respective provinces. In political terms the most obvious competitor with the local government would be the federal members. The authority which the British government continued to exercise under cabinet government was tolerable in part because the British government dealt with, and through, the local cabinet. Although the colonial cabinets had in the past held only limited powers, they had participated in decision-making and had political control of their provinces. Macdonald's scheme to ignore the provincial governments would upset the political practices of twenty years' standing. His intention to preserve the existing forms of provincial governments while depriving them of many of their political privileges under the cabinet system was a dubious and devious subterfuge. He was supported by Tupper, who felt that on issues involving the form but not the substance of provincial governments the delegates should not 'shock too largely the prejudices of the people in that respect.'[14] However judicious in the short term, it ignored the long-term consequences.

The proposal to strip the provincial governments of their functions and transfer effective power to the central government was not accomplished easily. Difficulties were encountered particularly in establishing the upper house, because it was supposed to be the defender of provincial interests, yet representation was calculated on a regional basis rather than on strictly provincial lines. Thus, Nova Scotia was allotted ten seats out of the twenty-four assigned to the Maritimes. In a further attempt to limit the influence of the provinces, the members of the upper house were to be appointed by the governor-general-in-council. If some system had been designed to allow the provinces to participate in the selection of their representatives, the upper house might have been guaranteed a more active role. Such a procedure might have encouraged the development of provincial rights. However, senators selected by one provincial government might well have become opponents of its successor, and the upper house might have emerged as a check on the provincial governments rather than as an extension of their power. Many delegates at Quebec, of course, were determined to deny any real power to the provinces, as they were unwilling to create a powerful second chamber.[15] The minor role for the upper house increased the importance of representation in the lower house. The delegates decided to have representation based on provincial population, which would give the Province of Canada dominance in the new lower house. Quebec was allotted sixty-five members, and the other provinces were to have representation proportionate to that of Quebec. By this procedure Nova Scotia would have nineteen members out of a total of 194.

In devising the financial terms of union, the delegates faced the problem of creating a formula that would suit the diverse conditions of the various provinces. One particular problem for Nova Scotia was that it relied upon a county form of government; Halifax, with a population of some thirty thousand, was the only incorporated city in the province. In the absence of municipal bodies, the legislature bore responsibility for local matters of importance. Unless there was to be a complete reorganization of local government in the province, some means had to be found to meet this financial burden. The problem was compounded because the province derived approximately 80 per cent of its revenue from customs and excise duties which, under the proposed scheme of union, were to be taken over by the federal government.

To compensate for the loss of revenue by the provinces, the delegates devised a subsidy which was intended to make up any difference between the anticipated provincial revenue, using existing methods of taxation, and expected expenditures after union. For convenience they decided to base the subsidy on population. It was to be an annual payment of eighty cents per capita based on the 1861 census, which would provide Nova Scotia with $256,000.00.[16] Although this formula was likely to provide Ontario with a surplus, there was serious doubt whether it would meet the needs of Nova Scotia.

As part of the financial terms of union the delegates decided that the federal government would assume the debts of the various provinces. Politically this would cause difficulty since many Nova Scotians were convinced that the Canadians were spendthrifts. If the federal government were to take over all the debts of the provinces, there were likely to be complaints from the Maritimers that they were being forced to pay for Canadian extravagance. There was little doubt, at least, that the various provinces had followed different policies with respect to the funding of public works, the chief source of public debt. Opposition to this scheme might have been reduced if there had been a feasible means of giving some credit for the various assets which the federal government would also take over from the provinces. No alternative evaluation emerged, however, and the delegates finally agreed to set an arbitrary debt allowance of $25.00 per capita, which for Nova Scotia would amount to $8,000,000.00.[17] Since Nova Scotia's debt in 1864 was $4,850,000.00, this seemed generous. But just before he left for Quebec Tupper had called for tenders on a railway to run from Truro through the coal fields to Pictou.[18] He was also determined to build a railway from Windsor to Annapolis. These two projects were likely to push the provincial debt up to, or even beyond, the debt limit.

The suggested terms of union, both economic and political, were thus marred by serious faults. Some of these were seen by R.B. Dickey, the only merchant in the Nova Scotian delegation, who objected to the centralist tendencies of the proposals. He would have preferred the formation of a colonial free-trade bloc, whose members could co-operate on such matters of common concern as the construction of the Intercolonial Railway.[19] Unmoved by the prospect of creating a vast new nation, Dickey saw colonial union as harmful to the status and interests of Nova Scotia. Despite his refusal to agree to the terms of union,[20] he failed to dissuade the other Nova Scotian delegates and they accepted the proposals. As they prepared to return to Nova Scotia, Dickey's position was but a mild indication of what was to come.

DISCONTENT IN NOVA SCOTIA

The Nova Scotian delegates returned to Halifax in early November, and within three weeks Tupper knew that he would have difficulty carrying the scheme.[21] One of the first to oppose him was the governor, who may well have resented some upstart colonials from Canada threatening his own hope for maritime union. In his view the Quebec scheme solved no problems of the Maritimes but created new ones because it would establish petty governments which could offer no scope for ability or challenge to ambition. As for the proposal that the lieutenant-governor become an agent of the federal government, MacDonnell, as a professional colonial officer, may have been amused at the notion that colonials could fill his position. He took himself and his office sufficiently seriously to consider dismissing his government if it persisted in demanding colonial union.[22] However, when the Colonial Office supported union he was effectively prevented from taking any action.[23]

Tupper's first concern was not with MacDonnell but rather with the political climate of the province. As Conservative premier Tupper could propose a bold programme of reforms because, for the first time in over a decade, the ministry had an overwhelming majority in the House of

Assembly. Tupper, son of a Baptist minister and a graduate in 1843 of the Edinburgh medical faculty, had represented Cumberland county in the assembly since 1855. He was officially opposed in the assembly by A.G. Archibald, a member of a prominent Nova Scotian family who had practised law in his native province since 1839 and had first been elected to the legislature in 1851 for the county of Colchester. He had served in two Liberal ministries. Tupper also had to deal with the Liberal leader of the council, Jonathan McCully, who, like Archibald, was a lawyer but, as editor of the *Morning Chronicle*, indulged himself in the polemical newspaper wars of the period. Tupper did have the support of the two Liberal leaders on the issue of union, but neither McCully nor Archibald felt constricted in attacking other policies adopted by him. This created an ambiguous situation, particularly in the early stages of the discussion on union, because criticism of union tended to be intermingled with attacks on other government policies. Although the government had been in office only a year, it had provoked serious opposition through changes in the education system which had resulted in significant increases in local taxation. Complaints about these changes, as well as the government's railway programme, surfaced during a by-election contest in Annapolis to replace J.W. Johnston.[24] Tupper, in an unsuccessful attempt to save the seat, tied confederation to his programme of railway construction. The prompt and spirited protest from McCully[25] against this use of union for party purposes was scarcely realistic since defeat for the Conservatives, by inference, would be a setback for union. In the long run Tupper's refusal to form a coalition with the Liberals on the question of union probably helped the Conservative party. Tupper thus followed a different course with respect to the Liberals than did Macdonald in the Canadas, but the result for the Liberals was much the same.

Had Tupper entered such a coalition he may have had to mute other policies – and this he was bound not to do. Despite the opposition to the school reforms he had introduced in 1864, he had every intention of making further changes in 1865. Many of the opponents of school reform were members of the Conservative party, but they were unlikely to desert to the Liberal party in large numbers on this issue because the Liberal leadership itself had supported some of the key parts of the school legislation. Tupper was also determined to begin construction of several railways, including a line to Pictou, another to Annapolis, and a third through his own county of Cumberland which would eventually form a link in the Intercolonial Railway. Some Liberals protested that the province could not afford these railways. The proposal for colonial union, however, made it possible for Tupper to proceed. The resolutions of the Quebec Conference provided for the proposed section of the Intercolonial, and threw in, in effect, three million dollars to help construct the other two railways. Even this sum might be insufficient, but without it there was no real opportunity for Tupper to proceed with all of his projected railways unless he forced the province so deeply into debt that it would have been unable to attempt any further projects for years to come. Without colonial union, then, Tupper's own political career was uncertain because his ambitions exceeded provincial realities. Colonial union would help him carry out some of his plans and also provide him with the wider stage he so obviously thought he needed.

Construction of the railroad from Truro to the New Brunswick border, which would later form part of the Intercolonial Railway, would be tangible evidence of Canadian goodwill and would provide Tupper with significant political benefits. Tupper's arrangements for an immediate start on the project, made while in Quebec, were cancelled, however, by John A. Macdonald, who feared the political repercussions in the Province of Canada if Canadian money were committed before Nova Scotia agreed to union.[26] An engineer, Francis Shanley, did carry out a survey of the projected route,[27] but Macdonald continued to refuse to make any other concessions to Tupper.[28] Tupper was undoubtedly too impatient, but he needed help if he were to bring his province into union.

Some influential people in Halifax were prepared to provide Tupper with assistance to carry union. When he held a public meeting to explain the proposal, Bishop Binney of the Church of England, Archbishop Connolly of the Roman Catholic church, and three judges of the Supreme Court all agreed to support the scheme. On the opposition side were ranged an increasing number of merchants, some of them former Conservatives, who were fearful that political union and tariffs would compromise their independence. Although many of the merchants had little political experience, they were able to finance an organization which sent out speakers and distributed printed material.[29] The supporters of union organized their own society, but, despite the abundance of talent available to the confederates, it did not prove effective.[30]

As the struggle over union developed, both its opponents and its supporters made heavy use of the newspapers. Outside Halifax the opponents had a definite advantage because the county newspapers, save the Pictou *Colonial Standard*, rejected union. In the city, however, the anti-confederates were at first supported principally by the *Acadian Recorder* and the struggling but lively *Citizen*,[31] while the confederates had the support of four leading city papers,³² including the official organs of the two political parties. This situation began to change when William Annand returned to Halifax from England in December and decided to oppose union. Annand, whose thin voice and halting manner made him a poor public speaker, wielded a considerable influence because of active political experience which stretched over thirty years and an acute, cunning intelligence. He persuaded his son, Charles Annand, who had bought the *Morning Chronicle* from him the previous July, to dismiss McCully as editor and to change the editorial policy of the *Chronicle* and his other paper, the *Novascotian*.

Annand's decision to oppose union was significant but Tupper was much more concerned about the opposition of Annand's long-time associate, Joseph Howe. Throughout his long career in public life, Howe had always been a disturbing influence in the province. Whether it had been his spirited attacks on the local oligarchy ruling Halifax in the 1830s or his sometimes convuluted efforts to alter the political institutions of the province, he had always managed to be unpredictable and a figure of suspicion in the eyes of the respectable folk of the city. Capitalizing on an earthy sense of humour and a sometimes rakish charm, he managed to lend an air of reform to his crusades while never losing touch with an essentially conservative tradition in provincial politics. Tupper, therefore, had reason to fear Howe's influence in the province and he quickly convinced himself that Howe was behind the growing opposition to union; he tried to have the British government instruct Howe to abstain from political activities while he retained his British commission as fisheries commissioner under the Reciprocity Treaty.³³ Tupper exaggerated Howe's role, although Howe did prepare a series of twelve articles, 'the botheration letters,' which first appeared on 11 January and ran until 2 March. Many people immediately recognized his style,³⁴ but his authorship was not acknowledged until the end of February.³⁵ Despite these articles Howe could scarcely be held responsible for the growth in opposition to union, since it began before his position was known and continued to grow after he left the province in the spring of 1865.³⁶

Howe's stand was condemned by the unionists, who tried to prove that he was acting out of purely selfish motives. One unionist who viewed Howe with bitterness was W.A. Henry. The latter, who still effected the style of an Irish gentleman by carrying white riding gloves and riding crop with an Irish setter at lead,³⁷ was a forty-six-year-old lawyer who had represented Antigonish county in the assembly since 1841. Although he had long been prominent in the Liberal party and had been a member of the Liberal government in the early 1850s, he had broken with Howe over the Roman Catholic crisis of 1857. In Henry's opinion [Howe] 'could not get over the mortification of seeing this great change accomplished without his assistance or aid. And if it were the work calculated even in the minds of every one to benefit the Country still if he were not the head of it, he would not permit it if he could prevent it ... He is acting the part of a *traitor* as he always was ...'[38] For his part, Howe did not understand Tupper and regarded him merely as an ambitious speculator, who leapt from expedient to expedient, hoping that patronage would be a panacea for all problems.[39]

Howe himself had spoken of the possibility of colonial union in the past, but he had devoted much more attention to the idea of a reorganization of the empire. He had wanted to strengthen the colonies so that colonials might participate in the empire as citizens rather than remain as colonials. Indeed, the attempts by McCully and others to prove that Howe had previously supported the idea of union were highly ironical since in the 1850s the Conservatives had advanced the proposal as part of their campaign against responsible government in Nova Scotia. While the new proposals for colonial union avoided the negative overtones of the original Conservative policies, their emphasis on founding a new North American nation continued to conflict with Howe's interest in the empire. Moreover, Howe was offended by the obvious subordination of his province within the proposed union; his feeling of patriotism for Nova Scotia was probably the cause of his suspicion of Canadian motives. These doubts were shared by the Halifax mercantile community, but not his interest in transforming the British empire. Howe's relations with the merchants had not always been amiable, and he had lost much of their support by carrying out certain policies, such as building government-owned railways, in the 1850s. The attempt to identify him as the instigator of the opposition to union obscured the fact that many of the merchants had opposed him in the election of 1863 and now had their own reasons for opposing union. Although Howe expressed several of the popular objections to the Quebec scheme, he was not the natural spokesman for some of those interests which were causing Tupper such trouble.

In considering the question of colonial union the Nova Scotians recognized that it would affect the total development of their province. One of the principal themes expounded by the advocates of confederation was that through union the colonies could increase their strength to the point where they could assume such national functions as self-defence.[40] To lend credence to this argument, they stressed the danger of attack from the United States once the Civil War was ended. This appeal was most likely to influence those who distrusted the North, and it was noticeable that men such as Archbishop Connolly, who advocated colonial union, were active supporters of the South.[41] The fear of military attack from the northern states reflected not so much an assessment of the existing situation in the United States as the general political attitude of some supporters of union.

Although the slogan 'in unity there is strength' had some appeal, it was unlikely that colonial union would improve the military position of Nova Scotia. The Canadians would undoubtedly prefer to share with the Maritimes the financial burdens of any fortifications built in the Province of Canada. They might even anticipate the despatch of militia from the Maritimes to help defend the extended border of Canada. The Canadians could do little to protect the Maritimes, however, since the latter required a naval defence. Nevertheless, the confederates contended that unless the colonials undertook part of their own defence, the British government would withdraw its protection from the colonies.[42] In supporting confederation, Archibald balanced his appeal to 'the position and dignity of freemen' to provide for their own security with predictions that the comfortable relations with Great Britain were undergoing a rapid change.[43] The opponents of union were forced to admit that the colonies should contribute to their own defence, but they did not see confederation as the only solution.[44] There was also the possibility that once colonial union was brought about, Great Britain would withdraw the bulk of its military forces from British North America.[45] Were that to happen, and the talk of creating a new nation made it seem possible, then union might worsen the existing military position of Nova Scotia.

All parties in Nova Scotia were agreed that union would alter the tie with Britain, although they differed on whether union was a response to this change or a cause of it. In many ways the changes in imperial trade policy, which had so deeply affected the other British North American colonies in the 1840s, had passed Nova Scotia by. Reassured by the sight of British men-of-war, Halifax had been immune to those brief flights of annexationist fervour for the United States which had struck the mercantile communities in Saint John and in Montreal. Although Howe had spoken of imperial federation, others had comfortably accepted the imperial connection without reflection. Taking the British presence for granted, it probably came as a shock for some to have to consider the problem of imperial relations. They would have been in a far stronger position if they had made some tangible move to redistribute the cost of their defence before the Civil War had begun.

The confederates' proposal of relying on the Canadian solution to the problem of self-defence seemed foolhardy to many Nova Scotians and particularly to the merchants. It seemed scarcely credible to them that an inland province, which had shown itself unsympathetic to the Maritimes in the past, would provide a policy suitable for their mercantile economy. The merchants, and particularly the respectable West Indian commission merchants of Halifax, were less concerned with military issues than with economic policies. Oriented towards the ocean, they did not share in the enthusiasm for developing a continent, particularly when it meant being subordinated to the Canadians, who were trying to develop their own manufacturing industry. Because of differing priorities, the Canadian tariff was higher than that of Nova Scotia, and it included items important for the carrying trade of Nova Scotia.

The Canadian tariff system could not be ignored but the confederates were forced to fall back on the claim that the issue had been misunderstood and could be adjusted to meet Nova Scotian interests.[46] The confederates tried to move the discussion beyond the narrow question of tariff rates by dwelling on the economic development of the province. Any harm to the mercantile economy of Nova Scotia by confederation, they asserted, would be far outweighed by the positive development of manufacturing within confederation. Once the barriers to interprovincial trade were removed, immigrants would be attracted, and this increase in population would lead to a further increase in industry.[47] Emphasis was placed on secondary manufacturing, and two shoe factories which had recently opened in Halifax were cited. But even more exciting, according to the confederates, was the virtually unlimited future for the development of heavy industry based on provincial deposits of coal and iron.[48] The belief that a nation's position rested on its manufacturing industries was widespread,[49] so it was perhaps not surprising that the promoters of a new nation should be interested in developing its industry. In contending that manufacturing would take place because of union the confederates were in effect combining an appeal to nationalism with a belief in progress.

The diversity of opinions about the economic effects of union was fully matched by opinions on the consequences of the proposed federal system of government.[50] For some Nova Scotians such a system was inherently republican in nature and had already been proven a failure in the United

States.[51] Complaints against the federal system appealed particularly to those who believed that the lower house of the legislature expressed the will of the people. Embedded in this opinion was the further idea that parliament was the proper vehicle for the propertied, reputable elements of society to exercise political control of the state.[52] Since the mandate of the lower house came from the people, the creation of five parliaments, as proposed by the Quebec Resolutions, would lead to endless, irreconcilable conflicts, because they all would derive their authority from the same source. For proponents of these ideas to be told, as they were repeatedly, that a federation was the only practicable form of union[53] merely seemed to indicate that union was not feasible. The Liberal view of the supremacy of parliament embodied an inherently unitary view of society. It assumed that those who controlled the political processes were in basic agreement with one another, for without some harmony in principles and interest there could be no unity in the state. Thus the proposal to neutralize conflicting interests by establishing a federal system was regarded not as a realistic compromise but as a clear indication of future disunity. In a federal union, some opponents concluded, was the strong inference that sectional interests would only be neutralized, and never erased.[54] Were union to function properly, sectional interests would have to give way to a common set of interests which would be properly expressed through one parliament. This commitment to parliament, with its assumption about the nature of society, helped prevent the opposition to union from becoming a purely sectional, negative, and inward-directed movement. A belief in parliament and an acceptance of the imperial tie provided a basis for co-operation beyond the limits of the province. Each of these concepts was to influence future events.

During the long months of debate on the proposal for colonial union there was a marked tendency to examine the scheme from the very narrow view of provincial interests. Much time was spent in estimating how much taxes would be increased by union and which local interests would be damaged.[55] A similar approach was adopted by some Canadian advocates of union. A.T. Galt, for example, was not above suggesting to a Canadian audience that Canada had secured the best of the bargain with the Maritimes.[56] Indeed, MacDonnell was of the opinion that the tendency of the Canadian ministry to appeal to the sectional interests of their own province was one of the prime reasons for opposition to union in Nova Scotia.[57] Support for union thus did not always indicate a broadsighted vision nor did opposition to it necessarily indicate a reactionary sectionalism.

16 Nova Scotia and Confederation

THE RETURN TO MARITIME UNION

The growth of opposition in Nova Scotia made it doubtful that Tupper could either cajole or force the legislature into approving Union during the session of 1865. His position was further weakened as increasing antagonism to union in New Brunswick threatened to delay the scheme. Union without New Brunswick scarcely seemed feasible, so all Tupper could do for the moment was to try to prevent the opposition from taking action against union until the results of an election in New Brunswick were known. Although he probably would have preferred to make the Quebec Resolutions official government policy, one government member threatened to resign if he did.[58] Circumstances thus dictated that he mark time. When Lieutenant-Governor MacDonnell opened the legislature in mid-February, the Throne Speech simply indicated that the subject of union would be referred to the legislature.[59]

The election in New Brunswick strengthened the demand that the people of Nova Scotia be provided with a similar opportunity to decide on union. Tupper was under no legal obligation to go to the polls until 1867 and he had no intention of holding an election one day sooner than necessary. His refusal to submit the question of union to the polls appeared to some people as one of the worst features of the entire proposal.[60] Indeed, did the legislature have the constitutional right, as opposed to the power, to alter the constitution without the consent of the electorate? Joseph Howe was particularly disturbed and he insisted that to refuse an election was to deny the essence of self-government.[61] Colonial union, he repeated, was abhorrent because the confederates intended to carry it by methods which would deny the political freedom which had been granted Nova Scotia in 1848.[62]

Even without the risk of an election, Tupper faced a formidable task in trying to win over opponents within the existing legislature. Some of them might have been swayed if changes had been made in the Quebec Resolutions. Yet once the legislature began altering the terms of union there might be no end to constitution-making. Lieutenant-Governor MacDonnell, therefore, quickly blocked a suggestion from Governor General Monck that the various legislatures be allowed to alter the resolutions.[63] But he objected just as strenuously when it was reported that John A. Macdonald had stated that no amendments to the resolutions could be admitted.[64] There was already sufficient distrust of Canadian motives without encouraging the notion that the Nova Scotian legislature would have no voice in shaping the constitution of the united provinces.[65]

Rather than have each legislature approve the specific terms of union, MacDonnell suggested that the only feasible alternative would be approval in principle. This would prevent it from approving the specific results of a conference which it had not sanctioned in the first instance.

From the opening of the legislature it was doubtful that a majority could be found to support union, and the opposition increased as the session progressed. The members may have been impressed by more than two hundred petitions against union which were submitted to the legislature, most of them from the eastern counties. Although some of the signatures were undoubtedly fraudulent, the thousands of names on the petitions revealed a strong antipathy to the scheme.[66] Any further reason for not publicly admitting defeat was removed when the New Brunswick general election resulted in the rejection of S.L. Tilley's government and the formation of a new ministry opposed to union. Lieutenant-Governor MacDonnell saw this confederate defeat as a splendid opportunity to advance the discarded maritime union. He found Tupper willing to revive the idea, for he regarded it not as an alternative to the larger scheme but as a useful tactic to keep alive the idea of colonial union.

On 22 March 1865 Tupper finally introduced a resolution into the assembly to authorize the government to renew negotiations for maritime union. This was merely a ploy to gain time and Tupper, making no secret of his intentions, moved the resolution which read in part that the assembly 'while regarding with favour the proposed Union ... does not under existing circumstances deem it advisable to come to any decision at present.'[67] Tupper had to retreat from his support of confederation and substitute a phrase which merely indicated that confederation was impracticable under existing circumstances.[68] Debate continued because some members refused to accept the inference that maritime union was but a stage towards the larger union. As the month of April wore on, the lawyers in the assembly became restive since the Supreme Court began its spring session on 2 May. Finally, on 21 April, Tupper accepted a proposal from Archibald that all reference to confederation be deleted from the resolution.[69] The members passed the amended resolution without division, and the legislature quickly rose.

At the Colonial Office the return to maritime union was met with distinct coolness. Edward Cardwell, the colonial secretary, was afraid that maritime union would strengthen the opposition to confederation.[70] He wanted confederation implemented, and he was uninterested in the political realities of the colonies. MacDonnell was therefore curtly warned not to take any further action on maritime union.[71] The instructions were effective; when MacDonnell discovered that the New Brunswick legislature was discussing maritime union, he quickly visited Fredericton and arranged with Lieutenant-Governor Gordon to bury the subject.[72]

Some Nova Scotians still hoped that if they could only present their arguments to the Colonial Office the British government would reject the entire scheme of colonial union.[73] The bias of the Colonial Office, evident in its reaction to the revival of maritime union, altered the situation. It was one thing to oppose a scheme advanced by colonials but quite another to reject imperial policy. Many Nova Scotians saw confederation as a proposal which would injure their political and economic interests. The fact that a federal system would result in the domination of their province by the Canadians merely made the proposal more unacceptable. Yet under existing circumstances such considerations were not relevant because there was no plausible alternative to union for Nova Scotia. The subordination of Nova Scotia within union was but a recognition of an existing situation. Britain's determination to divest itself of responsibilities in British North America was working to the advantage of Canada, not Nova Scotia. Provincial interests might receive little consideration from the Canadians, but in the 1860s they would receive even less from Great Britain. Confederation did offer a solution to this problem of imperial relations, but many Nova Scotians were unwilling to consider this question or to accept the secondary importance of their province.

2

Approval of union in principle

NOVA SCOTIA, THE CANADIAN GOVERNMENT, AND THE
COLONIAL OFFICE

By the summer of 1865 the political situation was serious though not yet critical. Some commitment of the province to union was needed in 1866. If the legislature could not be moved then, it was unlikely that any action would be forthcoming during the 1867 session which would be followed by a provincial general election. The apathy must have been particularly galling to Tupper since any real change in the Nova Scotian attitude was likely to be in reaction to events outside the province. Tupper could hope for little from the Canadians since they were so engrossed with their own interests and priorities. Properly used, however, Canadian insensitivity could be turned to the advantage of the confederates.

The strongest weapon upon which the confederates could rely in 1865 was undoubtedly the support of the Colonial Office. Although its officials were reluctant to recognize the reality of colonial interests, they, and the British government in general, remained solidly behind the proposal. The confederates could expect that in time pressure from the Colonial Office would force their opponents to give way. This likelihood was increased by the rapidly changing situation in the United States which was creating new difficulties for Nova Scotia.

The close of the American Civil War, a war which for long had been viewed with apprehension by many Nova Scotians, might strengthen the case for colonial union. But should the coming months pass without some mark of hostility from the United States, one of the principal arguments of the confederates could fall to the ground. Nevertheless, there was likely to be some tension, for the United States government had already given notice that it would abrogate the Reciprocity Treaty in March 1866. By this treaty, which had been originally signed in 1854, Nova Scotia was able to send such natural products as coal and fish duty free to the United States. Cancellation of the treaty might well reduce the level of exports from the province and thereby affect the economy of the province. In addition to free trade, the treaty had also quietened the old issue of fishing rights by allowing American fishermen access to the inshore waters of the province. Both the issue of trade and of fishing rights extended beyond provincial borders and would involve Great Britain and other colonies in British North America. The resulting situation was likely to indicate Nova Scotia's dependence and thereby work to the advantage of the confederates.

Tupper realized that the most critical decisions affecting union were being made in London. He was sorely tempted by an informal invitation from A.T. Galt and George Etienne Cartier, when they passed through Halifax in April, to accompany them to England.[1] Yet as much as he wanted to be involved in any discussions, he feared that his departure would spark rumours of some conspiracy to drag Nova Scotia into union.[2] By June his caution had evaporated, and, with W.A. Henry, he set sail for England, ostensibly to arrange for construction of a railway to the New Brunswick border. While more of an excuse than a reason for the trip, immediate construction of the railway, part of the proposed Intercolonial Railway, was seen by Tupper as one means of circumventing charges of Canadian bad faith.[3] Tupper did succeed in securing a contract with a British firm[4] and in September finally got a promise from Macdonald that any act of union would contain a guaranteee for the building of the Intercolonial.[5]

Although Tupper devoted a considerable amount of effort to his railway schemes, he did not neglect to enquire into the more significant question of trade relations with the United States. He pressed the colonial secretary, Edward Cardwell, to include Nova Scotia in any negotiations concerning renewal of the Reciprocity Treaty. On enquiring into the matter Cardwell discovered that the Foreign Office had already instructed the British ambassador to consult only with the governor general. This exclusion of the Maritimes from any negotiations was consistent with developments since the late 1840s. The manner and the extent to which they would be consulted would depend entirely on the governor general and his constitutional advisers. The Canadian government took its dominant position for granted[6] but Tupper objected to being placed in a secondary role, particularly on issues of such significance to Nova Scotia.

Approval of union in principle 21

From the Maritimers' viewpoint, the willingness of the British government to include colonists in certain imperial policy decisions was benefitting the Canadians at their expense.

The colonial secretary was finally persuaded to include the Nova Scotians.[7] But as it would be awkward to have all colonies participate in each stage of discussions with the British ambassador, the Foreign Office proposed that the colonies hold a trade conference to decide on a common policy.[8] Such a conference did not differ greatly from a proposal made earlier by Monck. Although the trade conference was to decide on policy, the Canadians would still have primary responsibility for carrying it out. The Nova Scotian wish for partnership would not be fully met, but a conference summoned under the auspices of the British government would at least appear to establish the principle of equality among the colonies. Tupper first learned of this proposed conference, which was subsequently held in Quebec on 15 September, when he met with Cardwell early in July. On returning to Halifax in August he claimed that the colonial trade conference was his proposal.[9] Later, in a report presented to the assembly, he added to his own version of events by contending that the Canadians had tried to prevent the other colonies from being consulted.[10] Tupper may have risked strengthening the antagonism towards the Canadians in Nova Scotia in order to give them a reminder to consult with the Maritimers in future. Indirectly, however, he was returning to a theme advanced in the session of 1865 – that in the long run Nova Scotia had no position in the empire separate from the Canadians.[11] Although the Nova Scotians might force the Canadians to consult with their neighbours in special cases, the only way to ensure continuous co-operation was through political union. Once Nova Scotia had representatives in the Canadian parliament and members in the Canadian government, the province would be in a better position to protect its interests than under existing circumstances. The arguments with the Canadians over reciprocity (even without Tupper's distortions) actually appealed to provincial self-interest. These clashes emphasized that there was no logical alternative to union in view of evolving imperial policy, which was gradually extending more rights to the North American colonies.

It was apparent that Nova Scotian politicians would not accept union willingly, but they might be forced into an acceptance of the scheme. Early in 1865 some had hoped that Great Britain would not continue to thrust union upon a hostile province. Cardwell, however, had no intention of altering his policies. In a blunt despatch he instructed MacDonnell to inform the Nova Scotian legislature that 'the Colonies must recognize a right and even acknowledge an obligation incumbent on the Home Government to urge with earnestness and just authority the measures which they consider most expedient on the part of the Colonies with a view to their own defence.'[12] In writing his despatch he could be sure that many in Nova Scotia would be moved by imperial sentiment.

Cardwell again showed his determination when he appointed MacDonnell to Hong Kong, thereby ensuring that he would not have to find a position for a permanent official when colonial union did take place. He named Lieutenant-General Sir William Fenwick Williams, KCB, hero of Kars, to replace MacDonnell. Williams, a native of Nova Scotia, had just completed a tour as commander-in-chief of British North America and, as a serving military officer, would not need a colonial position after Confederation.[13]

PASSAGE OF THE UNION RESOLUTION

The first obvious break in Nova Scotian opposition to union appeared in the fall of 1865 when William Annand printed an editorial in the *Morning Chronicle* calling for a new colonial conference to consider union once again.[14] What Annand had in mind was not clear, and even if he had been explicit he might not have been believed as he had a reputation for being devious. In making his proposal, however, he was probably influenced by the belief that Great Britain was determined to implement union. If colonial union really was inevitable, then it would be wise for the opponents of union to seek to alter the terms as much as possible. It was quite possible that the antagonists could, with a measure of pragmatism, place themselves in a position where they would have to be consulted about union and where they could have influence once union took place.

There was little danger of Nova Scotia being forced into union as long as New Brunswick remained adamant, but if New Brunswick opted for union, Nova Scotia would be exposed to the full pressure of the British government. Three days after Annand issued his call for a new conference, George Brown, a leader of the Ontario Grits, arrived in Halifax. Brown's visit was not directly related to the editorial, but his presence in the Maritimes was connected with a shift in the New Brunswick political situation.[15] Tupper apparently decided that Brown, as a prominent member of the Liberal party, would be the best man to follow up the suggestion for a new conference. An invitation to meet Brown at Tupper's house was sent to Annand and William Miller. Miller, a thirty-year-old lawyer, had first been elected to the assembly from Richmond county in

1863 as an independent; although one of the original opponents of union, he was beginning to think that union was inevitable. He did not accept the invitation, but Annand, who agreed to discuss the general situation with Brown, was advised that should the Liberal parties in the various colonies co-operate, they would be able to control the new union.[16] Anand, however, perhaps not greatly interested in Canadian politics, made no commitments, and put aside, for the time being, his proposal for a new conference.[17]

During the course of these rather desultory negotiations Tupper suffered a humiliating defeat in a Lunenburg by-election.[18] This setback indicated that resentment against union remained high but did not seriously endanger Tupper's plans to carry union through the legislature. Leading anti-confederates, particularly Miller and Annand, were modifying their opposition, if only by default. Annand, through the *Morning Chronicle*, again proposed that Great Britain authorize a colonial conference to consider new terms of union.[19] Much of Annand's willingness to discuss the idea of union apparently was based on his doubts as to how long his colleagues would continue to resist the blandishments and pressures of the confederates. The opponents of union in the assembly had various reasons for their stand, but were not united and had not even agreed on a leader. Although many were Liberals, some were members of the Conservative party, and thus were subject to pressure from Tupper. Several might well be won over through a continued appeal to their loyalty to the empire, while others risked the anger of their constituents if they thought that Tupper could carry a union resolution through the assembly. Annand tested their determination when the legislature met at the end of February 1866 by suggesting that those Liberals who opposed union should depose Archibald as their party leader and form a new party with the Conservative anti-confederates. The proposal was rejected[20] and Archibald continued as leader of the Liberal party even though most of the Liberals were opponents of union. This refusal to forget old party divisions left the anti-confederates in the assembly divided and brought into question both their ability and willingness to resist pressure to support union.

Rebuffed by the Liberal caucus, Annand was receptive to a suggestion from Williams that he should propose in the assembly that a new conference be held on colonial union. This overture to Annand followed a long period of apparent inactivity on the part of the Nova Scotian government, which had left both Monck and Lieutenant-Governor Gordon dissatisfied. The Nova Scotian government had not been willing to raise the question of union in the legislature until the New Brunswick situation had been somewhat clarified. Unfortunately, the New Brunswick legislature was not scheduled to meet until 8 March, some two weeks after the opening of the Nova Scotian legislature. Gordon, involved with his own schemes to entrap his premier, wanted Williams to help him by making the first move.[21] Williams was not to be hurried,[22] but the situation in Halifax soon appeared to be sufficiently favourable for him to make the long-awaited overture to Annand.

It was by no means certain that Annand could persuade many of his colleagues to try for new terms of union. Nor was it certain that he had a clear objective. At one point he had proposed that the anti-confederates should help organize a new colonial conference, which they could then frustrate by an endless series of proposals.[23] At another time he mentioned the possibility of a Maritime conference to precede one in England called to devise new terms of union.[24] If Annand's real concern was the possibility of betrayal by some weakening anti-confederates, then the use of obstructive tactics in a conference might be sufficient to block union. But if any defections from anti-confederate ranks were due to pressure from England, and not just personal weakness, it was vain to hope that attempts to obstruct a conference would succeed. If the anti-confederates were unable to prevent union from being approved by the assembly, they were unlikely to be able to block a conference. Annand was probably interested in arranging for some anti-confederates to attend a new conference, which would be held in England, where they could force through some changes in the terms of union. He also wanted to act in unison with the anti-confederates of New Brunswick, and to this end he decided to visit Albert Smith, premier of New Brunswick, to arrange for a joint policy. Gordon, however, fearing complications if Annand intervened, wired Williams to stop Annand from sailing to Saint John.[25]

Annand's proposed trip to New Brunswick coincided with reports of a threatened Fenian invasion of the Maritimes. Williams followed Gordon's lead and called out the militia on 17 March.[26] The sight of militia being mustered in Halifax may have been reassuring, but the real defence of the province lay in the British fleet. Another danger was created by the ending of the Reciprocity Treaty, which raised anew the question of American entry into the inshore waters. The Nova Scotia government adopted the view that, since the United States had abrogated the treaty, the inshore waters should be barred by the British navy to American fishermen. If this were done, the Americans might decide to renew the trade treaty, and in the meantime the Maritimers would not have to compete in their own waters with the Americans. In wanting to exclude the Americans, the Nova Scotians were revealing their automatic reliance on British aid. Use of British power for what was an essentially colonial issue affected their view of union, for in appealing to England the Nova Scotians had to consider their own responsibilities towards Great Britain.

In view of British restiveness about the burdens of colonial defence, it was uncertain whether the British government would follow colonial wishes on the fisheries. If Britain refused it was possible to conclude that the only feasible course for Nova Scotia, no matter how inadequate it might be, was to accept confederation. Such an argument was certain to be controversial and was likely to be less effective than a simple appeal to loyalty. For the sake of confederation, as well as for the protection of provincial interests in the fisheries, Tupper knew it was important that he persuade the British to exclude the Americans from provincial waters. As a means of reducing the cost to the British treasury he suggested that some of the required patrol vessels be provided by the colonies.[27] The Nova Scotian government did purchase a small ship and, on 19 March, Williams issued a proclamation prohibiting Americans from fishing in the inshore waters of Nova Scotia. The order was never to be carried out, however, because Cardwell had already decided against the exclusion of American fishermen. 'Her Majesty's Government,' he informed Monck, 'does not feel disinclined to allow the United States for the season of 1866 the freedom of fishing, granted to them in 1854 ...'[28] The Canadian government, recognizing the realities of the situation, decided that a system of licences should be adopted for American vessels fishing in the inshore waters. On that same 19 March Monck suggested to Williams that the Nova Scotians administer a licence system and use any fees collected for the protection of the fisheries.[29] Since many in Nova Scotia wanted to put pressure on the Americans by totally excluding them from the inshore waters, any compromise in the form of a licence system was bound to rouse hostility. Tupper, wanting to avoid any public debate, proposed that the entire fisheries issue be immediately discussed at a colonial conference to be held at Fredericton. The proposal was rejected by Monck, who replied that 'it is likely there would be a difference of opinion on the subject between your advisors and mine and that such differences might have a prejudicial effect on the Union discussion. I am anxious therefore to have that safely out of the way before we proceed to consider the Fishery matter ...'[30] Although the fisheries were of more direct importance to the Maritimes than to Canada, the Canadian government informed the Colonial Office of its licence proposal.[31]

The lengthy campaign to break the anti-confederate opposition to union finally brought tangible results when William Miller, on 3 April, rose in the assembly to propose that a conference be held in London to discuss union.[32] How Miller had been recruited by the confederates was unclear but he had probably carried on negotiations with Tupper through Samuel MacDonnell, a Conservative member for Inverness county, who seconded Miller's motion.[33] Although Miller had been an outspoken and conspicuous opponent of union, he, as well as MacDonnell, were political newcomers without any marked degree of political influence. Thus, while Miller served the confederates' purpose, Tupper would have had more success in destroying the anti-confederate opposition if he had converted Annand. The latter, however, rejected the idea of a new conference and condemned Miller. Annand may have been swayed by Howe, who had just returned to Halifax from Washington and still believed that union could be blocked. Nevertheless there remained a strong suspicion that in attacking Miller, Annand was acting out of pique at having him seize the initiative and presumably any political rewards. If this was the case he had only himself to blame since Tupper was pressed for time and was never noted for patience.

Miller had been prepared to make his motion in the assembly earlier but had been delayed by a sudden controversy, led by Archibald, over the Pictou Railway. Construction of this work had originally been granted to a number of contractors who had political influence in Colchester and Pictou counties. Work had progressed slowly and in order to have the project completed prior to the general elections, scheduled to take place in 1867, Tupper had secretly granted the contract to Sandford Fleming, who had been serving as chief engineer of the province.[34] In making this agreement Tupper ignored the provincial statute which stipulated that all public works had to be let out for tender.[35] Although Archibald launched a vigorous attack on Tupper in the assembly, the government was not worried about being defeated.[36] Yet, according to the later testimony of Miller, when James McDonald, member for Pictou and financial secretary, returned from a long trip to the Caribbean during the debate on the Pictou Railway, he threatened to resign. Such a resignation would have delayed the arrangements for union, if not toppled the government itself. McDonald relented only when informed of Miller's intended conversion on union.[37] Thus Miller wrote to Tupper in 1870: 'I might have defeated your government in the Pictou Railway Question, which would probably have been a serious matter to you ...'[38] Had it not been for Miller, therefore, Nova Scotian entry into union might have been delayed by an unnecessary incident, which had no direct bearing on confederation.

It was perhaps because of such blunders as the Pictou Railway affair that Tupper was distrusted by many of his associates. Some politicians refused to accept his promises, and, in making the final arrangements to carry union, he had to rely on the political influence of Lt-Gov. Williams. At least six opponents of union were seen driving up to Williams' residence before defecting to the union side. Three of these men were later appointed to the Canadian Senate.[39] In order to take 'the sting out of the opposition,' Tupper promised that the anti-confederates who dropped their opposition to union would be members of the delegation sent to London.[40] He also had to negotiate with Archibald and McCully, who were afraid that he would use confederation to strengthen his own party at the expense of the Liberals.[41] Although Tupper promised them various perquisites, including a number of Senate seats, they were not satisfied until they received word from Williams that he would guarantee, as a gentleman, that the Liberals would receive a share of the patronage.[42]

By 10 April Tupper was sufficiently advanced in his preparations to introduce into the assembly the following resolution:

> Whereas in the opinion of the House it is desirable that a Confederation of the British North American provinces should take place:
> Resolved: – That the Lieutenant Governor be authorized to appoint delegates to arrange with the Imperial Government a scheme of Union which will effectively assure just provisions for the rights and interest of the Province; each Province to have an equal delegation, Upper and Lower Canada being for this purpose considered as separate provinces.[43]

The motion discreetly avoided any reference to the Quebec Resolutions; thus the members were being asked to commit Nova Scotia to a union with Canada without discussion of the specific terms. By this time, however, the members may have been less concerned with the details than with the broad implications of colonial union. This attitude was expressed by the Right Reverend C.F. Mackinnon, bishop of Arichat, who wrote in a letter to Tupper: 'Although no admirer of Confederation on the basis of the Quebec Scheme; yet owing to the present great emergency and the necessities of the times, the union of the Colonies, upon a new basis, we receive with pleasure.'[44] But there was little reason to assume that the Canadians would abandon the Quebec Resolutions or devise a new basis for union. After all the rhetoric expended on denouncing these terms in

Nova Scotia, some members may have found it easier to speak of new terms without too close an examination of the inevitable. Some felt, however, that there would be no basic changes at all. McCully was definitely of that opinion and wrote privately to Tilley: 'But we have all felt & I still feel that with some trifling alterations it is the Quebec scheme & little else we can hope to have secured ...'[45]

Rather than continuing to question the advisability of union, most of the remaining opponents in the assembly were reduced to demanding that any terms of union be submitted to the Nova Scotian electorate for approval. This appeal to democracy was not only a popular cause in itself but avoided potentially dangerous arguments which might produce charges of disloyalty. The assembly rejected the proposal for a referendum, however, by a vote of thirty-one to eighteen and accepted Tupper's resolution by thirty-one to nineteen.[46] With the opposition in the assembly splintered, the anti-confederates in the council gave way without a struggle. Although they did not know it, they could not have blocked passage of the union resolution because Williams had the power, granted most reluctantly by Cardwell, to add new numbers to the council if needed.[47]

Voting patterns in the lower house on the union resolution tended to break down into a regional confrontation. Of the nineteen voting against union, sixteen represented the western counties – a region which had close ties with the United States and was not overly concerned with the fisheries dispute. Most of these opponents were identified with trade and, politically, had diverse party alignments: ten had been elected as Liberals, five as Conservatives, three as anti-confederates, and one as an independent. This contrasted with the supporters of union, who were mainly from the central and eastern countries and included only four Liberals and five Conservatives who had formerly opposed union. Ten of the eleven lawyers in the assembly supported union.[48] While a dozen merchants in the house voted with Tupper in support of union, there remained nonetheless a genuine fear by some merchants of the consequences of confederation. Some were moved by economic considerations, but others were undoubtedly influenced by party affiliations and general problems of imperial relations.

For a time it appeared as if the break-up of the anti-confederates in the legislature heralded a collapse of the agitation against union. Even Howe, completing his duties in Washington as fisheries commissioner, was dispirited. Sixty-two years of age, and with limited financial resources, he was strongly tempted by an offer to edit the New York *Union*. Writing to his wife he confessed: 'I am much inclined to accept – half inclined to throw up everything – come home and fight the battle of my own Country, in the dark hours that I see are closing round her. That would be the right thing to do, but we have had so much thankless care and labor, that I, for the first time in my life, hesitate between duty and interest. Poor old Nova Scotia, God help her ...'[49] He did finally accept the offer and, after signing a contract on 22 March, sailed from Boston on the same vessel as James McDonald. He arrived home to find that Annand was thinking of joining the confederates. Then Miller made his motion in the assembly, and Howe tried to convince Archibald that any proposal for union should be submitted to the electorate. Rebuffed by Archibald, he went to see Williams and met with a similar reception.[50] Convinced that his former friends had betrayed their public trust, Howe abandoned his new position in New York and resolved to regroup the anti-union opposition in Nova Scotia.

Appointing himself as the head of the opposition to union, Howe met with sympathetic members of the assembly. The first meeting was held on 20 April at the lodgings of Thomas Killam, who represented Yarmouth, and a second meeting convened five days later. Howe, convinced that it was the people's right to decide on union, was well aware that he would receive no consideration from the local government or from the existing British ministry. He could not believe, however, that all British politicians would deny that Nova Scotia had a right to decide on the nature of its own constitution at the polls. The best course to follow, therefore, was to gather evidence of the people's dissatisfaction with the idea of union and use it in Great Britain. There was also the chance that a new British government, one not committed to colonial union, might be formed. As his opening move Howe helped draft an address to the queen protesting against confederation. This address was signed by eighteen members of the assembly and five members of the upper house.[51] His real aim, however, was to reach the people, and to this end he helped establish the League of the Maritime Provinces, which became better known as the Anti-union League.

With the exception of Howe himself, the members of the executive were mainly drawn from the unofficial organization established in 1864 to oppose union. The revived society, which had a written constitution,[52] was concentrated in Halifax, but it soon fostered branches in various counties, particularly in the western area of the province.[53] Ostensibly formed to provide a voice for the people to speak out against the legislature, it echoed an eighteenth-century English belief that the people, through the instrument of the assembly, had a legitimate role in the system of government.[54] Since Howe firmly believed that the assembly had betrayed its role and ignored its responsibility to the people, it was entirely logical for him to conclude that the people must discipline their erring agent. In doing this, however, he provoked charges from the confederates that in establishing the people as separate and superior to the legislature, he had become a radical and a demagogue who was attempting to introduce democracy into the province. The claim that some anti-confederates were promoting the concept of popular sovereignty had some validity. From Yarmouth, for example, came the suggestion that each of the county branches of the Anti-union League should select delegates, who would meet in convention at Halifax.[55] Such an overt challenge to the supremacy of the legislature was too extreme for Howe, and the proposal was quickly dropped. Instead, the corresponding committees in various counties concentrated on holding meetings and circulating a petition which was to be taken to England by Howe.

The chief impetus of the Anti-union League was provided by Howe himself. He undertook a well-publicized tour of the western counties where the opposition to union was already established. Beginning at Windsor on 8 May, he slowly worked his way to Digby, where he spoke to over five hundred people.[56] His success in giving new vitality to the anti-confederates alarmed the unionists, who tried to discredit Howe and his league by issuing a bogus proclamation which declared:

> And whereas a further meeting with such improper and disloyal objects in view has already been held in Yarmouth, where resolutions have passed having a tendency to sap the loyalty of the people, entrap the unwary, and commit unsuspecting persons to principles and practices inconsistent with their allegiance to the British crown.
>
> ... This agitation would induce Her Majesty's Government and the British people to classify all who shall take part and countenance such meetings as *Fenian sympathizers*, disloyal to our common Sovereign and friends of Annexation to the United States.[57]

Public officials were warned to have nothing to do with the league, and the sheriff of Hants was promptly dismissed when he called a public meeting to discuss union.[58]

Responsibility for issuing the 'proclamation' fell on McCully, who was seen handing out copies in the Legislative Council. Exaggerated in language, the 'proclamation' nevertheless voiced the opinion of some unionists, including Williams, that Howe was directly or indirectly a traitor to Great Britain for disobeying British instructions. Opposition to union was particularly dangerous because, in Williams' opinion, union was the only means of withstanding a genuine military threat from the United States. Every opponent was, at the very least, unconsciously working to bring about union with the United States. There was, indeed, a slight but growing interest in joining the United States. According to McCully, while the union resolution was being debated in the assembly Thomas Killam 'got a map hung up & a pointer & proceeded to show that the natural home of B.N.A. was with & among the old Colonies ...'[59] Killam had actually stressed that he preferred to remain associated with Great Britain, but if a change in the position of Nova Scotia were to be made, it would be more rational to join with the United States than with Canada.[60] Under the strain of the moment it was easier for the confederates to view their opponents as veiled annexationists than to emphasize Howe's interest in imperial unity.[61]

With Howe marching through the western counties, Tupper preferred to avoid any issue which might add to public agitation. Unfortunately, he had to decide upon some policy for the fishery question. The Nova Scotian government was aware that the British ministry was not prepared to exclude American fishermen from the inshore waters, but it could not bring itself to accept the Canadian proposal of a licence system. The government was jolted into action when it received a despatch from Cardwell in which he praised the 'forbearance and good policy' shown by the Canadians in suggesting a system of licences.[62] Tupper, who doubted the efficacy of a licence system, also knew that it would be politically unpopular in the province, but it was evident that the British government would not alter its decision. 'I must distinctly inform you,' Cardwell wrote Williams in another despatch, 'that in a matter so intimately connected with the international relations of this country, Her Majesty's government will not be disposed to *yield their own opinion* of what is reasonable to insist on ...'[63] Tupper protested about the lack of co-operation from the Canadian government,[64] and made no move to carry out the Colonial Office instructions. The Nova Scotian government was finally forced to move when it received notification that the Canadians intended to issue licences immediately.[65]

In an attempt to cover up the Canadian initiative, Tupper tried to place responsibility for the licence system on Great Britain.[66] The anti-confederates, however, were not deceived about the role of the Canadians, and they saw in the licences another example of the dangers of union.⁶⁷ Although the lesson may have been harsh, the incident also showed that the Canadian assumption of leadership over Nova Scotia left the province with no feasible alternative to union. The Canadian government, without making an attempt to negotiate with the Maritimes, was already making decisions which affected Nova Scotia. Confederation, which would place Nova Scotia and other Maritime provinces in a position subordinate to the Canadians, would merely make formal a situation which already existed. One of the chief arguments in favour of colonial union was, therefore, this basic inequality between the colonies.

Since the Canadians refused to come to the Maritimes to discuss the fisheries, Tupper and Archibald announced that they were going to Ottawa to arrange for final details of the licence system. The real purpose behind their trip was more likely to convince John A. Macdonald of the need to go to England at once to arrange for union.⁶⁸ If the colonies moved quickly it would perhaps be possible to have the British parliament pass an act of colonial union before it was prorogued. Macdonald agreed to sail on 21 July, but on returning to Halifax Tupper learned that Monck refused to allow the Canadian government to leave, owing to the resignation of the Liberal government in England.⁶⁹ Tupper was deeply disturbed at this sudden twist of events because Howe had already left for England.⁷⁰ If left unchecked he might be able to create sufficient sympathy in the British parliament to have the new government alter Cardwell's policy on union. Convinced that Monck's policy of delay was placing the whole scheme of union in jeopardy, Tupper decided to follow Howe.

Without some drastic change in British policy there seemed to be little real need for concern. British determination to reduce its burden in North America by means of colonial union had finally had some effect on political attitudes. The sense of obligation towards England, enhanced by the problems of the fisheries and of the Fenians, served to emphasize the dependency of Nova Scotia on Great Britain. Although it was possible to conclude that union should be adopted out of a sense of duty to England, it was also possible to decide that union was necessary because of changes in imperial policy towards its North American colonies. In either case union would be regarded in Nova Scotia more as an inevitable necessity than a desirable destiny.

3

Passage of the Act of Union

THE COLONIAL DELEGATION IN ENGLAND

Two years after declaring that colonial union would not take place in the immediate future, Tupper had managed to commit his legislature to union. All appeared settled in Nova Scotia, the only conceivable threat being the provincial election in 1867. Tupper hoped to achieve confederation before that date and was impatient to leave for England. The British government was prepared to be more than co-operative but once again the Canadians were unwilling to consider the interests of their Maritime colleagues. The lack of co-ordination supported Tupper's often repeated view that union was necessary not because of the bond between the colonies but because of its absence.

Premier Tilley of New Brunswick endorsed Tupper's scheme[1] and on 19 July delegates from both provinces sailed from Halifax in accordance with the schedule previously arrived at with the Canadians. But when the Maritimers attempted to force the Canadians to follow them, they met with failure. Lord Monck categorically refused to move until he received explicit instructions on the matter from the new British government. His concern was unwarranted, however, as the new colonial secretary, the Earl of Carnarvon, had already arranged with Cardwell to have parliament approve a bill embodying the principles of union, with the details to be left to an Order-in-Council.[2]

When the Maritime delegates arrived in England without the Canadians, Carnarvon realized he would be unable to make any plans for union before the end of the parliamentary session. Tupper was undoubtedly encouraged when he learned of Carnarvon's support but he was still placed in an embarrassing position by the Canadians' refusal to proceed to England. Until they arrived late in the fall Tupper had little to do but check Howe – and he did not need the other delegates from Nova Scotia for that. In his company he had his attorney-general, W.A. Henry, his solicitor-general, J.W. Ritchie, as well as Archibald, McCully, and Alexander McFarlane, a lawyer from Cumberland.³ Tupper had attempted to keep his promise of including one of the original opponents of union in the delegation by inviting William Miller, but the latter had declined. Loath to return home to face taunts inspired by their useless trip to England, the delegates decided to employ their time in visiting Paris and enjoying the London theatre.

The discomfiture of the Maritime delegates pleased Howe, but he was even more satisfied over the fall of Lord Russell's government. Unaware that Lord Carnarvon had agreed in July to speed an act of union through parliament, Howe imagined that the new secretary was uncommitted on the question of union.⁴ Thus, chance appeared to be making his mission to block colonial union easier than he had first expected. To help him in his task Howe was accompanied by William Annand. Much later, in November, they were joined by William Garvie, one of the founders of the Halifax *Citizen*, who had moved to London to study law at Lincoln's Inn. The fourth and final member of the anti-union delegation was Hugh McDonald, 'a raw green politician from Antigonish,' who landed in England in December.⁵

After arriving in London Howe spent several weeks writing long letters to various influential people, particularly those he had met on previous trips to England. His initial efforts made little public impression, and he deliberately refrained from answering unfavourable newspaper editorials. Several weeks after his arrival, Cardwell could write Williams: 'I never heard (except from yourself) that Mr. Howe had come here at all.'⁶ A similarly weak impression of Howe's impact was shared by Carnarvon who stated in a letter to Williams: 'I cannot learn that he makes many converts to his anticonfederation policy.'⁷

During these weeks of apparent inactivity, Howe was actually busy preparing a manuscript, some sixty pages in length, which he sent to the printer early in September. He ordered 500 copies of this pamphlet, entitled, 'Confederation Considered in Relation to the Interests of the Empire,' and distributed them to newspaper editors and politicians. In this pamphlet he reiterated the familiar argument of the anti-confederates that the Quebec Resolutions would allow the Canadians to dominate the other provinces in the union. He stressed that union would not merely injure the interest of Nova Scotia, but that it was proposed to implement this scheme without allowing the people to vote on their own constitution. Howe probably expected that the exposition of Nova Scotian anti-confederate grievances would receive a sympathetic hearing from at least a few politicians. In an attempt to broaden his appeal he also dealt with the union issue from the viewpoint of imperial policy. In his opinion, one he had often repeated, the British support of colonial union sprang principally from a desire to abandon colonial responsibilities in North America. If Great Britain were to forget its duties to its colonies, however, he warned that Nova Scotia might consider itself released from its imperial bonds and decide to join the United States, rather than Canada.

Within four weeks Howe had sent out all the copies of his pamphlet. He followed this by another, 'The Organization of the Empire,' in which he developed his arguments concerning British colonial policy. Here the question of the North American colonies was presented in the context of the British empire, rather than merely as a factor in British-American relations. Howe proposed that instead of opting for a pragmatic response to the immediate problems of British North America, England should re-examine the entire question of the empire with a view to developing some sort of imperial federation.[8] This proposal conformed to his own long-held ideas, and it also suited his immediate needs. If only he could provoke sufficient interest in political circles he felt the British parliament might appoint a committee of inquiry,[9] which would force a postponement of union. A delay of a few months would be long enough to force Tupper to hold a provincial election.

Howe's pamphlets created some interest, and he carefully noted each favourable reference to his proposals in the various British newspapers.[10] Gratifying as public response might be, however, his real purpose was to convince the entire government itself or at least a sizeable number of the members of parliament. He did not appear to make any impact at all on the government. According to Tupper's later testimony, Carnarvon informed him at one point that some members of parliament, including John Bright, had decided to oppose colonial union because of Howe's campaign. But such success was short-lived, perhaps because of the counter campaign carried out by Tupper with Carnarvon's help and approval.[11] By late fall of 1866, although Howe continued to hope for a wave of support, it did not seem likely that he could delay passage of the Act of Union through parliament.

THE IMPERIAL ACT OF UNION

The Canadian delegates, who had experienced an additional delay because of Fenian raids into Canada West, finally arrived in London in

November. The London Conference, which was to settle the final terms for colonial union, began on 4 December. On the first full day of the conference Tupper presented the resolution on union which had been passed by the Nova Scotian legislature in 1866. Among the Nova Scotian delegates there was probably some hope, although little expectation, that the Quebec Resolutions might be substantially changed. Ritchie stated that it was his impression that all points were open.[12] This was scarcely likely, if only because the Canadian legislature had not passed a resolution similar to Nova Scotia's, despite Tupper's request that it do so.[13] The Canadian delegation had not shown any interest in deviating from the Quebec Resolutions and the conference in London, with scarcely any debate, adopted these resolutions as the basis of the discussions.[14]

Although the final scheme of union was to be based upon the earlier scheme, it remained possible to introduce minor changes. During their long stay in London the Maritime delegates had decided upon certain minimum changes in the terms of union. The first of their demands was that a clause be inserted in the Act of Union guaranteeing the construction of the Intercolonial Railway after union. Macdonald had already consented to this in September 1865, and it was difficult to see how the British government could have forced construction of the railway if the Canadian parliament had refused to authorize it. The Maritime delegates also demanded that the twenty-four Senate seats allotted to the three Maritime provinces by the Quebec Resolutions be retained even though Prince Edward Island had opted out of the scheme for union. Despite the strong opposition of at least one Canadian delegate, the twenty-four seats were divided equally between Nova Scotia and New Brunswick.[15]

The next request concerned the much-criticized financial terms. Since the original terms of union had been drawn up in 1864 the financial picture of Nova Scotia had changed markedly. The provincial debt, which then had been less than $5,000,000, had risen rapidly because of the cost of several public works and seemed certain far to exceed the debt limit of $8,000,000. This would cause difficulties because the interest charges on any surplus debt would be deducted from the annual federal subsidy to the province. This subsidy had probably been inadequate in the first place but Tupper had distorted the picture by increasing the level of government expenditures, principally through changes in the educational system.

From the beginning Tupper saw that he would not obtain any substantial changes in debt allowance. He therefore concentrated on small revisions, such as his proposal, which was accepted in part, that the subsidy not be based on a fixed figure but increase with the population of the province. The delegates' preference for juggling with figures rather than making substantive changes did add to the provincial revenue, but these increases were insufficient to meet provincial expenditures after union. In actual fact the financial situation was critical, probably far more than Tupper realized. Although he had a particular duty to his province, the entire conference shared responsibility for the financial crisis which developed in Nova Scotia after union.

The school legislation, which had done much to add to the financial problems of the province, also provoked a demand from Archbishop Connolly for the legal establishment of separate schools in the Maritimes. From the beginning of Tupper's reforms, Connolly had been insisting on the need for a separate school system. Although Tupper had been willing to grant the *de facto* existence of Catholic schools in Halifax and other regions,[16] he had consistently refused to compromise on the issue of state control of educational policy. The school system devised by Tupper was under the Council of Public Instruction, which was really the cabinet plus the superintendent of education.[17] Connolly was aware that no government could be formed without representation from the Roman Catholics, who made up 25 per cent of the provincial population. But he still insisted that the exclusion of the church from policy decisions concerning education was American in origin and 'the source of nearly the wholesale apostasy of that godless people ...'[18]

Connolly was determined to appeal to the Roman Catholic members in London on the separate school issue, and accordingly made trips to England both in July and December. The situation was complicated by the fact that Tupper was politically indebted to Connolly for his continued support of colonial union. From the very beginning of the debate on union Connolly had been an enthusiastic supporter, although the scheme had been initially opposed by the bishops of Saint John, Moncton, and Arichat. Although the latter two bishops had changed their position in 1866, Connolly's support was still significant because of his influence with the Irish. An Irishman himself,[19] Connolly was interested in strengthening British North America as a means of offsetting the influence of the United States, for, in his opinion, the Irish in British North America were far better off in matters of faith, social position, and material wellbeing than they would ever be in the United States. At the same time, his sense of the grievances suffered by the Irish at the hands of the British was behind his belief that confederation was a means of strengthening the colonies of North America to enable them to discard British tutelage. But he was not prepared to express such views in public and he warned Archbishop Lynch of Toronto that the Irish in British North America must compromise on all matters affecting business and politics and must never arouse the slightest suspicion of their loyalty.[20] Although Connolly would do his utmost to establish separate schools for the Maritimes within confederation, he would not sacrifice union for the sake of separate schools.

Connolly lobbied the delegates endlessly, particularly Hector Langevin, to whom he read a twenty-two page memorandum prepared by the Maritime bishops containing their appeal to have the Act of Union guarantee the right of minorities to establish separate schools. Langevin did not need converting, but there was little he could do. Tupper was still opposed, as was Archibald, and the Canadian delegation was unlikely to disturb its own carefully devised compromise for the sake of the Roman Catholics in the Maritimes. Finally convinced that the Canadians could not be moved, he capitulated gracefully by writing Langevin a letter demanding the various terms he knew the Canadians were prepared to grant. The Canadian proposal conceded the right of minorities to build separate schools if the provinces first passed the necessary enabling legislation. Once such legislation was enacted, a minority could appeal to the federal government if it felt that its rights were being infringed upon by subsequent provincial policies.[21] As worded, this provision only applied to Ontario and Quebec, and therefore provided no protection for Catholic separate schools in the Maritimes. By ignoring the appeals of Connolly the delegates were establishing one policy for Catholics in the Maritimes and another for those in Canada West.

The decision to leave the problem of Roman Catholic separate schools in the Maritimes at the provincial level, in one sense, ran counter to the strong tendency of the delegates at the London Conference to emphasize the position of the federal government. Not only did they want the federal government to retain the powers proposed in the Quebec Resolutions, but they also adopted several amendments which further restricted the power of the provincial governments. One such change, which was obviously caused by the dispute of the previous spring over the introduction of fishing licences, resulted in the coastal fisheries being placed under the exclusive control of Ottawa, rather than under the joint power of the federal and provincial governments. Another alteration, which was suggested by Tupper, relieved the provincial authority of the power to levy an export duty on coal.

When the conference finally finished its work on 23 December, the

Nova Scotian delegation decided to accept the conference report. This decision did not fully satisfy W.A. Henry, who would have preferred more weight for the Maritimes in the Senate and more power to the provinces in order to offset the dominance of the upper provinces within the proposed union. Nor was he content with the compromise on separate schools for Catholic minorities in the Maritimes.[22] His doubts about the proposed union did not interfere with the work of the conference but they did indicate that even within the ranks of the confederates there were disagreements which, after union, might easily lead to a splintering in the ranks.[23]

John A. Macdonald, as secretary of the conference, sent a draft of the report to Lord Carnarvon on 25 December. In order to make it more difficult for Howe, or others, to attack the resolutions, he suggested that they be kept confidential until the actual union bill was presented to parliament. Carnarvon readily agreed and even introduced the measure into the House of Lords so that he could speak to it.[24] The bill provoked little interest in the Lords and even less in the Commons.[25]

The strong support for confederation shown by the British government had long convinced Howe that there was no real possibility of obtaining a committee of enquiry. Yet still he hoped that he might appear before the bar of the Commons and 'strike a note of injustice or oppression that might thrill the House.'[26] When the bill finally passed through parliament almost without debate, Howe charged that the colonies were being treated with 'lazy contempt.'[27] He clung to his conviction that Great Britain, out of fear of the United States, was prepared to repudiate its imperial obligations. He could not bring himself to believe that England would really want to dispose of Nova Scotia. That colony was included in the union scheme, in his view, to provide the Province of Canada, which was the real centre of British concern, with frontage on the Atlantic as a preparation for eventual Canadian independence. He saw this policy of separation running throughout recent British decisions – the withdrawal of troops from North America, the refusal to exclude the Americans from the coastal fisheries in 1866, and now the support of confederation. The imperial tie, which Howe had defended throughout his long political career, was about to be repudiated, not by the colonies, but by England itself. But if England were to discard its unwanted colonies, then those colonies perhaps had no further obligations towards England. This view was summed up by a friend of Howe's who saw the passage of the union bill 'as a dissolution of the Compact Social & Political which has ever bound the People of Nova Scotia to the Land from which their Fathers came ...'[28] British support of confederation could thus be seen as a rejection of Howe's own career and a repudiation of the entire political tradition nourished in Nova Scotia since the American Revolution.[29] Nova Scotia, which for long had emphasized its difference from the United States, was now to be pushed into a North American future.

Although some of his friends in Nova Scotia feared Howe might not return to the province, he was resolved to take part in the affairs of Nova Scotia. Just what he planned to do about union was not clear. Possibly he might declare that since union was now the law of the land he must obey it. Yet, his opposition was far too deep-seated for him to accept such a course willingly. He could adopt a completely opposite policy and refuse to recognize union as a legal fact. He could then feel free to oppose it with all available means, regardless of the consequences to Nova Scotia. A more likely, and a much more responsible plan was to work within confederation until there was an opportunity to take Nova Scotia out of it. Even this policy was predicated on the assumption that release from union was a possibility; to hold out hope without any justification was to raise misleading and perhaps dangerous expectations. Howe, convinced as he now was that confederation was part of a far-reaching imperial policy, could not really believe that England would agree to release Nova Scotia from union. In view of his despair about England's betrayal of the colonies, therefore, he probably did not seriously consider the possibility of a repeal of the Act of Union.

Indeed, Howe's policy towards union in the spring of 1867 seemed vague and was probably not yet fully considered. To Stairs he wrote: 'we are powerless to do anything but to punish, if we can, the rascals who have sold the country.' The anti-confederates should send to Canada 'a body of men who will command respect and give us some chance of fair play, leaving the future to the action of the general Legislature which ... will soon be known ...'[30] Later he added: 'An idea had got abroad here that I am expected to lead the opposition at Ottawa. It would be a great mistake for our people to pledge themselves to oppose an Administration which is not in existence. ... All that they ought to do is to pledge themselves to co-operate and to take any line that, in their judgments will do most for the interests of our country.'[31] Once the bitterness over his defeat in England lessened, Howe might consider the possibility that Nova Scotia could escape from union, but as he well realized, success was impossible until Britain changed its policies towards British North America. Immediately following the passage of the Act of Union, at least, it did not seem that Howe was seriously considering any attempt to work for repeal, no matter now much he opposed union.

FINAL PREPARATIONS

With the union bill safely introduced into the British parliament, Tupper was free to return to Halifax for the opening of the Nova Scotian legislature on 16 March. Although the main struggle was obviously lost, the anti-confederates finally ignored their old party labels of Liberal and Conservative and selected Stewart Campbell of Guysborough, a fifty-five-year-old former Speaker of the assembly, as their house leader. During the session, Tupper, with a precision born of long practice and the confidence which came from success, proceeded to analyze the justification for union from the Nova Scotian point of view. With respect to the economy, he did not deny that there would be changes, but he presented them as advantages to be exploited rather than as threats to be avoided. Integration into the Canadian economy, he declared, would aid the province:

Under the Quebec scheme the power to levy an export duty of coal was left in the hands of the Local Governments. We have changed that ourselves ... I regard them [coal mines] as the great source of Provincial wealth and prosperity ... In fact, the possession of coal mines, together with other natural advantages must, in the course of time, make Nova Scotia the great emporium for manufactures in British America. We felt that in taking out of the power of any Legislature to double the amount of royalty, we were giving a guarantee to capitalists who might come in and invest their money in these coal mines.

Colonial union would thus create opportunities and remove obstacles for the development of manufacturing. It was also evident that his support for an active role by the federal government was advanced as a means of protection for provincial interests.

Tupper and his associates, who had used similar arguments before, obviously saw the coal mines as the basis of a new economy. At the same time they were forced to emphasize the existence of new possibilities because present Nova Scotian expectations and policies towards its mercantile economy would not be realized without union. This was particularly true with regard to the fisheries, where there was still resentment over the adoption of fishing licences in 1866. Some members cited the licences as an example of the policy which the Canadians would adopt within confederation. Tupper acknowledged the complaints but pointed out that Canadian domination was a political fact regardless of confederation. The fishing licences, he told the house, were '... a compromise suggested to the British Government by Canada. The Canadians were ready to licence the fisheries, and standing as we do to-day, we are at the mercy of Canada. If Canada falls, we must fall. We have no status by ourselves, we have no standing in relation to the Empire apart from Canada. As respects this question, it is well known that the voice of Canada has always been supreme, although we have the largest interest in the fisheries.'[32] Tupper had expressed such views before, but this statement, colder and more brutal, neatly summarized a realistic justification of union.

The attack on confederation, led by Campbell, was easily defeated after two days of debate by a vote of sixteen to thirty-two,[33] but the subject of union continued to arise during the session. With the advent of confederation, the provincial government, having fewer duties, could operate with a simpler structure. Tupper therefore reduced the size of the cabinet[34] and persuaded the House of Assembly to cut back its numbers from fifty-five to thirty-eight. At the same time a statute was passed to prevent members of the local assembly from sitting in the federal parliament. Tupper intended this move as a means of preventing local members from increasing their influence by dabbling in federal politics. He gave little thought to the relationship between federal and provincial parties because he assumed that the federal members would have undisputed supremacy in the province. Although the status of the provincial party would be related to the constitutional division of powers, it would also be influenced by the cabinet system of government which was in operation.

With the plans for reorganization of the government completed, the principal business before the assembly was the budget. This was of particular interest to members because of the clues it could provide about the future needs of the province. The account presented to the assembly only covered the fiscal year ending 30 September 1866, but it indicated that the marked increase in revenue was still insufficient to meet rising expenditures.[35] Tupper refused to divulge any information for the period since 30 September 1866, and it was later shown that for the nine-month period ending 30 June 1867 government expenditures exceeded revenues by $330,000.00.[36] It was easy to blame Tupper for extravagance, but much of the annual increase in expenditure since 1864 was caused by belated attempts to satisfy long outstanding needs. Whatever the justification, there was no doubt that this new level of expenditure could not be sustained with the financial terms which were calculated on the basis of government expenditures in 1864.

Among the costly projects which were pushing the provincial debt above the debt allowance was the eighty-five mile railway that was to run from Annapolis through rich farm land to link up with the government-owned railway at Windsor. The agreement made by Tupper in November 1866 with a British firm included a subsidy of $930,000.00 in 6 per cent provincial bonds and a loan of an additional $930,000.00, also in provincial bonds. When the terms became public they disturbed some members of the assembly because they far exceeded the original conditions approved in 1864. Dissatisfaction of the members was increased at the manner in which the company had abused its power of expropriation and had failed to begin construction on the agreed-upon date.[37] The difficulties were eventually smoothed over and the assembly voted the funds needed for the project.[38]

With the closing of the legislature on 6 May Tupper was by no means finished with his preparations for union. One important task was the selection of appointees to various positions, and particularly the Senate. The actual selection was begun in April, although not completed until May. Ostensibly Tupper was guided in his choice by the provision in the Quebec Resolutions, which he himself had proposed, that members of the existing upper houses would have first claim on the seats in the Senate. Such policy could not really be carried out, if only because there were only twelve Senate seats and twenty-one seats in the Legislative Council. There was also the claim pressed by McCully and Archibald that half of the Senate appointments should go to Liberals.[39] Six Liberals were eventually included in the list of senators, although one of these, John Locke of Shelburne, had opposed union. Tupper also had a political debt to several members of the assembly who in 1866 had abandoned their opposition to union. Three of these, Caleb Bill, John Bourinot, and William Miller, did receive Senate seats. Appointments to the Senate thus represented the various unionist factions, with a token representation of anti-unionists.

The list of senators also included six members of the provincial upper house and these appointments, combined with several existing vacancies, left Tupper with a number of seats to be filled. In June he appointed three Conservatives and three Liberals to bring the total membership of the provincial upper house to eighteen, which was the new limit established by the legislature during the 1867 session. With the new appointments the confederates would have eleven supporters, but to provide an even safer margin Tupper also selected Charles Campbell, a mine owner of forty-eight, with the proviso that the council must revert in future to only eighteen members.[40]

In his appointments both to the Senate and the provincial upper house, Tupper paid close attention to the existing political divisions within the confederate ranks. A similar feature marked the composition of the provincial government which was formed to take over from Tupper's ministry on 1 July 1867. Hiram Blanchard of Inverness, McCully's law partner, became attorney-general, while P.C. Hill, a former mayor of Halifax and a prominent Conservative, was appointed provincial secretary. Included in this ministry was John McKinnon, a brother of Bishop McKinnon of Arichat, who had served in Tupper's cabinet as minister without portfolio. Two other Conservatives were Charles Allison of King's and James McNab, a one-time Liberal, who had sat in the upper house since 1848. Rounding out the new government was Samuel Creelman, a Liberal who had been dismissed as chief gold commissioner by Tupper in 1863. The ministry thus carefully preserved a bi-partisan nature, but Tupper probably would have preferred a coalition between confederates and anti-confederates. Evidence that he had actually tried to effect such a coalition was provided by W.H. Townsend of Yarmouth, who later claimed that he had refused to help form a government of four anti-confederates and four confederates.[41] Had the confederates been willing to form such a compromise government, there was no evidence that their opponents would so willingly allow them to hold on to political office.

The new ministry did not include any of the prominent politicians who had been active in the struggle for union as it was assumed that they would take part in federal politics. Tupper and Archibald, as the two party leaders, were expected to fill the two cabinet positions likely to be allotted to the province in the federal cabinet. The actual formation of this government, however, was threatened by George Etienne Cartier's demand that he and two fellow French Canadians be included in it. If provision were also made for the representatives of the Irish Roman Catholics and the English Protestants of Quebec, then that province would have five ministers. The representatives of Ontario, in their turn, wanted one more seat than Quebec on the grounds that Ontario had a larger population. If both demands were met, Macdonald felt that the cabinet would be too large. He had decided to omit D'Arcy McGee, but this would leave the Irish without a representative in the government. After a week of negotiations, Tupper proposed that Edward Kenny of

Halifax, who had already accepted a Senate seat, be appointed to the government as a representative of the Irish, and that both he and D'Arcy McGee would stand aside.[42] This proposal allowed a government to be formed. Tupper's voluntary withdrawal was particularly generous since he diminished his appeal to those voters who were swayed by the political inducements a cabinet minister could provide.[43] Yet if he had not made his offer, the government would have been formed by George Brown, and Tupper's career was more secure with Macdonald than with Brown.

The formation of the federal cabinet completed the necessary arrangements for the new government. As 1 July came closer the confederates worked on plans to mark the event with fitting celebration. In Halifax a committee of fifty was set up, and on 1 July the streets of Halifax were lined with flags. A flag also flew over the governor's residence,[44] and a large demonstration was held on the Grand Parade. Elsewhere in the province the anti-confederates arranged their own mock demonstrations and their newspapers carried public notices condemning union. The *Morning Chronicle* came out with a black border of mourning and shortly after union a paper in New Glasgow printed a notice which read in part:

BORN

On Monday last, at 12:05 a.m. (premature) the Dominion of Canada – illegitimate. This prodigy is known as the infant monster Confederation ...[45]

Such demonstrations might be fatuous, but the protests still managed to disclose marks of real discontent that were to cause Tupper much difficulty in the future. Regardless of the complaints from the anti-confederates, Nova Scotia was in union and was to remain in it. Despite the various delays which had threatened to obstruct union to the point where Tupper would have been forced to hold an election, he had succeeded in carrying the project. While the hopes of some were the fears of others, all agreed that Nova Scotia had taken a momentous step which would drastically alter its future.

4

The federal and provincial elections of 1867

The general elections of 1867 in Nova Scotia, following up on that great confederation debate and implementation, were an anti-climax. The fierce three-year struggle had so exhausted some politicians that they were only too pleased to accept a seat in the Senate or in the Legislative Council. A feeling of lethargy was perhaps inevitable since in many respects the work of the original confederates was done. The election would be a comment on their work but it would be a comment after the fact. The federal and provincial elections were the opening of a new chapter, yet the confederates and anti-confederates alike continued to behave as if they were the close of the old.

The political leaders of Nova Scotia had known for some time that there would be a provincial election in 1867, but with the passage of the Act of Union they had to face an additional election for the federal parliament. Both contests were of great importance and both were bound to produce fierce competition, but it was not certain how the opponents of union would approach the question. If they looked on confederation from the limited viewpoint of their own province, they might conclude that the entire question should be determined by provincial attitudes. If they viewed Nova Scotia not as a country with complete right of self-determination, but as a colony in the British empire, the question of union would have to be considered in an imperial context. While the difference in viewpoint was primarily one of emphasis, one could lead to a complete rejection of union while the other would necessitate acceptance of it. The forthcoming election would provide an opportunity for them to develop their views on union and the results would influence the policy the anti-confederates might follow.

This question of policy was one of the first problems which confronted

Howe when he returned to Halifax from England in May. He made several speeches in which he stressed that the chief aim of the anti-confederates should be to defeat the confederates. This policy of revenge would punish the unionists for their past misdeeds and also prevent them from doing further harm to their province.[1] While this approach did not preclude future attempts to escape from union, it did suggest a certain acceptance of the fact of union. This impression was deliberately strengthened by Howe when he informed John Young, a pamphleteer in Montreal, that he would accept confederation because Nova Scotia could not 'fight the Queen's troops ...' Although his first goal would be to punish the confederates, Howe told Young that if he were then convinced the Canadians were disposed to act fairly, 'we may try the experiment, and endeavour to work the new system without much caring who leads or drives.'[2] A month later, when Tupper and Archibald were in Ottawa helping to form the first federal cabinet, Howe publicly emphasized his commitment to the fact of union. He indicated that he would go to Ottawa after the federal elections as he had already expressed his 'determination to bow to the paramount authority of Parliament, and try the experiment ...' He offered no apology for his opposition to union. He merely concluded: 'the task is over – that duty done. A new page is opening before us, on which is to be written the future of British America.'[3]

Acceptance of the fact of union did not prevent Howe from trying to alter the actual terms of union or from attempting to dislodge confederates from such public offices as the Senate. In order to alter the arrangements made by Tupper, he had to appear to keep his options open. He outlined one possibility in a major speech at Truro when he indicated that if the Act of Union were to be referred to the Judicial Committee of the Privy Council, the latter might 'decide that to sweep away the constitution of a self-governed province, in the summary manner which was adopted, is not the way in which British subjects should be treated.'[4] Although he raised the possibility of the Act of Union being thrown out by the courts, he warned he did not mean that Nova Scotia could evade the provisions of the act or that he was pledged to any specific course of action. He did not ever attempt to test the Act of Union in the courts himself, and he opposed those who proposed such action.

Howe was sympathetic to the attitudes behind the rejection of the Act of Union, but his principal object during the campaign was to punish the confederates. This emphasis tended to focus attention on the merits of union rather than foster debate on the policy to be followed in the future. This limited acceptance of union was adopted, in essence, by several of

Howe's associates. One of these, E.M. McDonald who owned the *Citizen*, advocated the modification of the Act of Union,[5] and when he decided to contest the federal seat in Lunenburg county he pledged himself to seek either repeal or an alteration in the terms of union. His commitment was not to a specific programme but to a vague policy that would 'give our Province its proper status as an independent member of the Confederacy: vindicate our right to self-government, and hurl from place and power the traitors whose chief goal is based on the dishonour of their country ...'[6] In committing himself to uphold the rights of his province McDonald was following Howe's lead, but in pledging to seek repeal first he went further than Howe in his public statements. Logically there was nothing incompatible in recognizing the fact of union as legally binding and working for its repeal by constitutional means. The fact that Howe took great care to state publicly that he accepted the fact of union indicated that he had more doubts about the possibility of repeal than had some of his associates.

Any suggestion that the Act of Union was unconstitutional could be twisted into a justification for actions that Howe would instantly oppose. It was evident, however, that his policy of revenge against the confederates was too mild for some anti-confederate politicians, particularly in the Pictou and Yarmouth regions. These men were beginning to deny the authority of the Act and to insist that only repeal would be acceptable. At an election rally in Yarmouth one candidate for office concluded that since union was unconstitutional, no member elected to the federal parliament should go to Ottawa, nor should Nova Scotia recognize the Act of Union.[7] Although Howe could be rash on occasion, he was not capable of advocating rebellion by denying the supremacy of Great Britain.

The notion that the Act of Union was unconstitutional did have some currency in the province because it implied that the people of Nova Scotia had the right to agree to their own form of government. This idea had appeal for the Liberals but it was too democratic for some Conservatives. An alternative theory was brought forward in a pamphlet by Martin I. Wilkins, an old Tory who still objected to the cabinet system of government. He attempted to rest his strained and rigid argument on the contention that the Act of Union was unconstitutional because it interfered with the right of the colonies to control their own taxation.[8] These arguments, from both Liberals and Conservatives, were cast in constitutional terms, but they were attempting to deal with a concept of nationalism which was being sharpened and brought into focus by the struggle over union. Awareness of a separate Nova Scotia was perhaps related to the fact that the overwhelming majority of politicians active in Nova Scotia at that time had been born in the province. The existence of this feeling, which had its parallel in the other colonies in British North America, suggested that as time passed union would become progressively more difficult to bring about. Although some politicians presented colonial union as a means for gratifying a wish for greater status, union could also be seen as a loss of colonial identity because it involved a merging of colonies. Assertions of Canadian self-identity might be interpreted as laudable signs of nationalism and protests in Nova Scotia against union as marks of simple-minded parochialism, but both embodied similar attitudes.

It was possible that those who advocated an extreme stand towards union during the election represented a small minority of the anti-confederates. Given the lack of a party structure which could select candidates or adopt an official party platform, it was inevitable that candidates would come forward as anti-confederates with a wide range of policies. The variety of opinion did reflect an obvious state of confusion among the anti-confederates and this raised the possibility that after the election Howe would find himself working with men who were sceptical of his policies.

The actual method used in the choice of candidates varied from county to county depending on precedent modified by expediency. In 1867 the selection was particularly complicated because the chief issue of the election, confederation, cut across previous party lines. Thus, in a number of counties factions of the old Liberal and Conservative parties had to effect some sort of coalition. The problem of adjustment applied to both of the new parties but was particularly acute for the anti-confederates, if only because there were far more opponents than supporters of union.

A lengthy dispute among the anti-confederate Conservatives and Liberals occurred in Pictou. It took six weeks and two meetings[9] of county delegates before Martin I. Wilkins was able to overcome the opposition of the Liberals and become one of the candidates for the assembly.[10] A similar conflict took place in Digby when A.W. Savary, a Liberal nominated for the federal seat at a series of meetings in various polling districts, was opposed by W.B. Vail, a local merchant and Conservative. Vail at first withdrew only to reappear, allegedly in response to a requisition signed by some 700 voters, as a candidate for the local legislature.[11]

Howe was less concerned about the possibility of future disputes with former Conservatives than with the immediate task of defeating the confederates. He therefore tried to reconcile the two factions. To prove that he accepted Conservative support he persuaded a Liberal to withdraw in favour of a Conservative in Queen's county,[12] and agreed to contest Hants county himself with two sitting members who were both Conservatives. After a county convention of fifty delegates had approved of the three candidates,[13] one of the Conservatives, James W. King, suddenly changed sides and opposed Howe as a confederate candidate.[14] The anti-confederates promptly selected another Conservative to stand for the local house. In an attempt to help the other two candidates Howe made two complete tours of his county, although one was usually sufficient for his election. It was apparent that in Hants, as elsewhere in the province, difficulty between the two factions within the ranks of the anti-confederates occurred throughout the campaign.

The frequent resort to public meetings and requisitions before the selection of candidates was intended to indicate that prospective candidates enjoyed support rather than to give the voters an opportunity to choose their candidates. Enthusiastic public support was welcomed but some candidates were prepared to proceed without any apparent public approval. This occurred in Yarmouth where Thomas Killam was refused a nomination for the federal seat at a public meeting.[15] He not only continued to campaign but forced an opponent, W.H. Townsend, to withdraw from the contest.[16] There was no province-wide party organization and in some cases there was no organization which could reconcile differences within counties. Formal party organizations would often have been redundant at election time as the influence of employer over employee and creditor over debtor was expected to carry considerable weight. Commenting on the use of influence in elections, one Halifax paper stated: 'We do not say that it is wrong for the employer to use a legitimate influence to secure the vote of the employed – he may do his best to persuade him that his is the right way of voting, he may, perhaps, go the length, legitimately, of asking his support as a personal favour.'[17] In practice the line between persuasion and intimidation was tenuous.[18]

Many Conservatives and Liberals accepted without thought the common assumption that those with wealth, education, and proper morals should control society. The tie between integrity and wealth was seen as intimate because only with wealth could a man attain the personal independence necessary to exercise his own judgment. The respectable elements in society were to debate policy and the duty of the ordinary voter was to select those candidates who would best provide the required leadership. If a voter disregarded the attitude of his employer, he was ignoring his subordinate status. The role of influence was varied and did not pass without challenge, but nonetheless was a significant feature of election campaigning. It was not considered unusual, for example, for Hiram Hyde, a government contractor, to use his woodcutters to try to break up a meeting of anti-confederates.[19]

Although candidates in the various counties found it helpful to have support from the provincial leadership, their success was largely affected by the amount of influence they could command in their own ridings. To some extent this gave them a degree of freedom which was misleading because, once elected, the members of the legislature had to adjust their position according to that held by the party leaders. During the campaign, however, the leader laid low, and Howe's campaign speeches were principally restricted to Halifax county, to Truro where he had a major confrontation with Tupper, and to Cumberland where he spent three weeks in the county being contested by Tupper. His campaign was interrupted by a recurrent illness,[20] but he did make one unscheduled public speech while visiting relatives in Digby to recuperate.[21] During the remainder of the campaign he devoted most of his efforts to his own county of Hants. The more robust Tupper made even fewer speeches. He also spent considerable time in his own county of Cumberland where he faced a serious challenge from William Annand.

One means of persuasion open to both party leaders was the province-wide distribution of printed material, such as pamphlets, election fly sheets, and regular Halifax newspapers. Not only were editorials of Halifax papers often reprinted in the various county newspapers but the papers themselves had a wide readership. In the nine-month period ending 30 June 1867 the Halifax post office handled 2,528,000 newspapers, a marked increase over the previous year.[22] Both political parties organized the distribution of Halifax papers, and they also tried to print and distribute their own newspapers. The confederates briefly flew *The Banner of Union* in July, but after a few issues they decided to use their money to purchase extra editions of regular papers instead.[23] Their opponents issued the *Gun-Boat*, but when this paper failed to appear on one of its regular publication days, the confederates counterfeited an edition containing anti-confederate lead paragraphs followed by union propaganda. This effectively sank the *Gun-Boat*.[24] The Halifax newspapers compensated, to an extent, for the lack of a provincial party organization. It was sometimes open to question whether the most important function of the papers was to convert the opposition or to persuade the party followers to accept a particular policy.

Tupper had one clear advantage over Howe in that he was able to rely on government patronage – in particular the allocation of work on provincial roads. According to established custom each county received a certain proportion of the funds allotted by the assembly for road work, regardless of whether the members from that county were government supporters or not. Government supporters, however, did receive preference in the allocation of any supplementary grants, and the government and its supporters controlled the appointment of supervisors to the actual work.[25] The local governments also authorized some of their supporters to borrow money on impending road grants. In addition to patronage from the local government, the confederates were able to suggest the possibility of favours to come from Ottawa.

Controversy always surrounded government patronage, partly because it provided the principal alternative to the system of influence controlled by merchants and employers. It was the government, rather than the existing political parties, which was able to challenge the authority of local factions, and the government party therefore enjoyed a definite advantage over its opposition. The actual amount of patronage available during an election campaign was limited, however, so the advantage was not insurmountable. Still, an effective party organization was far more likely to develop out of government patronage than out of the merchants' influence.

Tupper had enjoyed some advantages as government leader, at least until 1 July, but he also had to bear responsibility for his actions while premier. One major embarrassment was the Pictou Railway, which was officially opened on 30 May 1867 although it was not yet completed. Complaints against Sandford Fleming,[26] which included charges of poor construction and excessive profits, were not silenced by a laudatory report issued by an American engineer whom Tupper brought in to inspect the railway.[27] This criticism was potentially dangerous because the critics included known Conservatives, and their complaints reflected, at least in part, on Tupper himself.[28]

The major dissatisfaction over the Pictou Railway was confined to three or four counties, but agitation over Tupper's school policies extended throughout the province. The best co-ordinated campaign against the school legislation was led by Archbishop Connolly, who continued his previous attempts to secure the establishment of a separate school system. During the legislative session in the spring of 1867 Connolly called the Catholics 'a half-lifeless corpse' beyond the control of bishop or priest. But he told Tupper that were he to introduce separate schools, 'both Bishops and Clergy will solemnly pledge themselves to take up your case as their own and to procure nearly every Catholic vote in the Province.'[29] Connolly probably did not expect any concessions from Tupper, however, since he had refused all earlier appeals.

Creation of a separate school system in 1867 might have produced some enthusiasm among Catholic voters, but the real cause of their apathy to Connolly's appeals may actually have been union and not disappointment over the government's school policies. At the beginning of the debate on union Connolly's enthusiasm for the scheme had been in marked contrast to the attitude of several other bishops and Catholic politicians in Nova Scotia. In 1866 all the Catholic members of the assembly had endorsed the necessity for union, but the majority of Catholic voters retained their scepticism, particularly after the Fenian scare had faded away. The Irish and Scottish Roman Catholics felt no affinity with the French-Canadian Catholics and the long battles against Catholics in Canada West had failed to provide a bond of sympathy with that area. As for the Acadians, they probably felt few ties with Canada East, and there was little contact between the Catholic churches of Canada East and Nova Scotia. There seemed to be no reason why Catholic voters, as Catholics, should be favourable to union.

Opposition to the government's school policy was not confined to Roman Catholics, and throughout the province many people objected to the consequent increase in taxes. One of the more open confrontations occurred in Halifax where the city council first refused to vote funds to keep the schools open and then only gave way after lengthy negotiations with the government.[30] Some confederates, including Tupper, argued that dissatisfaction with government policies, and not confederation, resulted in the government's lack of popularity.[31] Tupper's government might well have been toppled over opposition to its school policies, but in the campaign of 1867 this issue gave way in the editorials and public speeches to the question of union. The school issue provided an excuse, but not an explanation, for the difficulties faced by Tupper. His arguments would have been stronger had all confederates supported his school policies and all anti-confederates opposed them.[32] It was the issue of union, not that of schools, which drew the line of political division in the province.

Although Tupper tried to reason away the opposition to union, he was quite aware of its widespread unpopularity. With the passage of union into law he was able to exploit the people's belief in order and argue that the law should be obeyed. This argument was adopted enthusiastically by the confederates. One paper declared that opposition to union was justifiable in 1866, but now that confederation was law and had 'by the highest authority recognized by us, been declared part and parcel of the statute law of the Empire [, our] duty then, the duty of every loyal subject and good citizen is to accept that law ... in a proper spirit.'[33] This linking together of loyalty and obedience to the law had appeal for some anti-confederates as well, and was cited by Townsend of Yarmouth as a justification for accepting union.[34] To Archbishop Connolly the refusal to obey the law of the land was not only disloyal but indicated a spirit of republicanism. Concerned by Howe's campaign, he wrote to him: 'Punish the *rascals* that sold the country if you can. Include myself in the number but do not I implore of you Americanize or in other words excite our Catholic people in the Province who are already inflammable enough as you well know.'[35] Howe promptly denied this charge.[36] There was actually little possibility that Howe would allow himself to disobey the law because of his opposition to union.

Among the many criticisms that surrounded the union issue there was great resentment over the Canadian initiative in 1866 in having a licence system imposed on the fisheries. Tupper knew that the arrangement would be renewed in 1867 and he hoped to reduce some of the complaints in Nova Scotia by having the Canadian government agree to double the fee charged for the licences.[37] Macdonald ignored the suggestion, but just before union went into effect Tupper doubled the fee without informing any of the other colonies or England.[38] This caused a flutter in the Colonial Office but achieved very little. The American fishermen probably realized that the British navy was not rigidly enforcing the licence system, and if they did decide to buy licences they could obtain them from the other provinces at the old fee.[39] Tupper's determination to act alone over the increase was a measure of the unpopularity of the system in Nova Scotia. In ignoring the opinion of the Canadian government he also indicated that he did not intend to follow Canadian leadership unquestionably, nor did he identify Canadian interests with those of Nova Scotia. Tupper's view that Nova Scotian interests could only be protected within union suggested that his policy contained a strong element of provincialism. Instead of protecting the provincial interests through the local legislature, he proposed to work through the federal government.

Tupper had every reason to be concerned about the election campaign. By mid-summer it was apparent that the anti-confederates were going to carry a number of seats in both the federal and provincial elections. The actual election campaign began when Howe returned to Nova Scotia in May, but it was not until the middle of August that Tupper announced the elections would be held on 18 September 1867. As a matter of convenience he decided to hold the federal and provincial elections on the same day, a decision that emphasized the tendency to unite the two elections into one campaign and to present the party candidates for the two houses on a common slate. The Nova Scotian elections were expected to be the toughest challenge facing the federal government and they were scheduled to be the last held in the Dominion of Canada. The federal government hoped that its anticipated victories elsewhere would influence some Nova Scotian voters to accept their fate quietly.

The confederates expected to suffer heavy losses, and as early as July Archibald thought that the anti-confederates would win over half of the nineteen seats allotted to Nova Scotia in the federal house.[40] This estimate seemed to be generally accepted by the confederates, at least up to a week before the elections. They were even more pessimistic about the outcome at the provincial level. A few days before the elections Edward Kenny, Tupper's replacement in the federal cabinet, forecast that the anti-confederates would form the next provincial government.[41] This sombre prediction was partially fulfilled when four seats were lost because the confederates failed to field any candidates in Cape Breton and Shelburne counties. They automatically lost another four when they brought in single candidates in the four double-seat counties of Antigonish, Inverness, Richmond, and Yarmouth. In the federal election the confederates allowed five seats to pass without a contest, in Cape Breton, Guysborough, Shelburne, Victoria, and Yarmouth. In four counties the confederates probably hoped to benefit from a contest among several anti-confederates for the same seat. At the federal level the anti-confederates managed to suppress their open divisions everywhere but in Digby, where the one federal seat was contested by two anti-confederates and one unionist. One severe weakness of the confederates, and it may well have been more a symptom of their problems than a cause, was that fifteen of the thirty-two members of the previous assembly who had supported union in 1866 did not stand for re-election in 1867. Six of the fifteen had accepted seats in the federal Senate or in the local Legislative Council. Of the remaining five, four were over sixty years of age and probably did not feel up to the rigours of a bitter contest.

By the time the Nova Scotians went to the polls they knew that Macdonald's government had secured a sufficient number of members in the Commons to remain in office. The confederates in Halifax took advantage of Macdonald's victory to argue that only confederates would have any influence in Ottawa.[42] P.C. Hill, a member of the local government who was contesting one of the three Halifax seats, asked Macdonald to send him a telegram expressing the 'pleasure which it would give the Governor General if the officials in the various departments under the General Government should vote for the union candidates.' The requested message was duly received and read at a polling booth in Halifax, and 'as far as these parties were concerned the telegram had the desired effect.'[43]

Hill faced real obstacles in carrying Halifax because he had to contend with the opposition of many prominent merchants and bankers. His victory depended to a major extent on whether Archbishop Connolly could deliver the bulk of the Irish vote. This vote had been sufficiently united in the past to swing the western division of Halifax county, which included the city, first to the Liberals and, since 1859, to the Conservatives. During the 1867 session of the provincial legislature Tupper had decided to remove the old division of east and west and allocate three seats in the local house to the entire county. This was really a gamble that the Irish vote would swamp the Scottish Presbyterian bloc in the eastern sections, which had gone to the Liberals for several decades.[44] Despite the opposition of Archbishop Connolly, the anti-confederates had managed to bring out Patrick Power, a wealthy dry-goods merchant who enjoyed considerable popularity among his fellow Irishmen, for one of the two federal seats. This division among the Catholics may have decided Tupper to abandon his plans to contest Halifax and return to Cumberland county. With Power as a candidate, Connolly contended that he simply had 'to interfere in the course of the election because of the mad course taken by some of the Roman Catholics in Nova Scotia.'[45]

As part of his contribution to the election campaign Connolly issued a public letter addressed to the Roman Catholics of Halifax, which to him meant the Irish community. He justified his speaking out on political issues on the grounds that the Irish were a minority led by their archbishop and priests, 'who for twenty-five years have been with them in religion, in politics, in education, in fever ...' This unity was now being challenged by Power, the archbishop charged, but had the Irish wished to change their political representative 'they need but hold a public meeting beforehand and adopt another candidate, as he, John Tobin, was chosen twelve years since by an unmistakable majority ...' Since this had not been done, Connolly contended that Tobin remained the nominee of the Catholic people of Halifax. As a final appeal to the Irish, Connolly closed his manifesto with the declaration: 'I will feel it a sacred duty of conscience to vote ... for *The Whole Union Ticket* ... and in honor of me, and still more for their own benefit, I ask my whole Catholic people to follow my example.'[46] His assumptions concerning the necessity for the Irish to act together as an ethnic pressure group, his attitude about the political role of the church, and his general belief in the political rights of an élite all provided ample grounds for controversy in Halifax County. On the whole his letter may have had little impact because most voters had probably already made their decisions. The bulk of the vote was cast for union, with some 800 votes for, 250 against, and 800 abstentions.[47] Although the Irish helped give the confederates a majority of 400 in the city, 'the one-sided vote of a few bigoted Presbyterians ...' in the eastern section gave the victory to the anti-confederates.[48] Elsewhere in the province the Catholics split even more openly on the question of union. However much it displeased Connolly, the disintegration of the Catholics as a unified political force made it dangerous for either party to write them off by dabbling in anti-Catholic polemics. By giving support to the anti-confederates, the Irish and other Catholic voters helped dampen controversy on political issues related to religion in the years immediately after union.

The confederates had not expected to do well in the elections but they were badly shaken when they realized that only one confederate, Tupper, had been elected to the federal house and only two avowed confederates to the local house. Tupper, who never publicly admitted to the slightest doubt of his success in any election, probably had faced a stiffer contest than he had first imagined. His opponent, Annand, who had left his own relatively safe area in Halifax, had conducted a bitter campaign which had been financed by Halifax merchants. Tupper beat off the challenge, 1368 votes to 1271, and helped carry H.G. Pineo, Jr, into the local house. The only other successful confederate was Hiram Blanchard, a member of the provincial government formed in July, who had run in Inverness which he had represented since 1859.

The initial reaction of the confederates was to claim that they had been the victims of wholesale bribery. According to McCully's tabulation, at least eight counties had been bought by the anti-confederates. The bribery had been so flagrant, he claimed, that at one of his open houses in Colchester, when Archibald had been giving away free liquor to prospective voters, the anti-confederates had bribed all his supporters 'before his very eyes!'[49] Connolly estimated that the anti-confederates had offered twenty pounds a vote and that Archibald 'had had to my own knowledge to spend several thousand, in fact all he had in the world so that in fact losing the election he lost all and is now to all intents and purposes a ruined man ...'[50] The bribery thesis was convenient, particularly since the anti-confederates had been supported by many of the merchants and bankers in the province,[51] but it was unlikely that any group could have financed a campaign as extravagant as that indicated by McCully and Connolly. The cries about corruption probably reflected to a large extent a refusal to accept the results of the elections and a sense of outrage at the voters who had rejected the leadership of the confederates. What the confederates realized was that they had been so badly defeated that any question of conciliation towards their opponents might well result in their own political eclipse. The same result was even more likely should some future settlement be arranged with the anti-confederates over the opposition of the Nova Scotian confederates. The refusal of the confederates to accept the election returns as a verdict on union therefore may have been an attempt to safeguard their own position and was likely to complicate an already difficult situation.

The confederates were not certain what the anti-confederates would do following their election victory. Before polling, several of the confederate newspapers had expressed the view that Howe intended to punish Tupper and his supporters.[52] After the election some of the confederates heard rumours that Howe intended to work for repeal. They did not take these stories seriously and thought that the whole notion of repeal would die away if only John A. Macdonald would find something for Howe to do outside of the province. The rumours about Howe's intentions, however, were true. Elated by the size of his victory, he was considering the possibility of obtaining release from union. No doubt he found personal satisfaction in pointing out to the officials of the Colonial Office that he had been right about Nova Scotia's attitude to union.[53]

In the immediate aftermath of the election Howe probably found it difficult to believe that England would disregard the obvious sentiments of Nova Scotia.[54] When he had time to recall his experiences in England earlier in the year, however, he decided that the British government certainly would ignore his province and reconsidered the utility of any serious attempt to gain release from union. His judgment was affected by the attitudes of the anti-confederates elected to office. Their opinions, as expressed during the election campaign, ranged from a demand for an immediate release from union to an acceptance of the fact that union was the law of the land and must be obeyed. The more extreme statements appeared most often in Pictou and Yarmouth counties, yet even in Yarmouth a very moderate candidate, Townsend, defeated a candidate who suggested that the Act of Union should not be obeyed.[55] Candidates who proposed an immediate flagrant disobedience of the law or who openly suggested that union with the United States would be preferable to union with Canada were not successful. This still allowed a wide variety of options with respect to union, however, and the very size of their victory encouraged some anti-confederates to adopt a more rigid stand on the necessity for repeal of union.

Discussion by the newly-elected anti-confederates of their future policies was affected by their lack of political experience. One-half of those returned to the federal house and three-quarters of those to the provincial house were without previous legislative experience. Lacking practical knowledge in the actual operations of the connection with England, they were tempted to exaggerate the degree of freedom open to Nova Scotia. The situation in the local house was further complicated by the number of former Conservatives elected as anti-confederates. Of the thirty-eight members, fifteen were publicly identified as Liberals and sixteen as Conservatives.[56] Howe assumed that he could continue to speak for all of his party, but it was open to question whether he could, as a federal member of parliament, speak for the provincial wing once they had formed a provincial government. This was particularly true since the strong Conservative bloc in the local house was led by Martin I. Wilkins. The latter had not only opposed Howe on every major public issue since the 1840s but was far more inflexible on the issue of repeal. There were serious divisions within the anti-confederate party, then, but there was also the possibility that these divisions could coalesce around the issue of union.

5

The repeal movement

THE GROWTH OF THE DEMAND FOR REPEAL

The victory of the anti-confederates in both the federal and provincial elections had been expected and, in itself, changed little. The extent of the victory was unexpected, however, and had important consequences, in part because it revealed the impotency of the confederate party in the province. The apparently overwhelming opposition to union could well encourage extremists who might believe that provincial opposition was sufficient to end confederation. Victory at the polls also brought with it the responsibilities of office. With their attention fixed almost entirely on the past, the anti-confederates had ignored such issues as the relationship between federal members and the provincial government. These questions could no longer be overlooked, and the method by which policy was formed and carried out could, as was shown in the coming months, be of equal importance to the policy itself.

The election results in Nova Scotia ensured that the opposition to confederation would become a critical issue between the federal government and the province. The Canadian prime minister, Sir John A. Macdonald, was unlikely to have sufficient sympathy for the opponents of union to allow them time to adjust to their new position. The possibility that he would not adopt a conciliatory tone towards the anti-confederates was strengthened by his dependence on the Nova Scotian confederates, who discounted any real danger to union and opposed any compromise with their opponents. Federal policy towards Nova Scotia was also likely to be influenced by Macdonald's well-known wish to subordinate the provincial governments, if not ignore them entirely. Such a policy would immediately raise the question of the proper role of the provincial government within union, as well as the relationship between the local ministry and the federal members.

The initial indication of how the anti-confederates would react to their overwhelming victory was provided by a caucus of their members-elect, both federal and local, in Halifax, on 6 October. Elated by their success, they agreed that the provincial legislature should petition the crown for release from union.[1] In view of many of their election pledges this was the least that could be expected, but there were also substantial signs that some anti-confederates would not be content with a perfunctory appeal to England.[2] Despite signs of a growing belligerency in the tone of the Halifax press, Howe maintained an aloof complacency. When Major-General Charles Hastings Doyle, due to become lieutenant-governor at the end of October, suggested that Howe should enter the federal cabinet, he replied that he could not do so until the British government had answered the Nova Scotian demand for repeal. 'Pending their decision,' he continued, 'I can take no office but while guarding my own consistency and honour will help you to do any good you can, without compromising you ...'[3] The implication of his reply was that he did not expect the appeal to England to be successful. This impression was strengthened when he borrowed a thousand dollars from his friend, W.J. Stairs, to attend the opening session of the federal parliament,[4] although he had not yet decided upon what course to adopt in federal politics. If he were to negotiate for a revision of the terms of union he might well have calculated that his bargaining position would be improved if he remained aloof from the political divisions of the Upper Canadians. At the same time he was at least willing to consider an alliance with the Ontario Liberals and informed George Brown that they might be able to make some form of arrangement once he [Howe] arrived in Ottawa.[5] Had Howe been convinced that repeal was likely, he would have shown his defiance by staying home or even have led another repeal delegation to England to petition the British parliament when it met about the same time as the Canadian parliament.

Before Howe went to Ottawa, Doyle, who had now replaced Sir William Fenwick Williams, accepted the resignation of the local ministry led by P.C. Hill and Hiram Blanchard.[6] John A. Macdonald had wanted the confederates to stay in office until they were defeated in the legislature,[7] but Hill and Blanchard wished to avoid the abuse they were certain to receive from the anti-confederates. Faced with the task of forming a ministry, Doyle, on the advice of Howe, asked Richard McHeffey, who had served in the legislature since 1838, to organize a ministry.[8] McHeffey attempted to do so but his efforts were rebuffed. Martin I. Wilkins then became attorney-general and leader of the government in the lower house and Annand became treasurer and premier of the province. Also included in the cabinet were W.B. Vail of Digby, a Conservative, as provincial secretary, and Robert Robertson of Shelburne, a Liberal, as commissioner of public works. Completing the roster were four men, including the deflated McHeffey, who served as ministers without portfolio.

Howe, who had not consulted with anyone before selecting McHeffey, later claimed he had not chosen Annand because he did not have a seat in the legislature. The objection was valid but obviously not insurmountable. The logical course would have been to make Annand eligible by appointing him to the upper house, even though there was some difficulty because the six new members elected in June had not been gazetted until September.[9] When the anti-confederates formed a government in November they were forced to accept the new members but they disregarded the reduction in size which Tupper had put through and appointed additional members to bring the total membership to the previous level of twenty-one. The confederates remained in a majority on the council but at least Annand was provided with a seat.

Howe's failure to consult with Annand was unfortunate as it provided Annand, and his son, Charles, who owned the *Morning Chronicle*, with a grievance against him. Personal enmity was strengthened when Charles Annand's claim for the position of queen's printer was contested by E.M. McDonald, owner of the *Citizen*, who had held the position under Howe's ministry from 1860 to 1863. A compromise was eventually reached whereby McDonald and Charles Annand shared the government printing. The younger Annand apparently held Howe responsible for McDonald's demands and at one point threatened that if he and his father were not properly looked after, they would join Blanchard.[10] It was unfortunate that relations between Howe and the Annands became strained for three of Howe's former opponents, Martin I. Wilkins, W.B. Vail, and John J. Marshall, who became Speaker of the assembly, held influential positions in the provincial wing of the party. Thus, from the very formation of the local ministry it was apparent that Howe's leadership would be questioned.

Overt signs of disagreement between Howe and the provincial ministry emerged with a resolution in favour of repeal passed by the provincial caucus in November, which read in part:

We in no way impeach the prudence or patriotism of the members-elect in having resolved to attend in the Dominion Parliament; but while we have confidence that they will not designedly compromise the rights of the people of Nova Scotia, we nevertheless feel bound to protest against their acceptance of their seats ... being in any manner construed into an acquiescence ... in the obligatory force of the British North American Act, as regards the rights of the people.[11]

Howe privately thought that the declaration was 'well written but somewhat overstrained.'[12] He undoubtedly did not miss the slur on his own policy or the point that the provincial wing was arrogating to itself the right to make policy for the entire party. The challenge to Howe was put more bluntly in the coming weeks when Wilkins categorically stated that any member who attended the Canadian parliament was recognizing the Act of Union, which he contended was unconstitutional.[13] Sparked by Wilkins, the campaign for repeal quickly became virulent. The anticonfederate press completely abandoned its earlier stand, and declared that it would be content with nothing less than repeal.[14] As the campaign for repeal grew, so did the possibility that Howe and his policy of moderation would be its first victims.

Had Howe remained in Halifax during November he might have been able to control some of the more violent outbursts. He was in Ottawa, however, for the opening of the first parliament of the new dominion, as were most of the other federal members from Nova Scotia. In his first speech in the House of Commons, Howe defended the anti-confederates' right to agitate against 'a mere act of parliament,'[15] although he did not pledge himself to join that agitation.[16] Perhaps made cautious by the mood in his province, he remained aloof from the government and made no attempt to act on his earlier suggestion to George Brown and co-operate with the Ontario Liberals.[17] He summed up his policy when he indicated that he would 'maintain an independent attitude as an anti-confederate, asking nothing and accepting nothing till the British Parliament decides for or against us and then will be governed by circumstances, after full consultation with our friends.'[18]

Just as Howe and the other Nova Scotians were ready to return to Nova Scotia, the government extended the tariff rate of the old Province of Canada to include the Maritimes. For Nova Scotia this meant that the *ad valorem* rate, which had been 10 per cent, was raised to 15 per cent. No particular attempt was made to adapt the new rates to the interests of the Maritimes; thus, a sugar duty designed to aid refineries in Montreal was retained, although it would injure the import trade of the West Indies merchants of Halifax.[19] No protection was included for Nova Scotian coal but the farmers of Ontario were protected by a series of duties on food items. It was the duty on imported grain, including corn, the poor man's flour, which proved to be the most obnoxious to Nova Scotia. Not only did Nova Scotia import all its grain but in the fall of 1867 many people were suffering because of a total failure of the fisheries industry.[20]

Protests against the tariffs were immediate and widespread in Nova Scotia. Some anti-confederates left a petition in the Merchants Exchange Reading Room calling for the removal of the duty on corn meal and then discovered that it had also been signed by several prominent confederates.[21] The increases seemed to confirm the prediction that Nova Scotian economic interests would be ignored within union. John A. Macdonald professed himself baffled at all the uproar, for if the poverty were as bad as they claimed, surely the Nova Scotians would be too poor to buy corn meal at any price. He saw nothing inequitable to Nova Scotia in a system which had originally been constructed exclusively by Upper Canadians and which favoured Canadian interests over Maritime interests. In his opinion the extension of the Canadian tariff system to the Maritimes meant that the same burdens fell upon every part of the dominion. As he told McCully: 'You must remember that we have got a distinct policy in view as to our dealings with the United States, and that policy must not be interfered with from any accidental poverty in one section.'[22] This policy towards the United States was the same one which had resulted in the Canadian initiative on the Maritime fisheries in 1866 and against which Tupper had struggled for two years. Although Macdonald's national policy appeared to dictate that the Maritime provinces should bear an undue proportion of the burden, there was no reason to expect that they would receive a proportionate share of the benefits. Macdonald could boast that he knew what was best for Nova Scotia, but he was soon to discover he would have to retrace his steps if he were to alleviate the problems he had aggravated, both before and after union.

When Howe returned home he was invited to give a series of speeches in favour of repeal. Starting at Dartmouth after Christmas[23] he surprised his audience by declaring that he was opposed to the public agitation for repeal. He indicated he would go to England if asked, but warned that he did not believe the British government would listen to opposition spokesmen.[24] Howe's pessimistic views caused considerable controversy among the anti-confederates in Halifax. The demand for repeal, reinforced by resentment at the recent increase in tariff, was far too strong for Howe to control. Rather than risk a complete loss of influence, he decided to accept the repeal programme as devised by the local ministry and bide his time until after the request for repeal was rejected by the British government. At a public meeting in Halifax he again disclaimed any responsibility for calling the meetings. He did, however, agree to go to London; and if the demand for repeal should be rejected, he promised to hold a 'war meeting' on his return to decide on future policy.[25]

Privately, Howe continued to try to moderate the agitation in order to prevent any public crisis. His immediate concern was to prevent the local ministry from trying to force Doyle to include some reference to repeal in his Speech from the Throne at the opening of the legislature on 20 January.[26] He was so concerned that he sent Doyle part of a draft speech expressing confidence in the continued loyalty of Nova Scotia to England,[27] which Doyle subsequently used. Before the legislature met the ministry submitted a draft copy of this speech to a caucus of the anti-confederate members. Two of them, Dr George Murray of Pictou and D.M. Dickie of Kings, wanted to include a declaration that the government would not work under the Act of Union. When the government refused to insert this statement, Dr Murray walked out of the meeting.[28] Similar radical demands were heard at meetings held throughout the province. Between 27 December 1867 and 17 February 1868 there were at least twenty-six public meetings, about one-quarter of which went on record as approving the use of any and all means to gain repeal. Although most resolutions were vaguely worded, one meeting proposed that if repeal were denied, the provincial government should seize the federal custom house.[29]

For many confederates such proposals to defy the law were tantamount to the deliberate encouragement of civil unrest and anarchy. Archbishop Connolly had long been convinced that the anti-confederate campaign would result in the breakdown of public order. By January 1868 he was appalled at what he regarded as a deliberate attempt by Howe, not merely to exploit the ignorance of the people, but to excite the rich (who were the natural protectors of social order) against union.[30] Connolly's fears of the consequences of the repeal agitation were shared by McCully, who predicted that 'expressions of disloyalty and discontent' would lead to chronic disorder in the province.[31] McCully perhaps felt his fears were justified when several companies of militia in Pictou refused to obey orders and, when constables tried to collect fines, they were attacked by a force of some two hundred men. The matter was taken up in the assembly by Hiram Blanchard who accused Martin Wilkins of inciting the riot when he told the militia men that the Canadian militia law could not be enforced in Nova Scotia. The charge was considered so serious that the assembly debated it in secret session,[32] and both the confederate and anti-confederate press refrained from discussing the incident.

The confederates were sufficiently disheartened by the turn of events in Nova Scotia not to have the stamina to stage a counterattack. They were unwilling to organize any public meetings because of their fear of failure, and their newspapers were left floundering as they unsuccessfully attempted to find a suitable policy. According to Doyle, the dominance of the anti-confederates was due to 'a very wide-spread belief, among people of *both* sides of politics, that there was a decided inclination during the last Session of a feeling among the Majority at Ottawa not to consult the interests of Nova Scotia: but, instead of doing so, of a wish to punish her for the hostile attitude she has assumed.'[33] Even Tupper realized that the situation had deteriorated since the September elections. Although in the previous fall he had been prepared to take Archibald's place in the federal cabinet, by March he had decided that acceptance of any federal office would merely weaken his influence in the province.[34]

The session of the legislature, which began on 20 January, provided the anti-confederate members with ample opportunity to develop their grievances. In protest against the Act of Union, the government did not present a budget and no legislative business was conducted. Instead, the members devoted much of their time to discussing fifteen resolutions which Wilkins presented on 5 February.[35] These resolutions, along with two amendments introduced on 21 February,[36] provided the basis for the petition to the throne which the provincial delegation would take to England. In substance the resolutions repeated the charge that the Tupper administration had exceeded its legislative authority in arranging for confederation. In his speech to the assembly, however, Wilkins laid down new arguments in defence of his view that the British parliament had no right to interfere with the constitution of Nova Scotia. He based his claim on the contention that the province was originally ceded to Queen Anne and her heirs by Louis xiv in the Treaty of Utrecht. Since that time Nova Scotia had belonged to the crown and it was from George ii in 1747, under the Great Seal, that the province had received its constitution. He concluded triumphantly that for any law to be binding upon Nova Scotia it had to be in conformity with this patent of 1747, and that required the consent of Nova Scotia.[37] Wilkins' enthusiasm for his academic exercise arose in part from his belief that he had succeeded in basing opposition to the Act of Union on an essential feature of the British constitution rather than on any doctrine which might smack of republicanism. Not all his government colleagues, however, shared his antiquarian bent or his tory beliefs, and they refused to incorporate some of his arguments in the petition to the crown. After a tedious debate the resolutions were passed but were not forwarded to the upper house since the confederates there still had a majority. After officially authorizing a delegation, which was instructed to seek only the release of Nova Scotia from union, the house adjourned on 25 February until 10 August.

With the legislative session ended, Annand, J.C. Troop of Annapolis, and H.W. Smith of Queen's joined Howe and his wife in England. Once assembled, the delegates began the task of meeting government officials and trying to create some concern among the members of parliament. More interest was shown on this occasion than in 1866, as at least five cabinet ministers were prepared to consider their case[38] and John Bright agreed to present their position in the House of Commons. Despite such surface signs, there was no change in the government's policy. The colonial secretary, the Duke of Buckingham and Chandos, had been prepared for some time to reject the request for repeal and had delayed making his refusal public only because he had learned that the Canadian government wanted time to conciliate Nova Scotia.[39]

As part of the new Canadian initiative, Tupper arrived in London bearing instructions to begin negotiations with Howe. The appointment of Tupper represented a change in Macdonald's policy towards Nova Scotia. Instead of pressing ahead with the integration of Nova Scotia into the Canadian system, he had decided to deal directly with Howe and offer concessions to his province. This decision followed several appeals from Nova Scotia to Macdonald, asking him to be less provocative in his behaviour. Macdonald's policies had also disturbed George Brown, who urged George Etienne Cartier to take some action to moderate the Nova Scotian opposition to union.[40] His decision to send Tupper was inevitable but there was always the possibility that Tupper would seize some opportunity to discredit or humiliate Howe. Macdonald did recognize this danger and admonished Tupper to adopt 'the most conciliatory tone with your Nova Scotian Friends.'[41]

Tupper's first move in London was to approach the anti-confederate delegates. When Howe returned the call, he and Tupper spent three hours trying to outbluff each other. According to Howe, Tupper thought 'the Canadians would afford us any terms, and that he and I, combined, might rule the Dominion. Of course I gave him no satisfaction but chaffed him all around the compass, and frightened him occasionally.'[42] In Tupper's version, Howe had been impressed with the offer of concessions and patronage but had been sceptical of his ability to convince the people of the necessity for such a policy.⁴³ Tupper had a further opportunity to carry on his discussion with Howe when he, Howe, and Howe's wife were invited to the residence of the Duke of Buckingham and Chandos. After the Nova Scotians returned to London Tupper continued to meet with the Howes and W.H. Smith, who, thought Tupper, would take a 'patriotic view.'⁴⁴

Despite any private doubts that he may have had about the possibility of repeal, Howe continued to press the Colonial Office to release Nova Scotia from union. On 3 May 1868 Howe and Smith had an official interview with the colonial secretary, who made it quite clear that the British government had no intention of granting repeal.⁴⁵ John Bright assured them of the same thing, and also convinced them that parliament would not go so far as to establish a committee of enquiry. The delegates decided they had sufficient justification to disregard their instructions to seek only repeal, but they were still worried as to how they would persuade their province to accept the inevitable.⁴⁶ The most promising route was Tupper's offer of concessions, but Howe suspended all further discussions when he discovered Tupper was claiming he had been authorized by Howe to say that the anti-confederates would accept confederation quietly.⁴⁷ Howe was even more disconcerted to discover Tupper's stories were being supported by Doyle, who had arrived in London on 30 March.⁴⁸ Howe, with his penchant for currying favour with the influential and prominent, found it difficult to accept that he was not liked by Doyle. Actually, Doyle distrusted Howe, suspecting he might propose that Nova Scotia join the United States.⁴⁹

The official rejection of the request for repeal by the British government finally came in June in the form of a despatch from the colonial secretary to Governor General Monck. This despatch, based on a memorandum drawn up by Tupper in April, subtly suggested that the Canadian government was prepared to make concessions to favour Nova Scotian interests in such areas as trade, fisheries, and taxation.⁵⁰ The rejection of repeal was merely confirmed by the previously scheduled debate in the Commons. The only satisfaction which Howe was able to draw from the debate was that it was conducted 'with an earnestness that contrasted with the flippancy of 1867.' Nonetheless, the request for a committee of enquiry was rejected 181 to 87 and Howe made only perfunctory arrangements to have the subject processed in the House of Lords.⁵¹

The rejection of repeal by the British government did little to end the impasse between the Nova Scotians and Canadians. At least the Canadians were now prepared to negotiate concessions, though the form and composition of any discussions was yet to be explored. A solution was not likely to be easy as was shown by Doyle's misconstruction and distortion of Howe's earlier attempts to be co-operative. There had been some prospect that the talks between Tupper and Howe might establish some mutual understanding, but this was destroyed when Tupper, ignoring his explicit instructions to avoid the press, issued a public attack on the anti-confederates.[52] He succeeded only in antagonizing Howe and showing his unsuitability for further involvement in any attempts to solve the Nova Scotian political crisis. The only logical alternative was for John A. Macdonald himself to assume responsibility.

Macdonald's policy of conciliation involved not only negotiations with Howe but also changes in some federal policies which affected the province. When the Canadian parliament resumed its sessions in March, with all but three of the Nova Scotian members in attendance, Macdonald arranged for the reduction of the objectionable duties on corn, corn meal, and flour and of the preference given to the Montreal sugar refineries.[53] In addition, the government withdrew its proposal to extend the currency of the old Province of Canada and New Brunswick into Nova Scotia.[54] The existence of several currencies highlighted the problem created by different laws on a variety of subjects that had been enacted in the several provinces prior to confederation. Canadian law, for example, required the death penalty for more crimes than did Nova Scotian law, and the Canadian Franchise Act stipulated a higher property qualification than that of Nova Scotia. With confederation these differences had to be reconciled, which in practice usually meant that Canadian law was extended to the Maritimes. This naturally aroused resentment in Nova Scotia from both confederates[55] and anti-confederates. The extension of Canadian law to their province made them feel that they had been merely annexed to the Province of Canada.

The preference for the laws of the upper provinces was probably due in part to the fact that almost all of the federal civil servants in Ottawa were former employees of the Province of Canada. Of some five hundred civil servants in Ottawa, only two, who were employed as clerks in parliament, were from Nova Scotia.[56] No provision was made to compensate those Nova Scotian civil servants whose offices had been abolished because of confederation, but employees of the Province of Canada who found themselves in a similar situation were granted pensions by the Dominion of Canada.[57] This type of discriminatory treatment in favour of the upper provinces went beyond mere convenience or habit and helped to justify the Nova Scotian fear that their province would not be given equal treatment within union. Perhaps the best that could be anticipated under the circumstances was that the government would slow down the rate at which changes were being imposed on Nova Scotia.

On the whole Macdonald was pleased with his progress during the session in dealing with the problem of Nova Scotia. The anti-confederate members had introduced a resolution demanding the release of Nova Scotia from confederation,[58] and in view of the agitation in their province, this was the least they could do. But they were torn by internal divisions. Neither Annand nor Troop would admit unequivocally that repeal was impossible, while[59] Macdonald knew that several of the members were prepared to abandon their agitation if provided with a proper opportunity. This applied above all to James McKeagney, who had promised Bishop MacKinnon that he would not oppose the law of the land. Opposition to union, however, was so intense in his county of Cape Breton that he had been forced to make various public statements in support of repeal.[60]

Macdonald hoped to encourage the moderates within the ranks of the anti-confederates by offering concessions to Howe. He was, therefore, disturbed when Tupper informed him that on his arrival in Halifax he intended to hold a public meeting and offer Howe the choice of joining the confederates or face him in a province-wide speaking tour.[61] Tupper's curious notion that he could negotiate with Howe at the top of his lungs on a public platform in Halifax convinced Macdonald that Tupper must be removed from any further negotiations with Howe.[62] Macdonald was concerned about the matter of timing of any negotiations and an opportunity to intervene arose when he received an invitation from Howe, through S.L. Tilley, to visit Halifax.[63] Macdonald promptly made arrangements to attend, along with other federal cabinet ministers, a 'war meeting' of the anti-confederates due to open in Halifax on 2 August.

THE SPLINTERING OF THE ANTI-CONFEDERATES

On Howe's return to Halifax public opinion on confederation was divided and the available evidence could be read in various ways. This situation was well-illustrated by a large meeting of anti-confederates in Yarmouth on 25 July. One speaker at the meeting declared that repeal might not be won until the campaign was sealed with blood, and others urged that Nova Scotia should join the United States rather than remain united with Canada.[64] The latter proposal had been the editorial policy of the newspaper, *Bluenose*, which had appeared briefly in March in the neighbouring county of Digby.⁶⁵ The Yarmouth meeting seemed to indicate that the agitation would continue, but Archbishop Connolly, who was in the Yarmouth region at the time, reported that the resolution favouring union with the United States had been moved by a 'great friend' who had merely wanted to see how far the 'unwashed' would go.⁶⁶ This explanation was not entirely reassuring as the resolution had been passed at the meeting. There were signs of a genuine break in the agitation, however, and from Digby, A.W. Savary reported to Howe that his French voters 'deprecate any violence & indeed are rather in favour of abandoning all further opposition.' Savary was in sympathy with this view but 'endeavoured to keep the fire going ...' until a new government was formed in Great Britain.⁶⁷ The campaign, real or contrived, thus continued. Inevitably the tone became harsher and the proposals more extreme.⁶⁸ When one paper suggested that Macdonald should be met with violence when he arrived in Halifax, Howe intervened to check such verbal excesses.⁶⁹

If not handled properly the proposals for violence might precipitate some crisis, but with care they could be used as arguments in favour of abandoning repeal. Any politician attempting to curb the campaign, however, faced the possibility that he might have to bear responsibility for the failure of repeal. Macdonald, perhaps not fully sensitive to such dangers, on his arrival in Halifax urged Howe to take the bold step of renouncing repeal and entering the federal cabinet.⁷⁰ Efforts could then begin to moderate the agitation and negotiate concessions for the province. Howe realized that such a course would strengthen existing suspicions about his own motives and required much more public confidence in the goodwill of the Canadian government than existed in Nova Scotia. Anti-confederates believed that they would obtain more from the federal government by shouts of repeal than by confessions of failure.

Howe assumed that as party leader he could negotiate with the federal government not only for his party but also for his province. Yet this assumption had already been questioned by the provincial ministry the previous fall over the matter of repeal. The issue was certain to arise again, particularly since the local government was afraid to repudiate the repeal campaign but was opposed to having Howe arrange a compromise with the federal government without their participation. It therefore suited their interest to have Howe identified as much as possible with the repeal policy. When the party caucus met, Annand left it to Howe, as party leader, to propose some means of obtaining repeal. In his speech to the members Howe discounted the possibility of maritime union and categorically rejected any political union with the United States; he raised several possibilities, including a mass resignation of all federal and provincial members.[71] None followed up his proposals, as most of the members were undoubtedly thinking of the necessity of coming to terms with John A. Macdonald, who was then staying at the governor's residence.

Annand knew that Howe had met with Macdonald, but when he visited the governor's residence, he, and later Wilkins, were both turned away by Doyle.[72] Determined to participate in the negotiations, Annand received the authorization of the provincial caucus to act on their behalf and returned to the governor's residence.[73] He informed Doyle that his government was ready to consider any terms proposed by Macdonald, but he was again turned away.[74] In consulting only with Howe, Macdonald was attempting to separate him from the provincial wing. His intention was to weaken Howe sufficiently in the province so that he would be forced to rely on Tupper and the confederate party. Howe might have counteracted this tactic had he swallowed his pride and brought in Annand. It was also obvious, however, that he did not see the provincial government as the natural spokesman for the province. Instead, he accepted without question Macdonald's views concerning the supremacy of the federal government within confederation.

Twice rebuffed, Annand decided to do all he could to obstruct the negotiations between Howe and Macdonald. Politically, Annand was in a difficult position because most of those who took an extreme stand on union were members of the local house and not of the federal parliament. There was also the significant constitutional point as to whether the provincial government could deal directly with the federal government or whether it had to negotiate through the federal members of parliament. Any concessions from the federal government, including revisions of the provincial revenue, would immediately affect provincial policies for some time. By negotiating with Howe, Macdonald was forcing the local ministry to abdicate the prerogative of negotiating on matters of direct concern for the provincial ministry to the federal members. In effect, Macdonald was deliberately denying the essence of almost twenty years of cabinet government in Nova Scotia. In several respects Annand was being forced into opposition by Macdonald.[75]

In the anti-confederate caucus the members continued to quarrel among themselves until A.W. McLelan, federal member for Colchester, proposed that a committee, made up of the local ministry, six federal members, and three other anti-confederates, investigate the alternatives open to the caucus. This committee was no more capable of agreeing than was the caucus. Annand insisted that they consider only written proposals from Macdonald but after two days, with Howe, as chairman, casting the deciding vote, the committee agreed to listen to Macdonald, Peter Mitchell of New Brunswick, George Etienne Cartier, and Edward Kenny.[76] In speaking to this committee Macdonald adopted the approach that the members could continue to seek repeal and at the same time begin discussions to adjust the financial terms of union.[77] After the snubs he had received, Annand was not likely to be swayed by Macdonald's blandishments, even though Macdonald had proposed the very course favoured by some anti-confederates. Unable to reach agreement, the committee had no policy to recommend to the caucus. After passing a resolution, which may have been inspired by Annand and Wilkins, to continue the repeal campaign by constitutional methods, the caucus ended.[78] Officially, the party remained committed to the repeal policy and this would prove an embarrassment to Howe as he continued his discussions with Macdonald.

Before Macdonald left Halifax he reached an agreement with Howe that when the legislature was prorogued in the fall Howe would request Macdonald to send a list of proposed concessions which he could circulate among his friends. This delay would enable Macdonald to submit his proposals to his cabinet, but it also meant that for several weeks Howe would have no proof that Macdonald was willing to make any concessions.[79] In view of the widespread suspicion of Macdonald in Nova Scotia, this was a serious problem. The two men also agreed that, wherever feasible, all political appointments designated for Nova Scotia would be kept open for Howe's use once he had rejected repeal.[80] Howe and his supporters were thus to be treated on an equal basis with the confederates. Some of the confederates were not enthusiastic about co-operating with Howe, and McCully, a chronic complainer, characterized the decision about patronage as the '"Conciliation Policy" which is interpreted to mean that the friends of union can hereafter expect nothing and that a generous consideration required that it should be so.'[81] McCully's resentment raised the possibility that Macdonald's complicated manœuvring to gain a political majority in Nova Scotia might be obstructed or partially nullified by the confederates. Macdonald's plans actually could go astray if the confederates, the local ministry, or the followers of Howe did not act precisely as predicted, or some event developed an unexpected twist. A less complicated scheme, not as ambitious in aim, would have had better prospects for success.

When the anti-confederate caucus broke up, the provincial members had to attend the Nova Scotia legislature which resumed its session on 10

August. Wilkins, in a prologue to the session, moved a resolution that although the legislature did not admit that the Act of Union was binding, it would conform to it.[82] He then proceeded to introduce resolutions intended as a reply to the colonial secretary's rejection of the demand for release from union.[83] The long polemic delivered by Wilkins incited Hiram Blanchard, one of the two confederates in the assembly, to reply with a harangue of his own. Blanchard's provocative intervention precipitated further heated exchanges, which did no one any particular good.[84] His days in the assembly were abruptly terminated, however, when he was unseated by an election committee which had been set up the previous February. Not all the anti-confederates were convinced that the evidence warranted this action, but the government, determined to be rid of him, prevailed.[85]

During the debate on his resolution protesting the refusal to grant repeal, Wilkins, at the close of a long speech, declared: 'England will not draw the sword upon the people of Nova Scotia, and if they were not strong enough to resist the Canadians, and were determined to free themselves by force, they would obtain the aid of other nations.'[86] To the military mind of Doyle, these words smacked of subversion and he immediately requested Wilkins to supply an explanation. Wilkins replied that he was incapable of entertaining or expressing sentiments of disloyalty, but when he learned that the correspondence would be published he sent a further note that the political system of any civilized country would be preferable to that of Canada.[87] On learning of this correspondence with Doyle, the assembly went into closed session and, after attacking Wilkins, censured Doyle for interfering with the freedom of debate in assembly. Doyle met this challenge by insisting that his government, in not preventing the vote of censure, had failed to give him the respect due to his office.[88] Vail and Annand, alarmed that Doyle might dismiss the ministry, offered an apology and arranged to have the censure erased from the journals.[89] From its attempt to appease the governor it seemed that, in spite of its vacillations and indiscretions, the ministry was essentially moderate.

Wilkins' political difficulties were not yet ended. During the same speech which precipitated the crisis with Doyle, he had produced the legal opinion prepared in England on his brief as to whether the Act of Union was constitutionally binding on Nova Scotia. British counsel had stated, in strong terms, that the brief was bad law[90] and Wilkins had tried to suppress the report.[91] But Howe had urged Annand to publish the opinion because 'the most fatal consequences might result from teaching the people that they might lawfully resent a statute that had no validity.'[92] His vanity wounded, Wilkins proceeded to condemn the delegates, including Howe, for having deviated from the instructions issued by the assembly in March.[93] When he subsequently invited Howe and the other delegates to receive a vote of thanks for their efforts in England, Howe refused to attend until he had received a copy of the offensive speech,[94] and when Wilkins did not comply, Howe paraded his contempt by walking with a friend in front of the legislature while his fellow delegates were honoured at the bar of the assembly.[95]

It was inevitable that the local government would present itself as the protector of provincial interests. In this role Wilkins offered a bill to prevent the removal of the local militia from the province without the consent of the lieutenant-governor-in-council. Doyle was not prepared to accept the bill, and Wilkins finally declared it was of such little consequence that he would leave Doyle 'to be guided entirely by his own inclination.'[96] Doyle promptly reserved the bill, with the result that it would not go into operation unless approved by the governor-in-council within one year. The notion that the province had to be protected from dreadful Canadian conspiracies prompted a private member of the assembly, D.M. Dickie of Kings, to propose that a secret service fund of $50,000 be set up for use by the government.[97] This suggestion carried connotations of corruption and Dickie's resolution was altered to require a public accounting of the fund.[98] The changes, however, could not erase the words 'secret service' from the public records.[99] Despite such blunders, which reflected more zeal than discretion, the notion that the local ministry was the proper protector of the province remained one of its major defences.

Encouraged by the mistakes of their opponents, some confederates decided to strengthen their own position, and at the same time prove that Macdonald's policy of conciliation was wrong, by contesting a by-election in Inverness following the unseating of Blanchard.[100] The latter finally agreed to run after McCully, his law partner, had emphasized that a victory for Blanchard would do more to stamp out the repeal party 'than all the hollow negotiations on foot,' and allow the confederates to '... just snap their fingers' at their opponents.[101] Neither the urgings of McCully, nor those of Tupper,[102] however, convinced Macdonald that the confederates had any real influence in the province. He decided, reluctantly, that the province could only be pacified through Howe, and therefore refused to provide Blanchard with any aid.[103]

Denied assistance from Ottawa, the confederates raised funds in Halifax. McCully scoured the list of federal employees to find eligible voters who could be sent to Inverness on election day. Through the intervention of Archbishop Connolly he also received the support of four French priests in the county.[104] When touring the French-speaking districts, Blanchard attended mass, but when he crossed into Presbyterian areas he issued warnings that the 'pure ways' of the Scots were endangered by Acadian ambitions.[105] The repeal candidate, Hugh McDonald, a protégé of the Rev. Alexander Macdonald, had the support of the Scottish Roman Catholic priests in the county. He was a political novice, however, and in response to a cry for help the Anti-confederate League in Halifax sent E.M. McDonald of the *Citizen*. On arriving in Inverness McDonald surprisingly discovered that Blanchard was claiming he had the support of both Howe and McDonald.[106] Blanchard was eventually defeated by twenty-four votes, due perhaps to a blizzard which isolated a strongly confederate area on polling day. Although Blanchard's entry into the by-election had been intended as a rejection of any compromise with Howe, McCully was furious at the intervention of McDonald.[107] McCully's exercise in self-deception and lack of judgment suggested that he and his associates were unwilling to accept the consequences of their own political weakness in the province.

Even before the campaign in Inverness had begun, Macdonald had initiated the second stage of negotiations with Howe by sending him a list of subjects open to negotiation, which he was to show to his associates.[108] At one meeting, which included Annand and A.G. Jones, a federal member for Halifax, it was decided that Howe should make no further moves until the local government tried once again to gain repeal. Howe, who had endured numerous veiled insults, including a thinly disguised offer of a bribe from a Halifax merchant,[109] decided to continue with his own plans. The growing hostility between Howe and the local government dismayed Jones, who was related by marriage to Vail, the provincial secretary. He had never trusted Macdonald and he tried to persuade Howe that a divided party would be in a weak position to demand concessions from the prime minister. Furthermore, he warned, a split would be dangerous because some people in the local ministry were attempting to put the responsibility of failure on the shoulders of the dominion members.[110] The long, bitter struggle was placing a heavy strain on Howe, and he refused to listen to the advice. A few days after Jones's appeal, Howe came close to rejecting repeal publicly when he issued a denunciation of treason and filibustering.[111] A meeting between Howe and several members of the local legislature was hastily arranged, but the participants could only agree to allow each other to go their own ways without interference.[112]

In a futile effort to block Howe, Annand and Richard McHeffey visited Fredericton with the hope of reviving the project of maritime union as an alternative to confederation. While Annand was away, his son, Charles, published a letter in the *Morning Chronicle* which charged that those who opposed repeal were enemies of Nova Scotia.[113] As soon as he saw the letter Jones warned Howe not to reply because if he did 'it might place many of the Dominion Members in a false position and leave yourself without the strong and unanimous support you should have from them. ...'[114] From Colchester McLelan also sent Howe a telegram telling him not to answer and in a subsequent letter predicted, 'the locals will want nothing better than for you to reply now.'[115] The warnings went unheeded: Howe replied,[116] thus beginning a newspaper war which ripped apart the anti-confederate party.

In many respects Jones was quite right to fear a split of the anti-confederate party on the issue of repeal. It would undoubtedly place the federal members in an embarrassing political position and would enhance Tupper. Jones's warnings also indicated that Howe's rupture with his party would enable his opponents to contend that he had seriously weakened his own position in his negotiations with Macdonald. Jones wanted party unity, however, for the opposite reasons Macdonald had worked since August to divide the party. Macdonald's tactics appeared to be successful as Howe, in a series of letters to the press, systematically exposed the hypocrisy of the 'locals' in demanding repeal. His bitter attacks, which were answered by rumours and slanders, left no room for compromise.[117]

The only policy which the local government could propose to answer Howe's acceptance of negotiations was another delegation to England. Readers of the anti-confederate press were assured that a fresh appeal to the newly formed Liberal government of William Gladstone would certainly result in success. Few, if any, Nova Scotians were likely to believe this, and the local government was really left without a policy. Unwilling to be excluded from the negotiations with the federal ministry, however, they were forced to continue with their discredited proposals. As a result, they turned inevitably to suggestions of violence. There would only be one more delegation to England, one paper predicted, because if Nova Scotia was rejected again, an insurrection might break out.[118] Another printed a suggestion that Nova Scotia might even seek to join the United

States.[119] Such hints lent credence to Howe's comment to Macdonald: 'The widespread feeling in favour of Annexation to the United States now complicates matters a great deal. There are whole districts where the sentiment of loyalty is dead, where no "enthusiasm" can be worked by anyone.'[120] Undoubtedly the issue of confederation had placed a tremendous strain on the bond of loyalty, but much of the alleged preference for the United States was more a rejection of Canada than of Great Britain.

For over a year the confederates had been complaining of a growth of republican sentiment, by which they really meant a rejection of the Act of Union, and Howe had maintained that the 'locals' were just blowing off steam.[121] Now that he had decided to take a firm stand, his tolerant cynicism suddenly evaporated. One hostile observer, McCully, thought that Howe's real problem was that in the midst of this most difficult fight of a turbulent political career he suddenly discovered he had lost support in the province.[122] There was perhaps truth at least in the suggestion that Howe had miscalculated his own strength in Nova Scotia.

Preoccupied by his fight with the 'locals,' Howe was unable to prepare the Nova Scotian arguments for concessions from the federal government quickly enough to satisfy Macdonald.[123] Now that Howe had made his break, Macdonald wanted him to begin formal negotiations for concessions immediately and without including the provincial ministry. Macdonald had never encouraged Howe to include Annand,[124] and he continued to argue that the federal members were quite able to handle the matter by themselves.[125] As he explained to McLelan: 'the Local Legislature cannot be considered as representing constitutionally in any way the interest of Nova Scotia in its relation to the Dominion. You have been elected under the present constitution to represent Nova Scotia as to all those relations – the Local Government having no more converse with them than the Corporation of Halifax.'[126]

The successful implementation of Macdonald's plans would have effectively limited the political influence of the local government and curtailed the operation of cabinet government at the provincial level. If the federal government actually did exercise all of its powers pertaining to a province through the federal members, the provincial ministry would inevitably become an appendage of the federal party. A number of Howe's associates recognized that the local ministry would not willingly accept such a subordinate status. Howe finally agreed to invite Vail as one of the delegates. The local ministry, although reluctant to be put in opposition to any reasonable settlement, wanted to be recognized by Howe and Macdonald as representing the province. Vail, therefore, insisted that the invitation to act as a delegate be extended to him through the lieutenant-governor and that he be empowered to participate as the official representative of the provincial government.[127] Howe decided that Vail could either accept the invitation from Howe himself or stay home. On 12 January Howe, accompanied by McLelan, left Halifax to meet the Canadian minister of finance, Sir John Rose, in Portland.

6

Howe and the federal government

THE 'BETTER TERMS'

Arranging a settlement between the Canadian government and Howe was much easier than trying to bring together the differing factions of the anti-confederates. They might have been able to establish some internal unity if only they had found some precedent to follow or model to adopt. Unwilling or unable to recognize the legitimate interests of each other, they neutralized their essential political strength by indulging in internal conflicts. From another perspective they seemed to be the perfect victims for the machinations of the devious Macdonald, whose insistence on dealing with Howe was at once a reliance on the role of a leader and a deliberate exploitation of it. Yet, as Macdonald's tactics developed, it became obvious that his attempts to solve political crises through entrapping a leader and ignoring established institutions and attitudes could only be fraught with danger.

John A. Macdonald's campaign for the pacification of Nova Scotia took a significant step forward when Howe went to Portland to meet Sir John Rose, the Canadian finance minister, on 15 January 1869. Rose's involvement was a clear indication of Macdonald's intention to revise the financial terms granted to the province by the Act of Union. Such a revision would allow Nova Scotia to adjust to union without a drastic reduction in its level of public services or a dramatic remodelling of its provincial institutions and would remedy a basic flaw in the original arrangements. Such adjustments would not appease convinced opponents of union since the position of the province within confederation would remain unchanged. Nor would any who saw the provincial government as a legitimate protector of the province be pacified when Macdonald insisted that he would negotiate only with federal members from Nova Scotia. Macdonald's policies would, thus, ameliorate the financial position of the province, but they might not achieve a political cease-fire in Nova Scotia. Political peace would also be determined by the amount of antagonism to confederation that remained in the province and on the ability of the provincial government to maintain its political strength. This strength would depend on the appeal of the concessions arranged by Howe, as well as on the degree of acceptance accorded by the confederates to those anti-confederates who wished to follow him.

Although the proposed financial concessions were designed to serve political ends, there was no doubt that the financial terms of union could not adequately satisfy the existing needs of Nova Scotia. After one year of confederation Ontario was left with a budget surplus of $1,000,000, but Nova Scotia had to reckon with a deficit of $100,000.[1] The immediate problem would be eased when certain projects, undertaken during Tupper's administration, were completed. The long-term outlook remained bleak, however, since the provincial debt far exceeded the $8,000,000 debt limit, although the exact amount had still to be calculated. According to the terms of union the province would be charged interest at a rate of 5 per cent on any sum in excess of the debt allowance and this amount would be deducted from the provincial subsidy. Thus, the provincial revenue, which was already inadequate, would be further reduced. To rectify this situation on its own, the province would have to resort to the politically unpopular expedient of direct taxation, or to introduce municipal institutions which would meet the cost of some public services through increases in local taxation. As a third possibility, the government could cut back on its financial contribution on certain programmes, as, for instance, the new school system. Such a course would have particularly serious repercussions since in many areas of the province public services were already inadequate to meet existing needs.

Before going to Portland, Rose had the opportunity to read a detailed report on Nova Scotia's fiscal situation prepared by the federal auditor-general. According to this report the original financial terms had been adequate to meet the provincial needs of 1864, but they had not been changed sufficiently to provide for increases in expenditures since that date. The report also stressed that although the total sum of taxation collected in Nova Scotia had increased since confederation, the amount was still less than the sum required to finance all of Tupper's schemes even if union had not taken place. Tupper had inherited in 1864 a province which had not only imposed less taxation on a per capita basis than did the other provinces, but which had also provided fewer public works and services. He had increased the level of provincial expenditures but had not provided for increased revenue. Even with the tax increases which resulted from confederation, Nova Scotians still paid less taxes, on a per capita basis, than did the residents of the other provinces. Furthermore, the amount of taxes paid to all levels of government was insufficient to meet the total cost of governing the province and to pay for the capital works undertaken by Tupper. While it might be contended that the province should raise its taxation to the same level as the other provinces, this would ignore the original intention of the Act of Union to provide sufficient revenue to enable each of the provinces to meet its obligations without drastic alterations in its institutions. Since the financial terms did not enable Nova Scotia to do this, the auditor-general concluded that the Nova Scotian case for additional revenue was sound.[2] This opinion was certain to be controversial in some provinces but the alternatives were not without their own difficulties. If each of the provinces was required to raise the same amount of taxation, then some assessment should be made of the public services provided by each of the provinces. Furthermore, there would have to be some calculation of the amount of taxation paid to each level of government. The proposal of the auditor-general, therefore, seemed to be the most judicious, as well as the simplest to calculate.

The auditor-general's report, which Howe had seen before his departure to Portland, provided him with ample support for his claims for concessions. The chief difficulty was in devising some formula that would meet the provincial needs and yet not raise an undue amount of opposition in other provinces.[3] There was likely to be particular difficulty in disposing of the surplus debt. In his talks with Rose, Howe expounded the argument, popular with many Nova Scotians, that the method used by the federal government of merely totalling the liabilities, without making any allowance for earning power of the assets taken over from the provinces, was basically unjust. Much of the debt of Nova Scotia had been incurred by the construction of government-owned and operated railways, whereas much of the Canadian debt had arisen from grants or guarantees of bonds to private companies, and the assets, if any, remained private property. Furthermore, although the auditor-general had indicated that any assets should be credited to the account of the party responsible for the liability, the federal government proposed to keep all the items listed as federal property and still charge the provincial account with the cost of the item. This appeared to be inequitable and was particularly galling in the case of the new provincial building in Halifax, which was claimed by the federal government but had been completed at provincial expense after the Act of Union had been implemented. Howe's contention that the various debts of the provinces should not be treated equally seemed to be reasonable, but it would have been a most complex task to calculate the exact value of each asset taken over by the federal government. Rather than adopt this procedure, which would have to be applied to the other provinces as well, Rose persuaded Howe and McLelan to accept the same per capita debt allowance which had been granted to New Brunswick. This formula would provide Nova Scotia with a debt allowance of $9,188,756. In evaluating the provincial debt, Rose allowed special compensation for provincial notes and also for deposits in the provincial savings bank. After these were calculated, the provincial debt was set at $9,040,439.

With the problem of the debt allowance disposed of, Rose proposed that the annual provincial budgetary deficit be met by a special annual grant of $82,698, to be paid for ten years from the date of union. In defence of his proposal, Rose offered the argument that since Nova Scotia paid more customs duties per capita than did the other provinces, it should receive a special grant similar to the one extended to New Brunswick, which was also to run until 1876.[4] Rose's argument obscured the real point of the special grant, however – that it was needed to cover an existing deficiency in provincial revenue. Unless the province found some additional revenue, it would face further financial difficulties when the grant expired in 1876. The fact that Rose could not simply arrange for special terms for Nova Scotia to meet its particular situation was in itself indicative of the strength of provincial rivalries.

With the revised financial terms, money would still not be available in Nova Scotia to subsidize new public works of purely provincial importance. The inflexibility of the provincial budget provided a formidable obstacle to those seeking better public provision for such groups as the poor and the mentally ill. Given the previous resistance to tax increases in the province, further demands for expenditures were likely to result in various types of pressure being applied on the federal government. These could vary from an outright insistence on further grants to an attempt to gain special treatment for favoured projects. Whatever the form, they would prove to be a continuous source of tension between the federal and provincial governments in the coming years.

THREE BY-ELECTIONS

The discussions begun in Portland between Howe, McLelan, and Rose were concluded in Ottawa, and the financial terms were approved by

Order-in-Council on 25 January.[5] For John A. Macdonald these terms were principally a means of persuading Howe to enter the cabinet. Before Howe had left Halifax, however, he had assured E.M. McDonald that he would not accept office until he had discussed the proposed federal terms with his associates in Nova Scotia.[6] Although Howe was probably unaware of it, Tupper was also of the opinion that Howe's followers should be drawn into the negotiations before he publicly accepted any terms to end the agitation against union.[7] At first Macdonald agreed that Howe should 'be the messenger of his own arrangements,'[8] but he nonetheless persuaded Howe to remain in Ottawa until a reply to the request of the Nova Scotian legislature for repeal was received from the British government. Owing to a delay in sending the petition, the reply had been prepared by the government formed by William Gladstone in December 1868.

The overdue despatch finally arrived on 30 January 1869 and it contained the anticipated rejection of repeal. On the same day Macdonald announced that Howe had accepted a cabinet position as president of the Privy Council and revealed the terms of concessions to Nova Scotia. This move proved to be a major blunder, because it put the entire responsibility for quietening the agitation in Nova Scotia on Howe. Macdonald, intent on ensnaring the most prominent and most capable member of the anti-confederates, underestimated the political appeal of the provincial ministry and overestimated the willingness of the confederates to accept Howe and his followers. Howe, in his defence, later complained that his health would not have withstood the rigours of a second trip to Ottawa in wintertime in order to be sworn into office. He had also been subjected to continuous pressure from Macdonald, McLelan,[9] and Jones,[10] and was anxious to show that he was able to arrange for important concessions to his province without any aid from those critics who had hounded and maligned him. Howe agreed to address a public rally in Montreal, but an urgent appeal from Halifax reminded him of his duty to his followers and he quickly set out for home.[11] When he arrived on 8 February he found that the local ministry had already organized its campaign to discredit him and the concessions made by the federal government.

Attempts by the provincial ministry to neutralize the effect of any terms arranged by Howe had begun as soon as he left for Portland. This tactic had been started by Vail who had requested the anti-confederate members, both federal and provincial, to reaffirm their loyalty to the policy of repeal adopted by the anti-confederate caucus in August 1868. This petition proved insignificant because only seven federal members signed it, and four of these soon declared their support for Howe.[12] A more effective means of combatting Howe was found, however, when on 25 January a Repeal League was formed in Halifax. One-half of the council of twenty-four were Halifax merchants who had been prominent supporters of the anti-confederate party. Only one member of the league council, Jeremiah Northup, was a supporter of Howe, and he resigned after Howe entered the federal government.[13] The purpose of the league was generally to organize and finance the campaign against Howe, and particularly to contest the by-election which Howe would have to face because he had accepted a cabinet position. A secondary purpose was to preserve party unity throughout the province. In this it was not notably successful because branches of the league apparently were established in only a few of the western counties.[14]

The anti-confederates continued to protest, sometimes with considerable vehemence, that they still supported the repeal policy. At the same time they fully recognized, and sometimes publicly acknowledged, that it was futile to pursue this policy any further.[15] A logical alternative to the repeal of confederation, which was adopted by some in the province, was to declare that the only course left to Nova Scotia was union with the United States. This annexation sentiment, although existing in the province, did not animate the policy of the provincial ministry. The main objective of the ministry was to force the federal government into extending it a degree of political recognition and influence. John A. Macdonald recognized the nature of the provincial ministry's demand to some extent when he indicated that were Howe to be defeated in the Hants by-election, he would have to 'accept Annand's terms and surrender the local patronage.'[16] Annand certainly wanted political power, but this trait was not entirely unexpected in a premier of a province. Nor was it unreasonable for the provincial ministry to expect that it would have a political role in its province. The quarrel over the 'better terms' was thus a debate on the role of the provincial government and the nature of confederation.

The anti-confederates might well continue to doubt that the concessions offered by Ottawa were really the best which could be arranged. Nor could they be enthusiastic about working with the confederates or even be sure that the confederates would co-operate with them. In their uncertainty about what they should do, they needed time, but Howe, obstinately insistent on doing everything himself, did not give them time. The local government was enraged because Howe had taken 'too much upon himself *without consulting them*,'[17] and Howe's own friends felt that they had been 'dragged through the dirt, and are left sprawling there by him.'[18] The decision whether to follow Howe was particularly difficult for E.M. McDonald, who was not only the federal member for Lunenburg, but also the queen's printer to the provincial government. McDonald knew that the local ministry would dismiss him the instant he declared his support for Howe, and the loss of the printing contracts would make it difficult for him to keep alive his newspaper, the *Citizen*. Furthermore, his political position in Lunenburg was weak as he had entered the county just prior to the election of 1867 and any declaration for Howe would be opposed by the two county members who sat in the local legislature. Despite desperate attempts to find support,[19] he was rejected by both the anti-confederates and the confederates. Tupper wrote him off as an 'incorrigible blackguard,'[20] and H.A.N. Kaulback, who had been defeated by McDonald in the 1867 election, dismissed him as 'the most contemptible man in his party.'[21] In rejecting McDonald, however, the confederates were jeopardizing the success of the federal concessions because they showed other anti-confederates what they might expect if they should follow Howe.

When McDonald finally did announce his support for Howe, he was, as he had anticipated, promptly dismissed as queen's printer. As his replacement Annand wanted to appoint Hugh Blackadar, whose paper, the *Acadian Recorder*, published bitter editorials with provocative hints that the province might join the United States. These editorials, which were probably written by Martin I. Wilkins,[22] succeeded in thoroughly antagonizing Doyle, who refused, as he told Annand, to approve the appointment of anyone dealing in sedition. Doyle had to give way when he was presented with a written promise from Blackadar 'that nothing calculated to sever the connection hitherto existing between this Province and Great Britain should appear in the journal under his control, while serving as an officer of the Crown.'[23] Promises did not, of course, guarantee performance, but such readily given assurances suggested that Blackadar did not take his own rhetoric overly seriously.

Many confederates, still convinced that the basic issues involved in the debate over confederation were loyalty to England and preservation of the social order, remained cool to the coalition with Howe. Although Tupper accepted the necessity of the agreement with Howe, he had not been actively involved in the negotiations since his return from England. It was difficult for him, however, to sit as an observer and there was a touch of resentment in his criticisms of the tactics adopted by Howe and Macdonald.[24] He did realize, though, that Howe had made a serious error in not drawing the local government into the negotiations with the federal government. Nonetheless, once the 'better terms' were announced, he strove diligently to bring the confederates into line behind Howe. Although he had some success, memories of old battles and personal feuds continued to obstruct any immediate acceptance of Howe by the confederates.[25] At one point it even looked as if some confederates might organize an open rebellion. This occurred when a Halifax newspaper, the *Unionist*, which had been previously owned by Jonathan McCully, began to denounce Howe and the 'better terms.' In one issue an editorial declared: 'We are Unionists to the backbone, and as such, we have the boldness to declare that, Mr. Howe's presence in the Dominion Cabinet – with Repeal on his lips – is a direct insult to every true Unionist ...'[26] The real author of these editorials, in Tupper's opinion, was W.A. Henry, who had continued to oppose the conciliation policy.[27] Henry may not have written the editorials but they undoubtedly expressed his views, as well as those of other confederates. The provocative editorials in the *Unionist* soon ended, but many confederates accepted the coalition with Howe in a sullen mood.

As the by-election campaign in Hants got underway, it quickly became apparent that Howe needed help. Although his opponent, Monson H. Goudge, was a former confederate and a merchant with no prior political experience, he proved to be a capable speaker[28] and, with the aid of some of Howe's former Liberal supporters in the county, began to wage a most effective campaign. To compensate for this division in the ranks of those who had supported Howe in 1867, Tupper, and other prominent confederates, tried to bring over their own followers to Howe, but the Irish Roman Catholics were not willing to forget their quarrels with him. John Tobin, a prominent Irish merchant of Halifax, was sent in to settle the dissension. When his mission proved unsuccessful, Archbishop Connolly decreed that the two Irish priests in the county, who were behind the opposition, should 'spend the early half of next week with me. I think it better the Doctor [Tupper] too should be at them and all will be right please God.'[29] Nothing further was heard of the unruly priests of Hants.

On his tour through the county Howe was accompanied by George Johnson of the *Halifax Evening Reporter*. The overall organization of the campaign was managed by Jeremiah Northup, a Halifax merchant who sat in the local legislature. Northup, who had been raised in Hants, was particularly useful because he had long been interested in the shipbuilding industry of the Maitland area and also because his brother had been associated with various agricultural societies. Despite the aid he was receiving, Howe felt the strain of the extremely bitter campaign. Often in the past Howe had managed, when in the midst of a serious struggle, to place the immediate dispute in the perspective of principle. Now, when he needed to weld together reluctant anti-confederates and suspicious confederates, he seemed to remain mired in the despair of his inglorious defeat in the long battle against union. Instead of preaching principle, he spoke of bribing his opponents and tempted his supporters with offers of patronage. At one public meeting he flourished a telegram from a Halifax merchant which pledged a donation of £1000 to the anti-Howe campaign, and he promised that for every dollar spent by his opponents he would spend two.[30] At another meeting he suggested that Hants would not be harmed by having a representative in Ottawa where there were '300 to 400 offices to dispose of.'[31] Such tactics, coming hard on claims that Howe had sold out his province for the sake of office, could do nothing but harm to his cause.[32]

For fifteen days Howe toured Hants. He held meetings in large drill sheds with as many as five hundred people present. These meetings lasted from two o'clock in the afternoon until past seven in the evening.[33] When the public speeches ended, he had to meet the local voters, plan the schedule for the next day, and do most of the writing for an election fly-sheet, the *Hants Gazette*. This schedule, coupled with the rigours of a typically cold and wet Nova Scotian February, finally brought on a severe case of bronchitis. On 3 March Johnson tried to postpone a scheduled confrontation with Howe's opponents. Vail agreed, but Annand, Jones, and Thomas Morrison, a member of the local legislature for Colchester, refused. During the speeches Howe lay on the stage, wrapped in his great coat, while his opponents stood about him, denouncing his cheap theatrical tricks.[34] For the next two weeks Howe was confined to bed, too ill even to write a letter. His breakdown, Tupper calculated, was opportune because it aroused a feeling of sympathy for Howe which had previously been missing.[35] And under the direction of the faithful Northup, Howe's election committee continued to tour Hants while he attempted to recover his strength in Halifax.

Tupper had persistently stated that Howe would win the by-election but as the contest developed he became aware of how difficult such a victory would be. He feared that Howe's campaign might be harmed by a federal by-election in Yarmouth to fill the vacancy created by the death of Thomas Killam on 15 December 1868. But with Killam's death, the *Tribune*, one of the two newspapers published in Yarmouth, decided to support Howe and the 'better terms.' Its circulation was limited, however, and it had never been a firm supporter of Killam and his policies. The most promising scheme to break the control of the anti-confederates centred around Nathan Moses, a popular merchant whose firm always delivered a sizeable percentage of the French vote in the Tusket region.[36] Unfortunately Moses wanted a seat in the Senate and he decided to throw his support behind N.K. Clements, a ship-owner and avowed confederate.[37]

Clements was not strong in the county but he did not want a former anti-confederate to run. Therefore he decided to contest the election himself, despite suggestions from John A. Macdonald that he stand aside.[38] In his campaign Clements depended primarily on political innocents[39] who had no more idea of running an election campaign than he had. He was unwilling to recognize that the confederates had always been a minority in Yarmouth and would remain so until they actively co-operated with the moderate anti-confederates. The opportunity created by the death of Killam to break the hold of the anti-confederates in the riding was thus ignored. Any hopes of victory which Clements might have had were completely destroyed when the anti-confederates, after a two-month search, brought out Frank Killam, the twenty-four year old son of the former member. Again the confederates complained of intimidation at public meetings[40] and promises of financial aid from local merchants were not kept. Once more Yarmouth appeared to be united against confederation.[41]

Yarmouth, which had been one of the first centres to oppose union, was also noted for its favourable attitude towards joining the United States. Thomas Killam had long insisted that although he was loyal to Great Britain, he would far prefer to join the United States than remain united with Canada. These views, which were shared by his son, could not be disregarded. To some confederates they were highly seditious, and the Killam group was held responsible for a pamphlet advocating union with the United States which appeared in February.[42] The Killams, like other shipowners in Yarmouth, were afraid that union with Canada would result in a disruption of their numerous economic ties with the United States. They also seemed responsive to the American attitude that a man's social and political position should depend on his ability, particularly in the economic area. Some did prefer to unite with the United States rather than with Canada but many, including Frank Killam, were unable to discard totally their allegiance to Great Britain. Hints about joining the United States were thus essentially an index of their dissatisfaction with confederation and were not intended to indicate support for a particular policy. During the election campaign Killam continued to maintain that he opposed confederation but would attempt to gain 'as our right, a fair share of Dominion appropriations.'[43] If one year of agitation had forced the federal government to increase the provincial subsidy by $82,000, then it was his duty to his province to go to Ottawa and obtain even better terms.[44] Killam's campaign could give no immediate reassurance to the diehard 'repealers,' let alone to those who favoured joining the United States. Nevertheless his campaign was clearly a rejection of Howe's policy.

A victory for Killam in Yarmouth, which by March appeared to be a certainty, could easily sway voters in Hants, but there did not appear to be any way of postponing the election. John A. Macdonald decided he could not legally prevent the execution of the writ of election which had been issued on 1 February. Then, suddenly, the Nova Scotian attorney-general, Wilkins, informed Doyle that according to Nova Scotian law both elections had to be held simultaneously.[45] Wilkins may have intervened only to show he knew more law than Macdonald or may have hoped to force Howe to advance the date of the Hants by-election. The confederates had no intention of doing this but five days before the Yarmouth contest Tupper sent Wilkins' legal opinion, without any comment of his own, to W.B. Townsend, the sheriff of Yarmouth who was a known supporter of confederation.[46] Time was short but C. Schreiber, a surveyor for the proposed railway from Annapolis to Yarmouth, agreed to deliver the messages to Townsend. Travelling by coach, snow shoes, and horseback through one of the worst storms of the winter, he arrived in Yarmouth on the eve of the election[47] and persuaded the sheriff to postpone the election. Doyle's role in the incident could have provoked a quarrel with the cabinet because the governor had acted without the authority of his ministers. Before anyone could take exception to the governor's actions, however, Wilkins burst into print with a letter in which he assumed full responsibility for the postponed election.[48]

While attention was focused on Hants and Yarmouth, a third federal by-election became necessary when W.J. Croke, a young lawyer who represented Richmond county, died after an extended illness. Richmond was a particularly difficult county to manage even at the best of times because its peculiar mixture of Scots, Irish, Acadians, and Huguenots created many internal problems.[49] The confederates were particularly ill-prepared to contest Richmond in the winter of 1869 since the leading confederate in the county, Senator William Miller, was not prepared to help his party which he felt had consistently neglected and ignored him since 1867. Although he considered his seat in the Senate a dubious honour, he was not tempted by Tupper's suggestions that he should resign and contest the by-election.[50] The most he would do was to help organize an election committee made up of business and professional people.[51] He then invited W.A. Henry to stand as a candidate.[52] Henry was well known in Cape Breton Island through his extensive law practice, but because of his role as a Father of Confederation he was a prime target for the anti-confederates.

Henry's opponent was Isaac Le Vesconte, a Huguenot, who had represented the county as a Conservative from 1863 to 1867 but had not contested the election of 1867. Le Vesconte, whom Howe described as 'a queer fish on whom no reliance can be placed,'[53] exploited the anti-union sentiment in the county to its fullest. On at least one occasion he even promised that if he were elected he would not go to Ottawa.[54] He was not likely to suggest violence or union with the United States, however, as he enjoyed the support of several priests, including the vicar-general of Arichat. This support was of particular significance to his campaign because of the large numbers of Roman Catholics in the county. Some of the influence of the priests was neutralized, however, when Archbishop Connolly, at the urging of Tupper, brought pressure to bear on the vicar-general to remain neutral in the campaign. Nevertheless, shortly after the archbishop's intervention Le Vesconte was able to make a fresh appeal to the Roman Catholics because a new regulation removed discriminations against teaching nuns and brothers trained outside the province. This new order proved effective in Richmond[56] but once the contest was over, opponents of the measures within the government prevented it from being implemented.[57]

Victories in Richmond and Yarmouth would have cheered the confederates, but the critical contest remained that of Hants. A defeat for Howe would check Macdonald's attempts to establish political control in the province. With so much at stake, the by-election promised from the very beginning to be extremely costly. Howe estimated that his opponents would spend at least $20,000, which would be raised principally in Halifax. Some of Howe's friends could raise funds in Halifax and Sir Edward Kenny reckoned that he would be able to collect $4000 from the confederates.[58] Howe had no need to worry about money, however. He received $1425 raised by Sir John Rose in Montreal[59] and $11,575 drawn by Macdonald from the government's secret service fund.[60] Also, Alexander Mackenzie, a prominent Ontario Reformer, maintained that a levy of $1000 had been imposed on each cabinet minister and that some private members of parliament had each donated $100.[61] While these rumours of a general assessment on the cabinet may have been true, they may also have been deliberately circulated to explain the origin of Howe's election fund. If Mackenzie's claims were correct, however, Howe's campaign may have cost over $30,000 and the two parties together probably spent in excess of $50,000. This was a staggering sum in view of the fact that there were only some 3000 registered voters in the county.

It was apparent that a large percentage of the election fund was being used to buy votes. So extreme and open was the bribery that S.L. Tilley warned Howe to use care lest he be unseated by a parliamentary committee.[62] Outright buying of votes did take place but this was restricted to an estimated 130 electors who were openly offering their services to the highest bidder.[63] Much more common than direct payment for votes received was the device of paying generous amounts for goods and services. It was later contended, with a strong dash of hyperbole, that the Repeal League purchased 'pigs and cattle ... at fabulous prices to such an extent that it is expected the League will shortly open an Agricultural show. Shingles were bought at prices that gave the Goudge committee the monopoly of the market. Flour was to be had for the truckage ...'[64] Considerable emphasis was also placed on political patronage. The Goudge committee, because of the support of the local government, was able to offer road grants and commissions for work on the county roads. The cumulative effect was important, but many of the specific requests seemed small and insignificant. Tupper, for example, was asked to have a postman's salary increased to $100 a year both because it would be a simple act of justice and because it would bring Howe four or five votes from grateful relatives.[65] While many voters were wooed with offers of favours, some were subjected to threats and intimidation. One man who defied the instructions of a creditor and voted for Howe found himself jailed as a debtor.[66] This type of incident had been common enough in the past and little had ever been done about it. Yet the bribery and intimidation used in the Hants by-election was of a scope never seen before in a single county.

When three by-elections were finally held on 20 April a verdict was returned on the 'better terms.' The importance of the election in Hants, combined with the fierce campaigning, produced a turnout of almost 80 per cent at the polls, an increase over 1867. Howe carried all but one of the fourteen polling divisions in the county but his majority of 313 out of a total vote of 2141 was less than that of 1867.[67] This victory enabled him to continue with the task of pacifying the province by working through the federal government rather than through the provincial ministry. The victory of Frank Killam in Yarmouth, however, indicated that this course might have to be altered in detail. The only consolation which the defeated confederate candidate, N.K. Clements, could find in the results, and that a rather dismal one, was that one-third of the registered voters had stayed away from the polls.[68] Howe could not have been reassured by Killam's election, but the victory was more an indication of a demand for greater protection of provincial interests than a triumph for the extremists who would work for union with the United States. Paradoxically, the chief challenge to Howe's programme was probably in Richmond county where Henry was defeated by Le Vesconte after a vigorous campaign.[69] The latter would probably reject Howe's leadership but he was likely to do so in sullen isolation where he could do Howe no harm. Henry, however, who had considerable influence among the confederates, heartily detested Howe. Had he won the election he would have been in a stronger position to fan the smouldering dislike that many confederates still harboured for Howe and his followers. The election results of the three counties thus did not produce any clear alternative to the course proposed by Howe, but they scarcely represented a triumph for him.

It was significant that Howe, who had considered confederation as the ruination of Nova Scotia, would seek to protect the interests of his province through the federal government and would oppose so strongly the local government's position as the protector of the province. He did not see the question in that light and the by-election merely confirmed his belief that he was fighting the forces of disloyalty. He continued to believe that he could gain political mastery of the province through the power of the federal government without the slightest concession to his opponents. When he received a request for a position on behalf of a former supporter who had been involved with the Repeal League, Howe flatly refused to help him. 'The great Party now forming,' he informed his petitioner, 'will, I think govern this country for some years, and the fools who have tried to crush me, will, or I am much mistaken find themselves, before long, crushed under its weight.'[70] His bitterness was perhaps understandable, but the fact remained that the 'better terms' agreement had not been as successful as he believed.

LEGISLATIVE MANŒUVRINGS

With the by-elections over, the provincial government had to make some hurried preparations to meet the legislature which was scheduled to begin its session on 29 April. The ministry really needed more time to decide upon a policy towards confederation, but the session, which had already been postponed because of the government's preoccupation with the contest in Hants, could not be delayed further. There was even a faint possibility that the ministry would not be allowed to formulate a policy, as Doyle was under pressure from Howe to dismiss his government.[71] Doyle was reluctant to try such a potentially hazardous experiment,[72] and Tupper agreed that it should not be attempted without the possibility of finding a more reasonable replacement. Doyle tried to persuade two of the known moderates in the ministry, Vail and Robertson, to form a new government, but when they refused he decided to allow his existing ministry to work out their political differences.[73] The government did not find the task an easy one, and the Speech from the Throne contained no reference to a provincial policy towards confederation.[74]

It took two weeks of debate in caucus[75] before Wilkins was able to announce the government's new policy. With a gesture towards the more extreme members, he declared that Nova Scotia would never be content until it was released from union. Repeal of union remained the ultimate goal of the government, but, he hastened to add, it would not be achieved for some time because of the obstinate opposition of Great Britain. With the release from union somewhat delayed, it therefore became the duty of the government to seek greater protection for the people of Nova Scotia. As one means of achieving this end, he indicated that Nova Scotia and New Brunswick should together be granted a number of seats in the federal House of Commons equal to those granted to Quebec. To provide for additional protection of the province, the provincial legislature should appoint the provincial representatives in the Senate. The 'better terms' arranged by Howe would be accepted, but no settlement of the provincial claims would be complete until the role of the province was enlarged. As a guarantee of good faith and as a symbolic recognition of the ultimate power of the government, Wilkins pledged that no settlement with the federal government would be final until there was a reference to the people.[76]

Despite Wilkins' effort to conceal the intentions of the government behind the facade of irreconcilable hostility to union, the declaration of policy was a victory for the more moderate men in the ministry. W.B. Vail made no attempt to hide his view that the government's policy was an acknowledgment that repeal was no longer practicable.[77] He was immediately challenged by William Kidston, one of the seven who adopted an extreme stand, who denied that anything had changed in the previous eighteen months. Kidston was probably one of those who had never thought England would willingly grant repeal and who held that union with the United States would be the only feasible way out of confederation.[78] The appeal of the malcontents was limited, but they were able to show up the defects in the government's avowed policy. It did take a peculiar act of faith to believe sincerely that Nova Scotia could force the federal government to make the changes in the constitution demanded by Wilkins.[79] It was obvious, according to Chambers of Colchester, that the government was being hypocritical and attempting to deceive the people.[80] Yet much of the opposition to union had amounted to a demand that Nova Scotia should have more influence within confederation, either directly at the federal level or through a more positive recognition of the role of the provincial government. Although the specific demands outlined by Wilkins would not be met, they did clearly commit the ministry to seek some mark of recognition of the provincial government from the federal government.

The specific proposals might thus be unsatisfactory, but few of the members in the assembly were prepared to dispute their general direction and implied purpose. Even the two former anti-confederates in the house, Amos Purdy of Cumberland and Jeremiah Northup, who supported the 'better terms,' did not try to defend Macdonald's concept of federal-provincial relations. Rather, most members appeared concerned lest their support of the government's policies be construed as a betrayal of their province. After an extended debate the members approved the government's policies on union by a vote of twenty-five to seven.[81] Some of the more determined opponents of confederation, however, were not to be easily silenced. Following the vote on the government's policies, Dr Murray introduced a petition from Pictou county which requested that the legislature appoint a committee to determine what terms of union Nova Scotia could receive from the United States.[82] The petition caused such confusion and consternation that Murray finally withdrew it. He was not yet subdued, however, because he subsequently moved a motion that the house petition the queen either to permit Nova Scotia to leave federation or release the province from its allegiance to the British crown. This was too flagrant a case of disloyalty for the comfort of the government, and Vail promptly prevented debate by moving the previous question.[83]

Dr Murray's insistence on putting himself forward as the spokesman for the unconverted opponents of confederation posed a problem for Wilkins, who also represented Pictou county. Probably as a means of counteracting any impact Dr Murray may have made in Pictou, Wilkins decided to have the Act of Union tested in the courts. From a legal point of view Wilkins' case appeared unsound, and from a political view it appeared unwise as it would keep alive the agitation against union. The cabinet refused to approve of the proposal, but Wilkins proceeded to introduce it into the assembly, not in his capacity as attorney-general but in his role as member for Pictou. He angrily informed the members that a vote against his resolution was a vote for union. Enough members agreed with him to pass the resolution by a vote of sixteen to fourteen.[84] The next day, however, in secret session, enough members stayed away from the house to enable the remainder to rescind approval of the motion by a vote of fourteen to twelve.[85] Although Wilkins' resolution was defeated by a narrow majority, the majority of the members did indicate that they were no longer prepared to continue with the campaign to repeal the Act of Union. A number were obviously dissatisfied, but the overwhelming majority supported the government's plan to improve the position of the province within confederation.

Bitterness engendered by the issue of repeal seeped into the general conduct of the house during the session and some members engaged in open quarrels with each other. In the opening days of the session Vail took part in a running battle with the Speaker. When J.K. Ryerson also began to criticize the Speaker, the latter left his chair and walked out of the chamber.[86] The member who was most often in difficulties, however, was Wilkins. Not only was his attempt to keep alive the repeal agitation rejected but some of his other proposals were also turned down. The members capped their treatment of Wilkins by criticizing the manner in which he handled his duties as attorney-general. He was not humbled by this criticism and on one occasion publicly criticized the premier.[87] By the end of the session, however, it was apparent he would like to leave politics, but was determined not to resign until he received an appointment to the provincial Supreme Court.[88] Appointments to the bench, however, were made by the federal government, and it was unlikely that Macdonald would ever select Wilkins. He would probably remain within the cabinet, therefore, even though he was in open disagreement with some of his colleagues and was distrusted by some members of the assembly.

Disagreements among the members were to be expected, not only because of dissension over confederation but also because they had little in common except their opposition to union. There were few indications, though, that the provincial party might disintegrate. Although several members had objected to the government's policies towards confederation, they were unwilling to go into opposition or try to force changes in the personnel of the ministry. Of the seven members who rejected the government's provincial rights campaign, only one, William Kidston, actually left the government caucus.[89] There were also some members who would have preferred a more straightforward declaration of the acceptance of union by the provincial cabinet.[90] Supporters of the latter approach, however, were particularly unlikely to go into opposition. During the session only two members, Northup, who had conducted Howe's campaign, and Purdy of Cumberland actually supported 'better terms.' Northup had a measure of protection because of his friendship with Howe. When Purdy broke with the provincial government he discovered that his overtures to the confederates were rejected and found himself politically isolated in his county. What gave this incident an added significance was the fact that Cumberland was represented at the federal level by Tupper. The fate of Purdy therefore stood as a warning to the anti-confederates that they should either support the provincial government or face political extinction.[91] The continued survival of the party was partly the result of choice but a strong measure of necessity was also present.

To a major extent the survival of the local government and the provincial party was the result of the tactics followed by Howe and Macdonald in arranging the concessions to the province. Macdonald had intended as early as the summer of 1869 to break the anti-confederate party into federal and provincial factions as a means of establishing the supremacy of the federal government. However, he had miscalculated the strength of the provincial government and had neglected to consider the antipathy of the confederates towards their opponents. Although Tupper and other confederates had worked hard to elect Howe, they had not shown the same enthusiasm towards other anti-confederates. Thus, many anti-confederates, who were already uneasy because they wanted a larger role for their province within confederation, were discouraged from following Howe.

7
A time for reassessment

The strategy for bringing about the political reconciliation of Nova Scotia was unfolding slowly and with unexpected quirks. The federal government still enjoyed some initiative, but politically its policies had become diffuse. The resulting lack of focus helped foster a sense of dissatisfaction among all political factions in Nova Scotia. No one group had clear control or even any coherent policy. The mark of the time seemed to be equivocation and pragmatism. Yet the seriousness of the problems facing the federal and provincial politicians as they sought to establish policies suited to their new situation remained undiminished.

The final stage in confirming the revised terms of union for Nova Scotia was reached in the summer of 1869 when the federal parliament, with some hesitation, formally approved 'better terms.' The Liberal party mounted a strong attack on the terms and also on the government's management of the subsidy revision, which in turn made it difficult for the Nova Scotian members to favour that party. Moreover, the provincial government lost the support it needed at the federal level for the concessions it sought from Ottawa. If it were to be isolated in federal politics, the local government could easily develop the theme that it was the only true protector of the province. Adoption of this approach, however, would merely emphasize its separation from federal politics and prevent the development of a tie with the Liberals.

The revised terms of union were introduced into the federal House of Commons by John A. Macdonald on 4 June 1869 and debate began a week later. The terms of the bill followed the concessions previously agreed to by Howe and the federal cabinet and provided Nova Scotia with an increase in its debt allowance as well as a special addition to its annual subsidy, which was to be retroactive to the beginning of confederation and was to run for ten years. In an obvious attempt to deprive Annand of the advantage of being able to dispose of a relatively large sum of public funds, the amount which was due from July 1867 to July 1869 was not to be turned over to the provincial government until 1876. A more direct form of pressure was contained in another clause which stipulated that the federal government would withhold interest on the total sum spent on the new provincial building in Halifax until it took possession of the building from the local ministry.[1]

The question of how the Act of Union should be revised produced sharply divided opinions, with most of the attacks on Macdonald's methods coming from the Ontario Liberals. The latter contended that all the provinces had to be involved in any alteration of the constitution; and one member declared that the federal government could not unilaterally revise the Act of Union, because 'union was held to be a compact, or treaty between the Provinces, merely homologated by the Supreme Power.'[2] In bringing forth the compact theory the Liberals were mainly concerned with preventing the federal government from making future indiscriminate grants to other provinces, particularly Quebec. If the federal government were free to revise the terms of union, then it would be able to slide out of future political crises with grease from the federal treasury. As one means of controlling the federal government, a member suggested that the negotiations for the Nova Scotian subsidy should have been conducted by the dominion and provincial governments and then have been submitted to the provincial legislatures. Had these legislatures given almost unanimous consent, then the revised terms could have been sent for ratification to the imperial parliament without any reference to the Canadian parliament.[3]

The Liberals, in arguing that the provinces should control any revisions of the Act of Union, shaped their objections into a defence of federalism. This should have appealed to the Nova Scotian members, who wanted the provincial government to be involved in the negotiations for 'better terms.' The Liberal version of the 'compact' theory, however, gave the upper provinces a virtual veto power over Nova Scotia. The Nova Scotian members expected no particular goodwill from the other provinces and they wanted some doctrine which would recognise the interests of their province and provide a role for their provincial government, without subjecting Nova Scotia to the control of the other provinces. Members, such as Frank Killam of Yarmouth and Le Vesconte of Richmond who had recently run successful by-election campaigns in opposition to the 'better terms,' found themselves in opposition both to the Liberal party and the federal government concerning the methods used to arrange for concessions to Nova Scotia. Furthermore, they were even more dissatisfied over the amount of the terms. Some of the Nova Scotians took it for granted that their province deserved further concessions. However, Edward Blake, a leading Ontario Liberal, moved an amendment to the bill, which was quickly accepted by Macdonald, that the concessions were to be in 'full settlement of all demands on Canada by Nova Scotia.'[4] This amendment may have been good tactics in Ontario, but it reduced the appeal of the Liberal party both to the Nova Scotian federal members and the members of the provincial government.

One important question raised by Blake was whether the Canadian parliament had the power to amend the constitution. He was obviously on firm ground in his contention that the Canadian parliament could not amend an imperial statute.[5] But, actually the 'better terms' bill was simply an exercise of the spending power of parliament and therefore within the constitutional powers of the Canadian parliament. There was no legal impediment to parliament's allotting federal funds as it saw fit, and any such grant did not legally become a part of the Act of Union. Blake's argument that the 'better terms' bill was a challenge to the stability of the constitution, however, was strengthened by the insistence of the government that the 'better terms' were indeed to be regarded as an amendment to the terms of union. When seen in that light a significant number of members agreed with Blake that the bill should be sent to the British parliament. E.M. McDonald of Lunenburg urged Howe to accept this position,[6] but he refused, believing that the federal government was the true successor to those governments which had initiated the compact to create the colonial union. According to this version of the compact theory the original governments had ceased to exist the instant the federal government was created. Thus, by insisting that only the federal government could amend a flaw in the original agreement, Howe was really emphasizing that once the colonies had come together in union they could no longer fall back into their constituent parts.

The federal cabinet was determined to push 'better terms' through the house, and it did manage, by resorting to extended sittings, to dispose of the bill in only four days of debate. Although some of the Nova Scotians thought the 'better terms' were inadequate, none of them voted to reject the terms or supported the amendments moved by Blake. After passage of the bill, the mood of many members, particularly the Ontario Liberals, remained so hostile to Nova Scotia that Howe did not seek any special grants for public works in his province for the remainder of the session.[7]

Amidst such animosity, the Nova Scotian members had little reason to ally themselves with the Liberals. Yet unless they were going to remain isolated in the house, they had to become associated gradually with one of the major parties. The cabinet encouraged this development by identifying as a party supporter any member who voted for the departmental budgets. The test was painless and the rewards were control of federal patronage at the county level. Thus, it was not surprising that by the end of the session a majority of the Nova Scotian members were ranked among the supporters of the government.

In accepting the support of the Nova Scotian members without regard to their political antecedents, the federal government was taking a calculated risk that it would be able, over a period of time, to create a unified party in Nova Scotia. The task would be difficult in view of the distrust between the confederates and the anti-confederates, particularly at the county level. Many of the federal members had run their election campaigns in 1867 in conjunction with the local members and they continued to rely on their former supporters. When dispensing patronage they therefore often rewarded supporters who also aided the local members.[8] One result of this in several counties was that federal patronage was given to supporters of the provincial government and not to the confederates. In practical terms this prevented the confederates from making a serious attack on the provincial government. At the same time it discouraged the provincial government from having any serious ambitions on the federal level. Thus, there was marked tendency for the development of both federal and provincial parties, even though the federal party remained unstable because of the continuing animosity between the confederates and the 'compromisers' who followed Howe.

The frictions within the federal party were particularly acute at the end of the parliamentary session as various 'compromisers' received positions in accordance with the agreement with Howe. Each 'compromiser' appointed to office meant another supporter of Tupper denied a position. Tupper had agreed to this policy, but in practice each appointment was a blow to his influence in the province. In several instances his promises to various supporters were broken as some 'compromiser' was appointed instead. Tupper's frustration came to a head when he attempted to have his son-in-law, Captain R.D. Cameron of the British army, appointed as director of prisons in Nova Scotia. Howe had promised the position to James A. King, a Conservative who had opposed Howe in the 1867 election but, through Tupper's intervention, worked on his behalf in the 1869 by-election. Although King, a farmer, was probably little qualified for the position, Howe insisted that he be appointed. Tupper fumed at Howe's 'base ingratitude' and complained that his wife was so worried about her daughter that she had been confined to bed for a week. Macdonald, unwilling to overrule Howe, decided that Cameron should become chief of police in the North-West Territories.[9] This proved to be only a temporary solution because Captain Cameron was caught in the Riel Rebellion and Tupper had to scurry out to Fort Garry to protect his daughter.[10] Tupper, an indulgent parent, thus found his personal affairs, as well as his political position, obstructed and damaged by the political coalition with Howe.

Included in the offices made available to Howe was a patronage-rich position on the commission authorized to construct the Intercolonial Railway. This particular post was sought by A.W. McLelan, federal member for Colchester county, who, in order to be appointed to a salaried position, had to resign his seat and move to the Senate. This forced a by-election in Colchester, and McLelan immediately began to use his railway patronage to control the election. He did not care who his supporters worked with, as long as they agreed to uphold the federal government.[11] He succeeded in winning some followers,[12] but they showed a greater preference for working with supporters of the provincial party than with the original unionists in the county, led by A.G. Archibald. When a faction of the 'compromisers' endorsed F.M. Pearson, who refused to support confederation although he promised to give independent aid to the federal government,[13] Archibald decided he would come out as a candidate himself.[14]

Archibald had hesitated to return to active politics, partly because he had exhausted his personal finances in the 1867 election. The expenses now were unlikely to equal those of Howe's contest in 1869, but Archibald needed more funds than Tupper could raise in Halifax. Hiram Hyde learned of Archibald's difficulty and offered him $3000 if he would help Hyde settle a dispute over a government contract to provide fuel wood to the Pictou railway. The government wanted to cancel the contract and, although Hyde had not met his terms, he indicated he wanted $40,000 compensation. Macdonald advanced $3000 on the contract and Hyde turned the money over to Archibald, but Macdonald refused to complete the deal until after the election.[15] Hyde made a further donation of $1000 to Archibald in an attempt to hasten a verdict,[16] but it was not until after the election that the federal cabinet agreed to settle the contract for a little under $20,000.[17]

The actual election campaign followed a predictable pattern. Archibald toured the county assuring his listeners that the election would not take place until late fall. Then nomination day was suddenly held early in September. The Pearson committee was expecting this move and was ready to offer the usual favours. Their campaign chest consisted mainly of $4000 raised by the Repeal League in Halifax and another $4000 from the 1870 road money for the county.[18] Archibald was never seriously concerned about the challenge from Pearson, although he did spend a large sum of money 'which may not have been necessary and far exceeded anything contemplated at first.'[19] He succeeded in turning a deficit of 360 votes in the 1867 election into a plurality of 355 in the by-election. Archibald discounted the contribution made by McLelan and boasted that he had finally settled the question of confederation in Nova Scotia. His claims were exaggerated, but he had delivered another blow to the hopes of the provincial government. One fact which he had clearly demonstrated, however, was that continuing tension existed between the confederates and the 'compromisers.'

Despite Archibald's victory, the local government still had considerable influence in the province. Its political future was uncertain, however, since Doyle might dismiss the ministry if its position appeared to be deteriorating. Convinced that their offices were in jeopardy, the ministry felt compelled to make an occasional gesture of defiance against confederation. A suitable occasion arose in August during the Colchester by-election when Governor General Lord Lisgar decided to visit Halifax. A public meeting was called to make the necessary arrangements to receive the governor general, but Jones, supported by a noisy band of anti-confederates, broke up the proceedings. The *Morning Chronicle* joined in the criticism of the visit,[20] and none of the provincial cabinet ministers attended the official reception at the lieutenant-governor's residence. In retaliation for the criticism of the governor general, two of the military messes in the city cancelled their subscriptions to the *Morning Chronicle*.[21] The confederates also resorted to claims of sedition against Jones, who was charged with having stated that he would cheer when the British flag was pulled down from Citadel Hill and replaced by another.[22] The entire incident was ridiculous, but it also had an ironical twist, since during the American Civil War Jones had been noted for his support of the South.

The response to the staged uproar over the visit of the governor general satisfied Annand that he could still rely on discontent over confederation. He decided to seek disolution of the legislature, but Doyle refused to agree to a general election.[23] Annand made no real protest over this setback, perhaps because he would have been criticized by his own supporters if he had called an election. His purpose was probably served when he discovered that the confederates did not want a general election. If they were unwilling to face a contest, it was possible that the federal government might be willing to reach some sort of accord with the local government. Annand thought he had discovered a way to explore this possibility when he learned that Doyle planned to go to Ottawa early in October in order to meet Prince Arthur, who was then visiting Canada. Acting on impulse, Annand requested Doyle to find out if Macdonald would agree to the establishment of a joint committee of the federal and provincial governments to consider the constitutional changes proposed by the local legislature the previous June. Doyle agreed, but after he left Halifax he decided that in acting as an agent for Annand he was by implication supporting the provincial government. Doyle, as a military officer, refused to be identified with opposition to British policy. Moreover, in this instance he agreed with Macdonald that the provincial government had no constitutional right to discuss the powers of the federal government. On arriving in Annapolis he telegraphed Annand to determine what he would do if Macdonald declared that the constitution should not be discussed by the legislature.[24] In reply Annand indicated that any decision of a joint committee regarding the request for additional financial concessions would be submitted to the legislature. With respect to the constitution, Annand agreed that it would not be discussed in the legislature but argued that provincial ministers, as members of a joint committee, might deal with it if it arose in discussion. He urged Doyle to keep the whole affair confidential, however, because he had not discussed the subject with all the members of his cabinet.[25] Doyle received this reply in Saint John, and as he thought about the answer Tupper unexpectedly appeared. The two men agreed that Annand really had some devious stratagem and that Doyle should have nothing further to do with the mission. As a result Doyle developed a sudden case of 'sea-sickness' from crossing the Bay of Fundy which required his immediate return to Halifax, via the Bay of Fundy, to recuperate.[26]

Doyle's nervousness that he might be seen as a supporter of the provincial ministry did make it appear that he was acting as the conscientious agent of the federal government as envisaged by Macdonald. His primary concern, however, was probably to ensure that imperial policies respecting colonial union were carried out. On issues affecting union Doyle could be critical of Macdonald and on other issues he sometimes supported his ministry, or, as often seemed the case, had no particular opinion.

Doyle's fear of Annand's motives was unfounded, for Annand was determined to reach a settlement with the federal government. Shortly after Doyle's return to Halifax, the Executive Council, on 15 October, issued a formal minute of council calling for the establishment of a joint committee 'to arbitrate upon the unsettled accounts between the Province and Dominion,' as well as to review the entire case of debt subsidies and assets of Nova Scotia.[27] Significantly omitted from this minute was any reference to the subject of constitutional revisions which had bothered Doyle. Thus, in order to meet the possible objections of Macdonald, the government was prepared to disregard the resolutions passed by the legislature at its instigation the previous June. What the government wanted were some financial concessions which it could use to justify its opposition to the 'better terms' and also some device, such as a joint commission, which would be proof that it could deal as an equal, on at least a limited range of subjects, with the federal government.

Early in November Vail took this minute of council with him on a trip to Ottawa, but neither Howe nor Macdonald would commit themselves on the joint commission. The government had no intention of agreeing to a concession on a point they regarded as affecting the entire constitutional position of the provincial ministry. After delaying a month, Macdonald informed Vail that the 'better terms' act of 1869 prevented him from considering any new claim from Nova Scotia. If it were merely a question of settling accounts, however, then he would be quite prepared to consider any written communications or even private visits.[28] Thus the obstacle was not one of additional money, but the method to be used in arriving at any new adjustment. Macdonald was determined to adhere to his policy, adopted in the summer of 1868, of refusing to treat with the provincial government.

While in Ottawa Vail did manage to settle one or two small items in the province's favour, but despite support from McLelan[29] he had no success concerning a pier in his county of Digby which had been damaged in a storm. Since no provincial funds were available for repair work, Vail wanted federal assistance, but the entire question of federal aid to public works in the various provinces was still unsettled. Prior to union the usual practice in Nova Scotia had been for interested parties to raise money, perhaps up to two-thirds of the estimated cost of the project, and for the provincial government to contribute the remainder.[30] The provincial treasury could no longer handle such projects and the Nova Scotians automatically turned to Ottawa. In an attempt to find some policy to handle the different needs of the provinces, the federal government decided in 1869 to establish a commission to look into the question. The commission was not appointed until 1870, but even if guidelines had been established it was unlikely that Howe would have agreed to ease Vail out of a political embarrassment.[31]

In attempting to come to terms with the federal government, the local ministry was trying, however awkwardly, to move away from its old repeal policy. The provincial government had no real alternative to continuing its overtures to Ottawa, short of openly favouring union with the United States. Annand and his ministers had never favoured such a policy, but there were a few in the province who had. As repeal of the Act of Union became increasingly impossible, these people, identified in the press as annexationists, had to discard the slogans of repeal. The first avowed Annexation Society was formed in Halifax in June 1869,[32] although an anonymous writer to a Halifax paper claimed that such a society had been founded in 1868.[33] The origins of the society formed in June 1869 were obscure, but one account indicated it was composed of delegates from various counties. Supporters of the society were noticeably shy of publicity, and the only known name of the various officers was R. Wilson, probably a Halifax school teacher, who served as secretary. There were reports, published outside the province, that this group was merely the Repeal League in a new form.[34] The repeal society, however, included some of the wealthiest merchants in Halifax and, if they had become supporters of annexation, Doyle and some of the other confederates would have referred to it in their correspondence. Some members of the assembly attended a monthly meeting of the society in March 1870,[35] but it eventually passed away without benefit of an obituary column.

The Halifax Annexation Society was supposed to co-ordinate the campaign for annexation throughout the province, but one of the chief characteristics of this movement was its total disorganization. Robert McConnell, owner of the New Glasgow *Eastern Chronicle*, held a few meetings in Pictou in mid-summer. The first one, in which McConnell was joined by a tanner from New Glasgow, was held at Springville, a small farming community. McConnell estimated the attendance at 300 people. He then helped form the West River Annexation League at Durham, a few miles west of Springville, although he had to admit that the support was disappointing.[36] In promoting his annexation movement, McConnell was able to make use of his own paper and rely on the sympathy of both a federal member of parliament and one of the local members from the county. His principal appeal was to the farmers, and there appears to be little evidence to support any suggestion that a fall in coal sales, consequent upon the ending of the Civil War, produced an upsurge in annexation sentiment among unemployed miners.[37] Despite the decline in the coal market, optimism about the future of coal mining in the province remained high, as a number of new mines were being developed.[38] Some of these mines were owned by Americans, while others were financed by such Montreal capitalists as George Drummond, J.J.C. Abbott, and Sir Hugh Allan.[39] Some people in the coal-mining industry opposed confederation, but there is no reason to suppose that either the companies or the miners were particularly in favour of annexation. Indeed, as far as the miners are concerned it is probable that they took only a limited part in active politics at that time.[40]

During the fall of 1869 and the winter of 1870 McConnell arranged an occasional annexation meeting, but his activities made no particular impact on provincial politics. He might have had a greater influence if Yarmouth, long noted as the centre of annexation sentiment in the province, had taken part in the agitation. Throughout 1869, however, the supporters of annexation in Yarmouth remained quiet, and it was not until February 1870 that they began a series of four meetings.[41] If the annexation movement was the logical outcome of the opposition to confederation, then the height of this agitation should have occurred at the peak of dissatisfaction with confederation. Instead it occurred only after it was apparent that the provincial government had accepted confederation. Rather than leading to annexation, the opposition to union resulted principally in an attempt to preserve the interests of the province either through direct involvement at the federal level or by preserving a strong role for the provincial government.

Although support for union with the United States was limited, the agitation against confederation did make many Nova Scotians highly critical of Great Britain. The lesson of confederation, for some anti-confederates, was that England was willing to sacrifice its North American colonies for the sake of its own alleged interest. Such views had been heard in Nova Scotia since England had begun to support confederation. It was probably due to frustration, but as the campaign for repeal disappeared these complaints against England increased. One of the most extended criticisms of Great Britain appeared in the columns of E.M. McDonald's paper, the *Citizen*, and particularly in a series of letters written by a lawyer, Alexander James, under the pen-name of 'Bright.'[42] In one letter James wrote: 'If anything could rouse us to a manly sense of degradation of our position as colonists ... the forcible annexation of this Province to Canada by an act of the Imperial Parliament ought to be quite sufficient to satisfy us that we can enjoy neither honor nor safety under such a system.' He went on to say that England had the power to deprive the colonies of all their rights, even to the extent of propelling the provinces into a union with the United States.[43] Great Britain and the imperial tie were thus presented as a danger to the continued survival of the colonies rather than as their protector. Thus the only solution was to acquire the full rights of a self-governing people. It was an insult, continued the paper, that 'we cannot alter the constitution which is a basic right of free men. Every hour we remain in such a state is a time of degradation.'[44] This advocacy of independence, which was echoed by the *Morning Chronicle*, probably disturbed some of the confederates, but it actually enhanced the value of union because it meant that Nova Scotia would have to rely on the other provinces.

As 1869 drew to a close the political tone of the province underwent a gradual change and the politicians tried to adjust to confederation. Despite the federal government's refusal to co-operate, the local ministry continued to seek a replacement for its discredited policy of repeal. The feeling that the former policy had to be openly disowned appeared to be strong among party supporters, and especially among those who had financed the various costly and fruitless by-election campaigns. Thus, the government was perhaps attempting to stop the grumbling of its supporters when in December it reimbursed the old League of Maritime Provinces the sum of $6710.94, which had been raised in 1866 to finance the anti-confederation delegation to London.[45] The government claimed that this money was to be repaid to those who had donated money in 1866,[46] but actually the entire sum was kept by supporters of the local ministry and none was distributed to those who supported Howe.[47]

Nova Scotian reluctance to engage in any further defiance of confederation was reinforced in December 1869 by R.G. Haliburton, who believed that American politicians would try to encourage discontent in Nova Scotia by blocking trade with Canada. Haliburton, one of the original promoters of the Canada First movement,[48] was secretary of the Nova Scotian Coal Owners Association. He had been trying for some time to persuade the Canadian parliament to provide protection for Nova Scotia by placing a tariff on imports of American coal. At the same time he also wanted the American Congress to lower its tariff against Nova Scotian soft coal, but did not think this could happen until the repeal agitation was finally repudiated.[49] He persuaded Vail to have the government put pressure on supporting newspapers to come out against any talk of annexation. Haliburton's intervention particularly pleased Annand, who had a personal interest in increasing coal sales as he had recently acquired a valuable coal area on Cape Breton Island.[50] The need to develop Nova Scotian markets in the United States was also important to Annand, for he, like many other anti-confederates, considered that the Nova Scotian economy was dependent on the United States. He therefore decided that he should go to Washington as an official representative of Nova Scotia to attend American Congressional hearings on the tariff. When this proposal was raised in the cabinet, Doyle flatly refused to consider it, but Annand went to Washington anyway without formal authorization.[51] The fact that Annand was trying to disregard the constitutional powers of the province tended to overshadow the more significant point that he intended his trip as an affirmation of confederation.[52]

Annand's initiative on American duties on coal was probably influenced by his need to present the legislature, due to meet in February, with some new policy on confederation. The government was also concerned about the resolutions passed in the 1869 sessions calling for constitutional revision. Vail wanted proof that the government had been active, so he again pressed Macdonald for some concessions. He assured Macdonald that if the federal government would only come to an agreement on the new provincial building, as well as on the Digby pier, Vail would be able 'to convince the people that they are receiving something like justice in the financial point of view.'[53] Macdonald could see no reason for helping Vail fashion a new political strategy, and he was no more receptive to this appeal than to any previous one.[54]

Faced with Macdonald's refusal, the government had to meet the assembly with empty hands. But by 1870 the mood of the members had changed and they were no longer willing to engage in a violent outburst against Ottawa, nor so ready to condemn the local ministry for failing to protect the province.[55] They revealed this new attitude when they decided to amend certain pieces of legislation which had been passed the previous session and which Macdonald had ruled exceeded the powers of the province.[56] The silence of the members was in contrast to the objections raised by the *Citizen* the previous fall when it had protested against the federal government's scrutiny of every line of legislation passed by the province. If the right to veto by the federal government were to be exercised with any frequency, the *Citizen* had warned, then the provincial legislature would be a sham.[57]

The government did not seem to be interested in formulating a coherent theory of federal-provincial relations. Rather it appeared content to make haphazard gestures which could be taken as proof that it was the guardian of the province. Wilkins' proposal that the house establish a committee which would collect statistics and generally scrutinize the federal administration of the fisheries was typical of the government's approach.[58] The committee was appointed, but it did not submit a report and was not reappointed in 1871. Essentially the government wanted to participate in those areas which it happened to think at any given time to be important.

The government had some trouble in persuading the members to accept its policy, but after six or seven caucus meetings they decided to try again to reach a settlement with Ottawa.[59] This time, however, rather than asking for a joint committee which would discuss several subjects, Vail only requested that the question of the new provincial building be sent to arbitration.[60] Despite two appeals from Vail and support from Doyle,[61] Macdonald was not prepared to make any concession which would imply he had been wrong to exclude the provincial government from the negotiations for 'better terms.' He refused even to answer the new requests and the government had to restrain some of its more extreme supporters without any aid from Ottawa.

The most open challenge to the government came from Dr Murray of New Glasgow, who proposed that the assembly should embrace 'any opportunity that may occur of extricating the Province from the present confederation.' The government wanted to suppress Murray's resolutions, but it was forced to negotiate with him when it appeared that a number of members were prepared to support him. Some cabinet ministers, therefore, arranged with Murray that they would adopt the resolutions if the stronger clauses were deleted. In this revised form the resolutions amounted to the contention that if Nova Scotia were kept in confederation, it would be contrary 'to free constitutional principles, and natural and civil right and freedom.'[62] Carefully omitted from the resolution was any reference to a remedy for this awesome list of injustices.

Once the government had control of the resolutions, Wilkins scheduled debate for Saturday, 16 April 1870. This meant that there would be little time for debate since the assembly was due to close on the following Monday. Also scheduled for discussion on the same day was a controversial motion which condemned the entire commercial policy of the dominion.[63] The government's tactic worked because only half the members were present when Wilkins introduced the revised version of Dr Murray's resolution. Instead of hearing one of his familiar denunciations of confederation, they listened in surprise as Wilkins predicted that independence would lead to a republic, which would be unable 'to stand against a powerful military nation like the United States.' 'A policy of annexation,'

Wilkins instructed the members, 'would lead to the destruction of Nova Scotia and the collapse of the party.' The members accepted his warning and with little debate passed the motion without a division.[64]

The government knew quite well that some members were dissatisfied with its policy on union, but they in turn understood that there was no feasible alternative. During the session, however, the government had to contend with a religious quarrel involving schools which threatened to tear the party apart. This issue began when Theodore Rand, superintendent of education, ordered an investigation into a school, run by nuns, in Richmond county. The government had already decided to replace Rand but one government member, E.P. Flynn, a Roman Catholic and a representative for Richmond, pressed for his immediate dismissal. The government did not want a repetition of the religious quarrels of the 1850s and so decided to appoint a Baptist minister, the Rev. A. Hunt, who was the nominee of his cousin J.W. Johnston, in order to pacify the Catholics without unduly arousing the Protestants.[65]

Not all Protestants were appeased by the selection of Hunt and when Dr Murray attacked the ministry in the assembly, Vail exploded and stormed that Murray had given 'the government a stab in the weakest joint of their armour, and probed them to their very heart ...'[66] Doyle later wrote that the two men had called each other in plain language 'liars,' which would never have happened in the old days of 'coffee for one and pistols for two.'[67] Despite unrest among the members, Vail was able to impose party discipline, and the government was upheld on the Rand affair by a vote of thirty to three, with Dr Murray and Kidston of Victoria abstaining.[68] Although Vail tried to play down the religious overtones of the issue, the dismissal of Rand probably helped strengthen the government's appeal to Roman Catholics. The government thus emerged from the crisis stronger than it had been in some areas such as Halifax where the Catholic vote was important.

The only measure of any significance passed during the session was a bill which established the use of a secret ballot in provincial elections. Any ballot system would probably have been of limited benefit in the relatively small, stable population of Nova Scotia, where each man's political opinion was likely to be known by his neighbours. This bill was particularly defective because it did not provide for mandatory secrecy when the voter was depositing his ballot.[69] It was therefore principally a symbolic recognition of the right of each voter to participate in politics. Some members did not like the bill, and it passed principally because of a reaction to the unprecedented use of money in Howe's by-election. Some consoled themselves with the thought that the bill expressed the anti-confederates' belief that the authority of the legislature came from the voters as opposed to the confederates' reliance on force, intimidation, and Canadian money.

If the ballot bill had been really controversial, the government would probably have found some way to block it. This determination to avoid confrontation was behind the ministry's refusal to accept Wilkins' proposal to establish a county court system, which would function between the provincial Supreme Court and the 2000 justices of the peace. Although many of the justices could scarcely write their own names,[70] any attempt to strip them of their existing powers was certain to be opposed by members of the assembly, many of whom held the position themselves.[71] If Wilkins' bill, by some unlikely coincidence, did manage to pass, then the government would have to appoint some of the members to the new courts. This would force by-elections, which the government feared they might lose.[72] The cabinet, therefore, decided not to proceed with the measure, but Wilkins did relieve some of the pressure on the Supreme Court by bringing in a bill to add two judges to the bench.[73]

Although there were few bills of any significance passed during the session, the ministers might well have been satisfied with their work. They had persuaded a majority of the members to accept the fact of union and had avoided extended harangues about confederation. A somewhat similar development occurred in Ottawa, but here, as in Halifax, there was some resentment at the way in which confederation was forcing changes on the province. At one point William Chipman of Kings complained in the Commons that the consolidation of laws by the federal parliament was really an attempt 'to destroy, repeal or expunge the laws of Nova Scotia altogether.'[74] This feeling was shared by the confederates and, during the fall of 1869, Macdonald received bitter complaints from Archibald and Tupper about changes introduced in the Nova Scotian railway system.[75] Some changes were inevitable, but certain alterations, such as provision for a uniform currency, could be postponed for a time.[76] Several of the members were uneasy about the developments at Ottawa, but they were not yet able to arrive at any coherent approach to their political position in parliament, nor even to find out what it was.

Nova Scotia's relations with the rest of the dominion were particularly sensitive on matters relating to tariffs. The government had made a few concessions to the Maritimes in 1868, but no protection had been provided for coal mining, an industry which for many Nova Scotians was the key to future prosperity. In preparing the budget for 1870 the government decided to add a tariff of fifty cents a ton on imported coal. As soon as the budget was announced, the Ontario members raised such a furor in caucus that the government stated it would withdraw the proposed duty on coal, as well as a tariff of twenty-five cents a barrel on flour. This did not satisfy the Nova Scotian members, who declared that unless coal received protection they would vote against duties on all grain products. This move apparently had some effect and the government, after hurried negotiations with the Ontario members, reinstated its tariff proposals.[77]

In defending the tariff increases in the Commons, Tupper argued they were necessary to preserve the home market for Canadian products. There was no alternative to protection, he contended, because the United States had used high tariffs to close the American market to Canadian goods in an attempt to starve the Canadians into submission. Rounding out his arguments, he asked with a rhetorical flourish: 'Should we allow the best interests of the country to be sacrificed or uphold a bold national policy (cheers) which would promote the best interests of all our classes and fill our treasury?'[78] These comments echoed arguments which Haliburton of the Nova Scotian Coal Owners Association had been using for some time in an attempt to obtain some tariff protection for the Nova Scotian mines.[79] He found a ready listener in Tupper, who had not only shown a strong interest in coal mining as premier of the province but was part-owner of a valuable mining area in Cumberland county.

The actual amount of protection provided for the coal industry was slight, but it was significant that in debate Tupper relied heavily on economic nationalism to justify the tariffs. His resort to a national solution to promote interprovincial trade may have been designed partly as an answer to Annand's recent emphasis on the need for continental trade. Appeals to a 'national policy,' which Tupper had hinted at during the debates over confederation in 1865 and 1866, were becoming increasingly popular, but the controversy in the house over the tariff on coal showed the strength of regional interests.

During the parliamentary session the Nova Scotian members spoke only occasionally and then usually on matters of direct concern to their own province. Alexander Mackenzie tried to win over some of them, but he was frustrated when A.G. Jones of Halifax, one of the most outspoken opponents of Howe, failed to attend the session of 1870.[80] He also had difficulty in persuading the Nova Scotians to accept Liberal opposition to the 'better terms.' During the session of 1870 Edward Blake again criticized these concessions, and Mackenzie reassured the Nova Scotians that Blake was merely trying to prevent similar grants from being made to Quebec in the future.[81] His efforts were fruitless because by the end of the session only four Nova Scotians would attend a caucus of all opponents of the government, and two of these, Dr J.F. Forbes of Queens and Thomas Coffin of Shelburne, still felt a tie of loyalty to Howe.[82] Thus, most of the federal members were prepared to work with the government,[83] but it was by no means certain that they would prove to be reliable if the government needed their votes to stave off defeat in the house. For the time being, however, the 'better terms' appeared to have succeeded in bringing over a majority of the Nova Scotians to the government side of the house.

Any satisfaction experienced by the government over this result was probably marred by the existence of considerable dissension within the ranks of their supporters in Nova Scotia. Many confederates continued to feel that their claims for rewards had been disregarded because of the attempt to win over the anti-confederates. Not only had several anti-confederates been appointed to important offices, but in November 1869 Howe had been promoted to the position of secretary of state for the provinces. In the spring of 1870 Macdonald decided that Tupper, who shared the confederates' sense of grievance, should replace Edward Kenny in the cabinet. Macdonald's plans were delayed when he became seriously ill towards the close of the parliamentary session. Kenny remained in the cabinet, but was appointed as administrator of Nova Scotia while Doyle enjoyed a holiday in Ireland. Finally, in June, Kenny retired from the cabinet with the consolation of a knighthood. On 20 June Tupper took his place in the cabinet as president of the Privy Council and, as required by law, had to face a by-election. Tupper was not likely to find the contest a serious challenge because his opponents were badly split and demoralized. What the contest did confirm again was that a feeling of irritation, not to say disgust, extended throughout all political factions. Tupper discovered the strength of this feeling among his own supporters when he tried to enlist Alexander McFarlane, a former running-mate in the local house, as organizer of his by-election campaign. McFarlane agreed he would '*for this time* stand by and give you any aid I can,' but quickly added, 'I have long felt that our Province was but weakly represented in the Canadian Cabinet and that so far as the claims in interest of the Union party were concerned they were utterly destitute of influence ...'[84] Even with only partial support Tupper was able to carry the county by acclamation.

Tupper's entry into the cabinet helped soothe the irritation of some confederates, who were further reassured by Archibald's appointment as lieutenant-governor of Manitoba and the North-West Territories in May

1870. His selection, however, opened up Colchester county, and in the summer another by-election, the third federal contest in four years, had to be held. F.M. Pearson, defeated by Archibald in 1869, decided to seek the seat. Publicly he took the position that although he was opposed to union he would support the federal government. This was satisfactory to McLelan, and apparently to Tupper. Some local confederates still refused to accept any compromise, but their efforts to organize opposition failed when they were unable to obtain aid from Ottawa.

Pearson's campaign also offended some anti-confederates, who took their objections to Vail. Vail summoned Thomas Morrison, one of the 'compromisers' who had supported Pearson in 1869, to Halifax but Morrison returned in triumph, bringing with him an editorial from the *Morning Chronicle* which declared 'Unconditional and unceasing opposition to either government or opposition at Ottawa we look upon as sheer folly. Whoever is elected for Colchester – and the same remark will apply to all future elections – should be free and untrammelled, and prepared to sit independently upon every question that comes up for the consideration of the House.'[85] This acquiescence in the coalition between McLelan and Pearson was really an indication that the local ministry had no political ambitions outside of the province. In one sense Vail and Annand were expressing the view that the province stood alone within union and would have to depend on itself. Yet in professing complete neutrality towards federal politics they were really establishing a cover for informal co-operation at the county level with the 'compromisers' who supported the federal government. This undoubtedly had a practical attraction as it enabled the ministry to remain true to its professed opposition to confederation and still allow its supporters to enjoy federal patronage.

The local government's position was sufficiently unacceptable to Robert Chambers, one of the Colchester representatives in the local legislature, to persuade him to run against Pearson as an annexationist. Chambers, a Liberal and merchant by profession, was a rather pleasant old gentleman who considered it an insult to ask any man for his vote. He made some speeches in the county [86] and received the aid of a few county officials,[87] but he was unable to cope with Pearson's organization. On election day Pearson polled 1670 votes to only 268 for Chambers. Morrison later tried to represent Pearson's election as a great victory over McLelan, but Chambers dryly commented: 'if that can be called fighting I should like to fight myself, for the battle ended in a bottle of champagne and two or three dozen of port wine.'[88]

The coalition in Colchester provided a clear indication that the local government did not fear the opposition of the unconverted opponents of union. The government's policy suited its own particular needs, but it did not help supporters like A.G. Jones, who recognized the importance of federal politics and wanted to bring the Nova Scotian federal members over to the Liberals. Jones had helped arrange for Alexander Mackenzie to visit Halifax in July 1870,[89] but without the aid of the local ministry he was powerless. To be successful Jones would have to persuade the provincial government to face the realities of their situation.

The disagreement between Jones and the local ministry became public in November, during a by-election in Halifax to replace Northup, who had been appointed to the Senate. The government press began the campaign by asserting that it deserved the suppport of the voters because it had proven itself to be the protector of provincial interests within a confederation which was basically hostile to the province. Summing up this argument, the *Morning Chronicle* asserted: 'The local Government must of necessity be opposed to that of Ottawa in many things of the utmost importance. ... In matters of political opinions there never can be harmony between the two Governments. The members of that which rules Nova Scotia believe that the continuance of Union must prove a curse ...'[90] In placing the basic political division between Halifax and Ottawa, the local ministry was putting the emphasis on the relations between the governments rather than on political parties.

At a major political rally in Halifax, Jones countered the government's argument by pointing out that Nova Scotia had to be protected in Ottawa even more than in Halifax. It was in Ottawa, he emphasized, that the major decisions affecting Nova Scotia were made and the local government could never insulate the province against obnoxious federal policies. Nor could the Nova Scotian federal members form an independent bloc in the Commons without any tie with a Canadian federal party. The federal members, he warned his listeners, 'could do nothing but adorn the chariot wheels of one or another Canadian party.'[91] His arguments were promptly rejected by Patrick Power, the other federal member for the city. Power advocated the election of avowed opponents of union to both the federal and provincial houses. 'We have to depend upon ourselves,' he contended, because 'I can see no hope from the opposition coming into power at Ottawa; for they have opposed step by step and inch by inch every concession to Nova Scotia.' Even if, as Jones contended, the opposition to the 'better terms' was not based on Ontario sectionalism, Power did not see why Edward Blake should feel free to use Nova Scotia as a pawn in his quarrel with Quebec.[92] Actually Power was quite aware of the importance to Nova Scotia of federal politics, but he was in a quandary because he preferred to work with the federal government than with the federal Liberal party.[93] As a supporter of the local government, however, he did not feel free to admit as much, so he had to fall back on the old anti-confederation sentiment. His position might have been easier if the federal government had been more co-operative in the past towards the provincial government. There was no doubt that feeling in the province against union remained high but at least some of the contention that Nova Scotia stood alone in confederation was a specific reaction to the policies of both the federal government and the federal Liberal party.

The disagreement over the proper role of Nova Scotia within confederation overshadowed the actual by-election in Halifax. The Conservative candidate was P.C. Hill, a long-time supporter of union, who controlled the federal patronage in the city. His opponent was William Garvie, who after returning from his law studies in London a few months earlier had established a practice in Halifax. At the beginning of the campaign Howe was asked to support Hill, but he refused, partly out of loyalty to Garvie.[94] Thus, the election began as a struggle between the local government and the original unionists, but Garvie brought the 'compromisers' into the fray when he began to criticize Howe and to ridicule his former partner, E.M. McDonald.[95] This proved to be a costly blunder and helped defeat him. On election day Garvie lost by twenty-four votes, out of a total of 4290.[96] In contrast to the winning performance of the anti-confederates in the 1867 election, Garvie lost 200 votes in the eastern section of the county where J. Northup and other 'compromisers' had influence. In partial compensation for this, however, he received a larger share of the Irish vote in the city. Thus, the split in the Irish vote, which had begun in 1867, was still widening, although the bulk of the vote did go to the Conservative party. Garvie lost the election, but the margin of defeat was so narrow that the election did not result in any discernible shift on the political scene.

As a result of this by-election, the local government was unlikely to abandon its contention that the province was isolated within confederation. Its approach had some appeal to those who disliked confederation, but its main contention was that it had a right to be consulted by the federal government on matters of importance to itself. Its demands were limited, and on several occasions Vail and Annand had indicated they were prepared to accept a token gesture of recognition by the federal government. Given a warmer reception by Macdonald, or even by the

Liberals, the ministry might well have moderated its views about the hostile political climate. Any change, however, would probably have been limited because the local government seemed more interested in establishing relations with the federal government than with federal parties. Under cover of its form of provincialism, the ministry did permit an unofficial form of co-operation at the county level between its own supporters and the 'compromisers.' The polarization of Nova Scotian politics into federal and provincial parties was thus marked by the anomaly that several members who supported the federal government remained independent of the Conservative party. This produced tensions which were a potential threat to the political balance achieved by the 'better terms.'

8

The Treaty of Washington, Confederation, and Nova Scotia

THE PROVINCIAL LEGISLATIVE SESSION OF 1871

By 1871 the government and most of the members of the Nova Scotia legislature had accepted the fact of confederation. They were still dissatisfied at having been forced into union by Great Britain, they mistrusted Macdonald and his emphasis on the national interest, and, within their own province, they seemed incapable of forming a coherent and logical programme. In the year to come a British-American conference involving an issue of prime concern to Nova Scotians – the fisheries – demonstrated again that they must look to themselves for their own best interests; and the provincial election of 1872 returned the same government to power in the province.

For some years the provincial government had focussed its policy of confrontation with the federal government around the issue of the new provincial building. The local ministry insisted on retaining possession of this building until the federal government agreed to negotiate the allocation of its cost. The government's campaign had some political currency in the province, but Macdonald still refused to talk. He was able to ignore the provincial government partly because the federal Liberal party opposed any further concessions to Nova Scotia. However, this stand caused considerable antagonism in Nova Scotia and during a visit to Halifax Alexander Mackenzie tried to remove some of the ministry's irritation by promising to support the Nova Scotian argument on the provincial building.[1] Macdonald reacted to this shift in Liberal tactics by informing Annand that any further discussion of the building issue would be fruitless and that the issue would be settled in the forthcoming provincial election. The ministry was quite happy to accept this challenge and ordered 8000 copies of the relevant correspondence for use in the elections.² Macdonald's action was provocative, but it placed the responsibility for further concessions to Nova Scotia on the Liberal party. Thus, when the Liberals proposed in the Commons that the dispute be settled by arbitration, Macdonald was able to agree, without fear that the Liberals would be able to exploit this concession in Ontario.³ Macdonald was still not prepared to establish an arbitration board until after the provincial elections, but the provincial ministry had finally gained a small victory in its struggle with the federal government. The incident did establish a definite link between the provincial party and the federal Liberal party, but the provincial ministry was unlikely to acknowledge this bond prior to the provincial election.

It was the notion that Nova Scotia was under continuous attack within union that provided a convenient explanation for Wilkins' bill to prevent federal employees from being members of the assembly. He also used the same argument to justify a bill to disfranchise all federal employees in provincial elections. Although the bill would apply throughout the province, it would have the greatest impact in Halifax where it would remove about 250 names from the voters' list. Indeed, the bill had been inspired by P.C. Hill's election in Halifax the previous fall and was intended to ensure the victory of government candidates over Conservatives in the forthcoming elections.⁴ Employing ideas of class duties and responsibilities familiar to many of his listeners, Wilkins stated that since the servant had to obey his master, federal employees would have to vote as instructed by the federal government. It therefore followed, he concluded triumphantly, that the legislature, in depriving the federal employees of the ballot, was actually doing these Nova Scotians a favour as they would not be obliged to vote against the interests of their country.⁵

The disfranchisement bill passed through the assembly with little trouble, but it faced an uncertain reception in the upper house where the council was evenly divided into Conservatives and government supporters. There was a vacancy in the council and Annand broke the tie between the two parties by appointing his brother-in-law, Charles Dickie, to the seat.⁶ One member of the council, James McNab, however, had not attended the council for some time because of illness and his son, Peter McNab, offered his father's vote on the disfranchisement bill to whichever party would promise him a government position. He was soon in receipt of written promises from several leading Conservatives including Dr Parker, a member of the council, and the announced candidates for Halifax, P.C. Hill and M.B. Daly. It is possible that the whole campaign had been arranged by Annand, because Peter McNab promptly handed the correspondence with the Conservatives over to him. Annand soon had it printed and the citizens of Halifax were able to read assurances from Tupper that '... anything Hill engaged to do I will carry out.'[7]

The provincial government used the Peter McNab case as an example of the type of federal interference which the disfranchisement bill was intended to prevent. The affair was a tremendous embarrassment to the Conservatives in council and they were only able to amend the bill to include some provincial employees and to exclude some federal employees. These modifications, however, were insufficient to destroy the advantage sought by the provincial government in the Halifax riding.

The government's determination to disfranchise all federal employees was one indication of their lack of confidence in the Ballot Act. This measure, passed the previous session, had been presented by several members as a recognition of the responsibility of the legislature to the people. There remained considerable opposition, however, and both Wilkins and Vail were known proponents of the system of open voting. They therefore supported a proposal made by Henry Smith of Queens to abolish the secret ballot, which passed through the assembly by a vote of eighteen to fifteen.[8] Repeal of the Ballot Act, however, foundered in the upper house when a majority, perhaps out of sheer perversity, refused to pass the bill.[9]

The opposition to the secret ballot in the assembly irritated William Kidston, who believed that the basic lesson to be learned from the struggle over confederation was that the legislature had not been truly responsible to the people. As one means of preventing the legislature from ever again denying the people's will, he proposed that the upper house, as a centre of privilege, be abolished. He was not in favour of extending the franchise but did agree that those who had proven the right to be voters should have control of the legislature.[10] In Kidston's view, the anti-confederate party, as the 'People's Party,' should take immediate steps to ensure that the will of the majority prevail. His motion to abolish the upper house was supported by such members as Dr Murray of Pictou and Chambers of Colchester. It was significant that these three were also the most outspoken supporters of union with the United States. Kidston was answered by Wilkins, who denounced the tyranny of the majority and defended the need to protect social order and stability. In his opinion, Tupper's success in 1866 with union was not due to deficiency in the implementation of popular sovereignty but rather to the excessive centralization caused by the cabinet system. Although Wilkins mourned the passing of the old Family Compact, he did not suggest that the government's opposition to union committed it to altering the political institutions of the country. In rejecting Kidston's motion by seventeen to nine, the members also rejected the last attempt to use the opposition to union as a justification for majoritarian democratic policies.

By 1871 the government had not only rejected any association with radical political ideas but appeared unable to formulate a coherent and logical programme. Instead, it sought to mollify various groups and factions. The ministry's attempt to ignore the contradictions in its own policies was particularly evident in its school policies. Officially, the government continued to support the public school system established in 1864 and 1865, but at the same time it tolerated concessions to the Roman Catholics. When Dr Murray pointed out that the government was permitting 'de facto' Catholic separate schools in various parts of the province, he was read out of the party.[11]

Although the government seemed committed to a policy of conciliation, there was little doubt that it favoured the merchants and property owners. This support ranged from acting as a spokesman for the merchants in their fear of the recent changes which had swept the province, to the granting of generous plots of crown land and mining leases. These land grants to wealthy supporters upset Thomas Desbrisay, a lawyer from Lunenburg county, who from the opening day of the session attacked the government and forced it to publish a list of its grants which showed that in the course of a few weeks one family had received almost two thousand acres of crown lands.[12] Although the government had remained within the letter of the law by making most grants in blocks of five hundred acres, the total indicated that the intent of the law had been grossly evaded in order to reward its political friends. Vail and Wilkins were unhappy over Desbrisay's questions, yet he was too influential to expel from the party. The government finally agreed to tighten the regulations concerning timber lands, but the alterations were insufficient to pacify Desbrisay.[13] He could do little during the session of the legislature, but the coming provincial election might well create an opportunity for him to combine with other dissidents to embarrass the government.

The lack of a substantial official opposition party in the legislature, therefore, did not keep the government from criticism. Indeed, it is possible that the government was unable to maintain firm party discipline precisely because there was no alternative to the existing government. By the end of the session, however, the government seemed to be in control of the assembly. It was not vulnerable to attack on the issue of confederation, despite the considerable changes in its policy since 1868. A measure of just how much it had altered its stand on union was revealed by

Lieutenant-Governor Doyle at the close of the session when he instructed the members to foster 'a true and loyal regard for the institutions of the mother country to which we owe so much, and an answering attachment to the throne of England and the Sovereign who occupies it. While other countries are still suffering from the disastrous effects of the late war, and from the revolutionary spirit which has been awakened by it, we remain in the enjoyment of peace, plenty and security.'[14] Doyle had tried to include a similar statement in his speech at the close of the previous session, but the government had been afraid that his praise for the political institutions of England would be taken as oblique endorsement of confederation.[15] By the spring of 1871, however, the government had apparently decided that its acceptance of confederation had become so obvious that Doyle's speech would do little harm.

THE TREATY OF WASHINGTON AND NOVA SCOTIA

While the provincial legislature was still in session a joint commission, composed of five American and five British commissioners, met in Washington to establish harmonious relations between the United States and Great Britain. Included in the issues to be resolved were incidents arising out of the Civil War, commonly known under the generic title of the Alabama claims, which were of particular significance to Great Britain, and several matters concerning British North America. It was this combination of subjects which invited the suspicion that the British government would offer concessions on issues relating to North America in order to make the Americans more tractable on those which primarily concerned Great Britain. While the British government did not give the issues high priority, it did want the Canadians to be involved in the decisions in order to forestall any claim that the colonies had been betrayed by Great Britain. Thus, as a conciliatory gesture toward Canada, the British government included John A. Macdonald as one of the five British commissioners. Although he was supposed to protect Canadian interests, he nevertheless had to accept instructions from the British government.

The members of the provincial assembly were greatly concerned that the fisheries question was on the agenda for the Washington Conference. In 1866 the Nova Scotians had resented the Canadian initiative in implementing a system of licences for American fishermen; between 1868 and 1870 the Canadian government had gradually barred American fishermen from engaging in any trade in Maritime waters. Although the closing of Maritime waters to American fishermen suited Canadian interests, it disrupted the entire organization of the fisheries and placed the Nova Scotian merchants at a decided disadvantage to their American competitors.[16] What these merchants needed was an arrangement whereby American fishermen would have free access to Maritime waters and the merchants would be able to ship fish into the American market free of tariff. In the 1871 session P.C. Hill, the Conservative member for Halifax who had been elected the previous fall, tried to forestall a general criticism of Macdonald by moving a resolution which called on the federal government to gain full compensation for any concessions granted to the Americans. In reply, Martin I. Wilkins denied that the Canadians could be relied on to do justice to Nova Scotia. Canadian intentions, added W.B. Vail, were proven by the selection of Macdonald rather than Howe, who was thoroughly familiar with the value of the fisheries. He also took exception to the fact that Macdonald, when about to make decisions of vital importance to Nova Scotia, had not seen fit to consult with the provincial government. William Kidston even suggested that since England had indicated its wish to divest itself of its North American colonies, Nova Scotia should seek immediate entry into the United States.

At the actual conference in Washington, Macdonald's task was not made easier by the tendency of the American secretary of state, Hamilton Fish, to adopt a truculent tone towards Canada. Fish was even disposed to believe that if the British government could be persuaded to grant Canada its independence, the United States would soon bring its northern neighbour into line.[17] He opened the negotiations on the fisheries issue by offering a sum of money for the enjoyment in perpetuity of the Maritime inshore waters. He knew that Macdonald would reject these terms, so he offered as an alternative the free entry of salt, fish, coal, and firewood into the United States in return for entry into the Maritime waters.[18] He picked these items because they were of prime importance to New England and to the Maritimes, which were the two areas most affected by the fisheries question. In this way, the American secretary of state hoped to overcome Congressional opposition to any deviation from the protective tariff system.

The American offers, although influenced by American political pressures, did not take into account Macdonald's need to secure terms which would satisfy the upper provinces of Canada. His real objective was to obtain free trade in such Ontario products as wheat, livestock, and iron ore. The other British commissioners, holding dear their own belief in free trade, made no attempt to understand Macdonald's political problems and priorities. They indulged their own particular biases by urging

The Treaty of Washington, Confederation, and Nova Scotia 125

Macdonald to accept a cash settlement, accompanied perhaps by the elimination of the American tariff on Canadian fish. To forestall his fellow commissioners, Macdonald managed to secure a promise from the Colonial Office that the Canadian parliament would have to give its consent to those clauses of the settlement which directly affected Canada.[19] It was now essential for Macdonald to gain concessions of particular value to the upper provinces. He was therefore less than enthusiastic on 22 March when Fish revised his opening gambit and offered only trade concessions on salt, fish, lumber, and coal. Macdonald tried to gain time by demanding that the Americans open their coastal trade to Canadian vessels. He also persisted in his attempt to obtain terms of interest to the upper provinces, but on 25 March the other British commissioners decided to negotiate on the basis of the American offer.[20] Macdonald, supported by the Canadian cabinet succeeded, however, in persuading the British government to delay settlement of the fisheries question.

The delay was of doubtful value because on 12 April Hamilton Fish informed the British delegation that the American government would no longer consider making any concessions on lumber, salt, or coal. The Americans now offered the removal of the United States tariff on salt fish and a sum of money, in return for free entry into the inshore waters for an initial period of ten years, with two years' notice required for abrogation of the agreement. No definite sum could be set, however, as Congress was about to rise and the amount of compensation would have to be determined by arbitration at a later date. These terms disturbed Macdonald, but the British government decided the American offer would have to be accepted in order to settle the issue.[21] Macdonald considered resigning from the commission but on 8 May he signed the treaty along with the other commissioners. He thus failed in his attempt to gain terms of particular benefit to the upper provinces and in the process ignored the opportunity to gain terms of some value to the Maritimes. Hamilton Fish might well have withdrawn the terms relating to the Maritimes regardless of what Macdonald had done, but nonetheless Macdonald had spent much of the period of the negotiations trying to prevent his fellow British commissioners from exploring the possibilities opened by the initial American offers. The first reaction to the terms of the treaty in Ontario made it evident that Macdonald's efforts on behalf of the upper provinces were not going to receive much recognition. The reaction in Nova Scotia, while not particularly important to Macdonald, was not without some significance, especially since news that a treaty had been signed came in the midst of the provincial general election.

THE UNCERTAINTIES OF VICTORY

On 17 April, only three weeks after the close of the legislative session, the government agreed that the legislature should be dissolved and an election held on 15 May. In preparation for the election Annand decided that his cabinet, which had remained unaltered since 1867, should be reorganized. Some changes were to be expected, because Wilkins had been thinking of retiring from politics for some time. John A. Macdonald had considered appointing him to the bench but the consensus appeared to be that the government was weaker with Wilkins in it than out of it.[22] He therefore did not receive the appointment he wanted and had to be satisfied with the position of prothonotary of Halifax. To replace Wilkins as attorney-general Annand appointed Henry Smith of Queens. The latter, who opposed such innovations as the secret ballot, would appeal to the former Conservatives within the party, but he was much more flexible than Wilkins. In another change, Annand took the position of commissioner of public works and mines from the plodding Robert Robertson and gave it to William Garvie, who had been defeated in the Halifax by-election the previous fall. Finally, Annand promoted John Flynn, a Roman Catholic from Richmond county, from minister without portfolio to the newly established position of commissioner of crown lands.

In Doyle's opinion the changes in the cabinet made a decided improvement in the calibre of the government.[23] There was, however, no significant shift in the government's policy toward confederation. Confederation remained the most discussed subject in the newspapers, even though the government and its newspaper supporters did not hold out any possibility that Nova Scotia could be released from union. Actually, the *Morning Chronicle*, which was the leading government paper, had acknowledged for some time that union was a fact. Another paper, the *Acadian Recorder*, had been reluctant to admit this, but in April 1871 it declared: '... here is the fact staring us in the face that Union is an accomplished fact. What next? Can we have it repealed? Our belief – and we may as well say so once for all – we do not believe that it will ever be repealed. Admitting then for argument's sake, or for any other sake, that Union is fixed, settled and irrevocable, what it may be asked, have we to complain of in this political weather in which we live ... We complain then, that the Ottawa administration ... is essentially bad, dishonest, corrupt.'[24] A similar attitude was adopted by the *Citizen* which, owing to a recent change in ownership, had ceased to support the confederate party.[25]

The contention of the *Acadian Recorder* that Nova Scotia's complaint was with the corruption of the federal government provided a rationalization for a political alliance with the Ontario Liberals. The suggestion that Nova Scotia was threatened by specific policies adopted by a particular Canadian party did indicate that the provincial government was beginning to adjust its public policies to the growing, but still tenuous, ties with the federal Liberal party. During the election campaign, however, the provincial government press preferred to argue that although the federal government used corrupt means, it was really carrying out the basic aims of Ontario. The *Morning Chronicle* held that the acquisition of British Columbia and the construction of a transcontinental railway were really to satisfy the ambitions of Ontario, but the cost would be borne by all of Canada.[26] Essentially the contention was that any alleged national policy would disregard the distinct sectional nature of the country. Rather than assume extremely costly burdens of benefit to one region, the *Morning Chronicle* argued, in effect, that the federal government should support smaller projects which were adapted to the needs of the different regions of the country. The government press, however, did not suggest that the federal government would alter its self-proclaimed programme of nation-building. Instead, it preferred to present the upper Canadians as hostile to the Maritimes and determined to seek their own ends regardless of the cost to the rest of the country.

The government press really began to develop its contention of Canadian hostility when reports reached the province about the fishery clauses of the Treaty of Washington. The *Morning Chronicle* wasted no time in declaring that the exchange of the Maritime fisheries for an undetermined sum of money was a betrayal of the province. 'We have been robbed,' declared the *Morning Chronicle*, 'of our independent government by Canada and it is now proposed to take the bread out of our mouths. It will not be done quietly or without driving the Province to the verge of separation.'[27] The tone was strident, but the paper was careful not to indicate that separation of the province was a probability or that the treaty would not be ratified. Actually, as the confederate newspapers pointed out, the government press should have been satisfied with the proposed terms, because for some time it had been denouncing the federal government for disrupting trade by excluding American fishermen from the inshore waters. The federal fishing policy was now ended and economic ties with the United States were restored by the treaty.[28] The charge had some point, but many people in the province had long held exaggerated notions of the importance of the Maritime fisheries and had fanciful notions of the benefits to be gained from them. Although the government papers were still unaware of the details of the negotiations, they insisted that the settlement did not adequately recognize the full value of the fisheries. Macdonald's failure to secure sufficient concessions for the Maritimes, contended these papers, was due to Canadian hostility and was an entirely predictable result of confederation.[29]

Combined with the myopic condemnation of the Canadians was an equally harsh denunciation of the British government. Although the government press criticized the Canadians for the fisheries settlement, they simultaneously claimed that the entire treaty was a blatant betrayal by Great Britain of its North American colonies in order to secure peace with the United States. If the ultimate responsibility for the treaty was placed with the British government, then it was possible that Britain and not the Upper Canadians should be criticized for the fisheries settlement. The provincial press, however, made no attempt to reconcile its two arguments but continued to develop its analysis of British policy. According to the *Morning Chronicle*, the British decision to withdraw from North America had begun with its support of confederation and had been completed by its abject surrender of colonial rights to the United States in the Treaty of Washington. The treaty had not only given the Americans everything they wanted, but it was also 'a full acknowledgment of all the principles popularly grouped together under the name of the Monroe doctrine. The sovereignty of the United States over the whole extent of North America would henceforth be indisputable.'[30] If Nova Scotia could no longer depend on the protection of Great Britain, then one might argue that economic integration with the United States would be soon followed by political absorption. If true, it was possible that some attempt should be made to use the new confederation to forestall political union with the United States. There was too little time before the provincial elections, however, for the government to develop the implications of its stand on the treaty.

The treaty thus provided an opportunity for the government to argue that as the issues of 1871 were the same as those of 1867, the electorate should continue to support the government and the provincial party which had consistently protected the interests of the province against the schemes of the Upper Canadians and Great Britain. The notion that the isolationist position of the provincial government had served the best interests of the province was challenged by Joseph Howe in a series of five public letters which he wrote in Ottawa and had published in Halifax newspapers.[31] Howe would have liked to see the Annand government defeated, but he did not really think it was likely since Annand was supported by large segments of the old pre-confederation Liberal party. It was his continued attachment to the Liberal party that made Howe so bitter towards such former supporters as Dr Murray, who he felt had betrayed his friendship in 1868 and 1869.[32] Thus Howe was not in favour of a Conservative candidate in Hants county running against one of his old associates, even though this Liberal had opposed him in 1869.[33] The confusion in political alliances was again revealed when Howe brought some particularly bitter charges against another Liberal, William Kidston, who was seeking re-election in Victoria.[34] In attacking Kidston, who was already in serious trouble, Howe threatened the seat of John Ross, a supporter of the local government, who was the brother of William Ross, the federal member for the same county. William Ross, a wavering supporter of Macdonald's ministry, strongly objected to Howe's interference in his brother's campaign.[35] Ross's resentment illustrated how difficult it was for the federal party to use its influence against the provincial government and its supporters in the political climate of 1871.

Even if Howe had wanted to use the influence of the federal government to defeat the local government, it would have been impossible, because in several counties the federal members actively campaigned on behalf of the supporters of the local government. The election campaign clearly indicated that the 'better terms' agreement of 1869, which Macdonald had promoted as a means of cementing a coalition between the confederates and the 'compromisers,' was not working as anticipated. Although a majority of the federal members supported the Macdonald ministry, several of them used their influence and federal patronage to oppose the confederates. In Queens county the confederates wrote to Howe demanding that their federal member be deprived of his federal patronage because he was helping a supporter of the provincial government. To this demand, as to others like it, Howe replied that '... patronage in the several counties is given to the members of the House of Commons who support the Government of the Dominion, without reference to their political antecedents, or to their actions in Local Counties.'[36] Thus, the practical result of the 'better terms' was to prevent the federal party from taking any concerted action in provincial politics. Just how this situation would evolve would depend on future events, but as far as the immediate election of 1871 was concerned, it meant that the Annand ministry was an indirect beneficiary of the 'better terms' agreement of 1869.

The federal influence on the provincial election was therefore limited, particularly as the extended sessions of the high commission in Washington kept Tupper occupied in Ottawa.[37] Never inclined to ignore his own interests, he did find time to persuade Sir Hector Langevin to agree to the extension of the Intercolonial Railway to serve the iron mines in Tupper's county.[38] He had also been concerned for some time with stopping the growing breach between his party supporters and the Roman Catholics. He was particularly concerned about the attempts of Theodore Rand, the former superintendent of education, to convince the Conservative faction of the confederates in Halifax that the best way to carry the three city seats was to start an anti-Catholic crusade.[39] Tupper failed in his efforts to entice Rand to Ottawa,[40] but in appreciation of his efforts Archbishop Connolly used his influence on behalf of the Conservatives.[41] Just prior to the election Tupper returned to his county, but the lack of time restricted him to Cumberland and Colchester. Looking across the province he could gain a measure of satisfaction since the Conservatives had managed to field a relatively strong list of candidates. This, it was true, was partly due to the disastrous results of the 1867 election which had left a number of experienced, capable confederates on the sidelines.

On 16 May, after a month of active campaigning, the voters went to the polls. Of the thirty-seven sitting members of the assembly, thirty-two stood for re-election. Of these, ten were defeated, including the unfortunate Dr Murray of Pictou and Kidston of Victoria. The initial results of the polls indicated that the confederates might have from twelve to sixteen supporters. The successful candidates included such experienced men as James McDonald of Pictou, who had been finance minister in Tupper's ministry, and Hiram Blanchard of Inverness, who had been unseated in 1868. The election results were a set-back to the government, but they had probably anticipated the loss of a few seats and were undoubtedly pleased at the defeat of Dr Murray and Kidston who had caused considerable trouble in the assembly.

Some confederates, seeing a chance to gain office, now decided to pry loose some of the more disgruntled government members. The more optimistic confederates hoped they could topple the ministry, and they gained some confidence from an air of dissatisfaction which rippled through the ranks of government supporters. Both before and during the election campaign these members publicly criticized the government's general performance. One of the most outspoken was Thomas Morrison, who was upset at being deprived of his salary of $800 as immigration agent just prior to the election. Morrison promptly declared he was running as an independent and accepted a confederate as a running-mate in order to carry the county by acclamation.[42] Morrison was flamboyant but he did not enjoy the influence, or have the ability, of Alonzo White of

Cape Breton county. During the previous session of the legislature White had usually voted with the government, but only after he had criticized the ministers for their ineptness. Another critic, and one who had much more specific complaints than White, was Desbrisay of Lunenburg, who had harassed the government in its handling of crown lands. Given the proper opportunity, these members might well abandon the government.

Negotiations were left to E.M. McDonald, federal member for Lunenburg, who had a marked inclination for political intrigue. McDonald, working through James Eisenhauer, one of the two members for Lunenburg, tried to persuade both Eisenhauer and Desbrisay to help the confederates form a government. He carried on similar negotiations with Alonzo White, although there was no indication that he approached Morrison. But these negotiations were scarcely begun before Annand appointed Desbrisay and White to a commission to revise the provincial statutes,[43] and Morrison was restored to his position as immigration agent. Both White and Desbrisay contended that they were still free to make any arrangements they wished,[44] but within a few weeks the negotiations with McDonald came to an end. McDonald was probably not surprised when his manœuvres failed, but at least he had explored all the possibilities. The chance of success had always been slim because any arrangement would have involved a coalition between the confederates and anti-confederates. Alonzo White may have doubted the competency of the government, but this was probably not sufficient to make him work with the confederates. Nor was there any evidence that confederates such as James McDonald and Hiram Blanchard would be prepared to work with anti-confederates, even for the prize of forming a provincial government. This continued animosity between the confederates and anti-confederates, which the 'better terms' agreement had obscured but not obliterated, had been of considerable assistance to the provincial government during the election. Now, following the election, these same antagonisms helped keep its opponents divided and the Annand ministry in office.

Having succeeded in winning the election and counteracting McDonald's intrigues, the provincial government demanded that the federal government keep its promise to settle the new provincial building issue. After several months of negotiations, which included a trip by Vail to Ottawa, the two governments announced that the federal government was taking possession of the building and that an arbitration commission of three would decide the amount of compensation which the province would receive. As its commissioner, the federal government selected a judge from Prince Edward Island and the provincial government appointed James Duffus, a Halifax merchant who had been treasurer of the now defunct Repeal League. These two then named a Saint John merchant as the third and ostensibly neutral commissioner. Actually he was a relative of Vail and usually spent his summers at the Vail home in Digby county.[45] The bias of the commission was revealed in November when the commissioners awarded the provincial government $80,000, which was $14,000 more than it had originally demanded.[46] The squabble over the building had dragged on for so long that the original issue had disappeared from view, and the fact that the federal government had finally been forced to negotiate with the provincial ministry had lost much of its significance.

THE TREATY OF WASHINGTON AND THE YMCA

In the months following the provincial elections various newspapers in Nova Scotia offered intermittent comment on the Treaty of Washington. The Conservative papers in Halifax cautiously adopted the view that the treaty did not offer all that the Canadians had a right to expect, but it was probably the best that could be obtained and for the sake of Great Britain should be adopted.[47] This attempt to gloss over any defects of the treaty and to appeal to imperial loyalty was somewhat embarrassed by the disclosure that John A. Macdonald had not followed up the American offer of free fish, coal, salt, and lumber. The *Halifax Citizen* immediately contended that Macdonald's refusal proved that the Canadians were implacably hostile to Nova Scotian interests.[48] This type of charge raised the possibility that attacks on the treaty would continue to focus on the Canadian government and that the criticism would be promoted by specific interests with a special grievance against the treaty.

Any concerted attack on the treaty was likely to be aided and abetted by the coal-mining interests. In June 1871 the coal association of Halifax held a general meeting and decided to oppose the treaty until there was some provision in it for the free entry of coal into the United States. As part of its general tactics, the association made arrangements to support opposition to the treaty in the other provinces.[49] Yet six months later, when another meeting was called to discuss the treaty, R.G. Haliburton, the erstwhile supporter of economic nationalism, was the only member to appear.[50] The collapse of the opposition to the treaty by the association was partially due to a rise in coal sales throughout 1871. Perhaps the chief obstacle to further increases in sales was a shortage of experienced miners. With future prospects bright, there appeared to be little need to worry about the American tariff on coal.

The buoyancy of coal mining was matched by a general improvement in 1871 of the entire economy. Crops were the best in years, shipbuilding was active, and cargo rates remained high.[51] Perhaps most important of all, fish were plentiful and prices remained firm. This made the fishermen and merchants somewhat complacent about the treaty, particularly as it provided free access to the American market and allowed the merchants to trade with the American fishermen.[52] Since much of the quarrel over the fisheries had actually been between American and Maritime merchants, the approval of the treaty by at least some of the Nova Scotian merchants was significant. Without the wholehearted opposition of some economic interest, and particularly of the merchants, critics in the province were not likely to develop the theme that the Canadians had sacrificed Nova Scotian economic concerns. As a result agitation against the treaty was less likely to be directed against the Canadians than against the British.

One of the most convinced critics of the treaty was Joseph Howe, who firmly believed that Canada had been betrayed by Great Britain. In a letter to Sir John Rose, unofficial Canadian agent in London, he stated: 'Though mortified and ashamed at the conduct of Great Britain in the matter of the Treaty I am not disappointed. I always told my colleagues that both parties in England would throw us over and buy their peace at our expense, as the Russian woman flings her children to the wolves.'[53] He was equally plain spoken when he wrote to the governor general: 'I still think, as I have thought from the first, that the conduct of the British Commissioners and of the Imperial Government in forcing the signature of the Treaty was hasty, selfish and unfair, I might almost say pusillanimous. On this point I am afraid I can hardly change my opinion.'[54] Howe's criticism of the treaty was thus directed to the treaty as a whole rather than to the fishing clause alone and the treaty confirmed Howe's long-held opinion that England was retreating from North America.

Opposed to the treaty as he was, Howe was unprepared to credit the rumours that reached him by mid-summer that there was some support for the treaty in Nova Scotia. He decided to check the accuracy of these reports during a planned holiday in the province. In late August, just prior to leaving for Halifax, he informed most of the federal members, in a carefully phrased letter, that he was interested in hearing their views as to what policy the government should adopt on the treaty.[55] None of the federal members seemed to believe Howe's disclaimer that the government was not committed to support the treaty, and several members suspected that he was not interested in hearing their views.[56] As a result Howe's enquiries aroused suspicions that the government was weak, indecisive, and afraid of defeat.[57] The government's public silence as to its policy on the treaty thus encouraged some members to consider the advisability of joining the Liberals.

Although some of the replies which Howe received from various federal members were critical of the government, none indicated implacable opposition to the treaty. Indeed, Frank Killam of Yarmouth emphatically declared that he favoured the treaty in general and the fishery clauses in particular.[58] Others were not prepared to give such personal endorsement, but both Hugh McDonald of Antigonish[59] and Dr Forbes of Queens[60] believed that the fishery clauses were acceptable to the province. Thus, if there was not wholehearted support for the treaty, several members were of the opinion that there was a measure of acquiescence. Moreover, for some members the real question was not whether Nova Scotia would accept the treaty but whether Great Britain would allow a mere colony to upset an international agreement.[61] Thomas Coffin of Shelburne thought the treaty was perhaps satisfactory from Nova Scotia's view, if not from Canada's, but that in any event the whole question was a foregone conclusion because England would force compliance.[62] Thus, the federal members seemed willing to support the treaty because the terms appeared acceptable to the province and because they themselves were not prepared to face a confrontation with England.

The views of the federal members from Nova Scotia did not shake Howe's belief that England had sacrificed Canadian interests for the sake of its own security. His opinion did not become public, however, until February 1871 when he addressed the Ottawa branch of the YMCA. Adopting the tone of a survivor of life's battles, he outlined the perils the young men before him would face as they took up life's challenge. After instructing his audience to follow the path set aside for Christian gentlemen, he cautioned his listeners to strive to keep confederation together by creating a sense of unity throughout the country. Petty provincial attitudes were not only degrading, he warned, but were also dangerous because they would prevent the dominion from using all of its energies to meet the challenge of the United States. Canadians had to rely on themselves because Canada could no longer rely on British power to offset the American influence. The recent withdrawal of British troops from Canada and the entire comedy of errors over the Treaty of Washington, he concluded, were all part of a general British policy which might end with England repudiating its national obligations to its colonies.[63]

Howe's speech provided an explanation and a justification for much of his own policy of the past six years. Since his return from England in the spring of 1866 he had spoken on several occasions of his fears that England was determined to abandon its North American colonies to the domination of the United States. Although Howe felt that America's supremacy on the continent was a fact of Canadian life, he had also long contended that the American challenge could only be offset by attempting to create a strong dominion of Canada. Thus, his denunciation of British policy, which might have startled his audience, was a significant reason for his presence in the federal cabinet.

Although Howe in his YMCA address had repeated views often stated before, he now spoke as a cabinet minister on the eve of a debate on whether to rectify the clauses of the Treaty of Washington relating to Canada. The speech attracted considerable attention, and Howe encouraged discussion by having his speech printed as a pamphlet. Howe, who enjoyed being the centre of attention, dismissed his critics as mere partisans who were always inclined to fight over anything he might say.[64] Yet the controversy could not be ignored so easily, as Howe undoubtedly knew. In Ontario the Liberals naturally tried to use the speech to embarrass the government, but it also caused some difficulty in Nova Scotia. The confederates attempted to ignore the speech for as long as possible[65] and the *British Colonist*, the leading Conservative paper, never did refer to it. Not even the provincial government papers were certain how to handle it. The *Morning Chronicle* at first professed to believe that the speech presaged Howe's resignation from the cabinet,[66] but later it decided that the speech indicated that the government intended to abandon the treaty in an attempt to stave off defeat.[67] This editorial confusion was partly the result of the paper's own change in policy towards the treaty. In the spring of 1871 it had denounced the treaty as a betrayal of Nova Scotia by the Canadians. By 1872 the *Chronicle*, and other papers which supported the provincial government, had begun to insist that the treaty was unjust to all Canadians, and that the real villains were John A. Macdonald and the British government.[68] This shift in policy reflected, in part, a growing interest in forming a political alliance with the Ontario Liberals who had recently formed a government in Ontario under Edward Blake.[69] Thus, political influences were helping to determine that one of the legacies of the anti-confederate campaign would be a suspicion of British motives and a move towards increased Canadian control of its own affairs.

When the federal parliament began to debate the treaty in April, John A. Macdonald could expect to be pressed by the Liberals to declare whether Howe had expressed the government's policy. To support Howe was to expose the government to charges of disloyalty, but to repudiate him would make his position in the cabinet untenable. Macdonald tried to walk a line between these alternatives by characterizing Howe's speech as the 'wailing cry of a loyalist fearing that the colony was going to be forsaken (cheers).'[70] Macdonald's approach was clever but it did ignore Howe's premise that the imperial tie should be severed if colonial interests were to be damaged by British policy. Howe maintained cabinet unity in the Commons by defending the treaty as being the best possible arrangement under the existing circumstances, but his intervention in the debate was brief.[71] On second reading the treaty was passed by a vote of 122 to 15. Of the nineteen Nova Scotian members, only Jones of Halifax and Ross of Victoria voted against the measure. Two other members were paired, and S. Chipman of Kings and Howe were both absent from the house. The remaining members, including P. Power, who was Jones' colleague from Halifax, voted for the bill.

Had there been any widespread opposition to the terms of the treaty in Nova Scotia, more of the Nova Scotian members would probably have voted against the measure. Macdonald's attempts during the Washington Conference to secure terms of particular advantage to the upper provinces did not appear to have materially influenced the Nova Scotian attitude towards the treaty. Although only a few of the federal members were prepared to endorse the terms openly, most of them appeared to believe that their province could live with the treaty. Thus, the treaty, and a generally buoyant provincial economy, helped dispel the fear that confederation would cause the immediate collapse of the provincial economy. Combined with this acceptance of the treaty was the strong belief that any confrontation with England over the treaty would be disastrous. Although they bowed to imperial necessity, it was probable that some sympathized with Howe's contention that British policy was bringing about a basic alteration in Canada's position towards the United States. By increasing the fear and resentment of British policy, the dispute over the treaty made the members more conscious of the necessity of union. As far as Nova Scotia was concerned, the Treaty of Washington probably helped strengthen the bonds of confederation.

9

Maintaining the status quo

DRAWING PARTY LINES

Nova Scotians were concerned about the Treaty of Washington, but they did not get involved in much of the controversy surrounding it. There was debate in the province yet its impact on politics was diffuse. With anti-confederates such as Power of Halifax and Killam of Yarmouth supporting the treaty against the attacks of Howe and such confederates as T.C. Haliburton, there was no opportunity for the treaty to become the focus of any political programme. These convoluted reactions helped bring a pause in the debate on problems related to the treaty, including federal economic policies. Politicians in Nova Scotia seemed content in 1872 to deal with questions of local and provincial concern.

When the provincial legislature assembled on 23 February 1872 the government, for the first time since 1867, found itself face to face with an opposition party. Hiram Blanchard, the opposition leader, set the tone for the session when he made it clear he would scrutinize the past record of the ministry in detail.[1] While seemingly innocuous, this determination indicated a desire to ignore the old debate on union and concentrate on issues that were under provincial rather than federal jurisdiction. The emphasis on the past made it difficult for returning government supporters to defect to the opposition, but without such defection Blanchard could not hope to topple the government. Ultimately his attack on the administrative record of the government would prove futile since the ministry, through its domination of the assembly, could control access to the records.

In reviewing the government record Blanchard was influenced by the respectable constitutional doctrine that the ministry was responsible to the assembly. The ministry, according to Blanchard, had not since 1867 been responsible to the assembly because of the absence of an opposition party. He seemed content to cast himself and his supporters in the role of the conscience of the assembly while accusing the supporters of the government in both the present and past houses of dereliction of duty, if not actual corruption.[2] If, as Blanchard claimed, the government did have such a hold over its supporters, then it was not clear how an opposition could make much difference. Blanchard thought of the assembly as a gathering of independent members held together by the code of a gentleman. In his own conduct he showed a distaste for a party organization in the assembly and was selected as leader by three or four experienced members of the opposition before the legislature opened, without referral to the other members of the opposition.[3] Nor did Blanchard consider calling together a caucus of the opposition to determine policy and discuss strategy.

Blanchard's intention of examining the government's record was actually never implemented. One major difficulty was that the rights of the opposition were not properly established in the assembly. The provincial secretary and leader of the house, W.B. Vail, had no inhibitions about using the party caucus to enforce government policy. He was also quite willing to impose a form of closure on debate by moving the previous question.[4] Thus the advantage in the assembly frequently lay with the government, particularly as the Speaker, J.C. Troop, regarded himself as an agent of the government rather than of the assembly, and stated that it was his right and duty to reply to any attacks on the ministry of which he was a member.[5] It was of course possible for opposition members to raise issues in committee, but Vail believed that the government was not required to produce papers from which someone might pick 'something out of which a charge could be made against the government.' The attorney-general, Henry Smith, however, did say that papers could be produced on the request of a committee. Yet this was of little value to the opposition as government supporters were always in the majority on committees.[6] Members of the assembly were allowed to examine papers in the various departments, but they had to raise any points at issue in the assembly, where the government could use its majority to prevent debate. The government, therefore, was quite able to block the opposition attempts to examine its administrative record.

From the beginning of the session Vail was able to place the opposition on the defensive. This was particularly evident over the issue of the statute of 1871, which disfranchised a number of federal employees in provincial elections. The opposition, concerned because its supporters were the main recipients of federal positions, tried to have the measure repealed in 1872 but found itself unable to block an amendment which tightened the statute. It was little consolation to the opposition that this amendment, which had been discussed in government caucus, was not supported by the attorney-general.[7] Debate was bitter, but nevertheless the amendment passed third reading by a vote of twenty-three to thirteen.[8]

The most marked achievement of the session was not the ease with which the government suppressed the opposition but the manner in which the two parties combined to play down the issue of union. Blanchard managed to avoid federal issues and most of the time he did not discuss the merits of union. A similar tack was taken by the attorney-general, who refused to be drawn into a long debate over the Treaty of Washington. He also justified the refusal of the government to be identified with a protest against the treaty prepared by the government of New Brunswick on the grounds that it was a federal responsibility.[9] Later in the session Vail refused to support an attempt by Thomas Morrison to revive the post-office issue, which had been settled by arbitration the previous fall.[10] Not all the government supporters were satisfied with its acceptance of union and recognition of differing federal and provincial responsibilities. Vail did not want to give needless offence to these supporters, and he therefore moved quickly, for example, to delete a favourable comment about the Dominion of Canada which the governor had inserted into his speech to close the session.[11] In effect the government sought to avoid any positive endorsement of union, while continuing to work within the federal system.

Lack of controversy over union meant that the policy of the ministry towards provincial affairs was clearer than in previous sessions. One positive result was government interest in the provincial mining resources. Several new coal mines had begun production since 1864 under the direction of companies based in Montreal, the United States, and Great Britain, but a major obstacle to further growth was the lack of railways connecting the mining areas to inland markets or to harbours suitable for shipping. The most pressing need was for a rail link between Cape Breton Island and the Pictou branch of the Intercolonial Railway, but the local ministry did not have the money to subsidize a private company. An alternate solution was to seek aid from the federal government, yet the latter was more disposed to give the Pictou branch away than to extend it to Cape Breton Island. If a Nova Scotian tried to argue that his province should receive federal aid because of money spent on canals in Ontario, he was likely to be told that they were compensation to the Upper Canadians for the Intercolonial Railway.[12] This railway had originally been offered as part of the terms of union, but it was regarded as a political liability in the upper provinces.

If the local ministry had wished to postpone any action on railway construction, it could have taken the position that any extension was dependent on federal aid. In 1872, however, it developed a proposal to promote railway construction along designated routes in Cape Breton Island and in the Spring Hill mining area in Cumberland county. Any company undertaking the Cape Breton project would receive a grant of crown lands and one-half of the provincial royalty on all coal carried by the railway for forty years. A third railroad, to pacify Vail, to run from Annapolis, through Digby, to Yarmouth, was also included. The government measure passed through the assembly by a vote of twenty-three to nine,[13] but it remained to be seen whether any financier would be interested in such a speculative scheme.

The local ministry was bound to be greatly influenced by the general policies of the federal government and also by its relations with federal politicians within the province. This was particularly true as its most important political opponent was not Hiram Blanchard but Charles Tupper, always a favourite subject for attack, and the federal elections, scheduled for the summer of 1872, made him an even more inviting target. As part of a general campaign to discredit him, the government charged that as premier he had abused his position in connection with a Spring Hill mining area in which he was part owner. The charges, which were wrong in detail, did contain some substance of truth and were investigated by the committee of mines.[14] The day before the session was to close, the lone opposition member of the committee, H.J. Cameron of Pictou, took the report and the next day failed to appear in the assembly. Morrison, chairman of the committee, broke into Cameron's desk, and the Speaker ordered the house into secret session.[15] The doors were still closed when the members were summoned to attend to the lieutenant-governor in the Legislative Council chamber. The Speaker later ruled that the report had been officially received[16] and the government maintained that for the first time in the history of the province the assembly had impeached a minister of the crown. Further action on the case, it stated, would have to await action in the courts.[17] The federal election campaign was obviously under way.

LIBERALS AND RAILWAYS

Campaigning for the federal general election, which was scheduled to take place in Nova Scotia in mid-August, was hampered by the discontent which many confederates continued to harbour about the compromise of 1869.[18] The problem of lethargy was also serious for the local ministry, which was trying to develop its alliance with the federal Liberal party.[19] It was perhaps inevitable that as the opposition to union declined, interest in local affairs would take precedence over federal political affairs. Yet, unless the local ministry could establish some interest in federal politics, the voters might ignore federal political divisions altogether and vote for the government supporters regardless of party label.

Although the politicians were slow to begin, the newspapers were ready with their editorials. In preparing for the election, the newspapers supporting the local ministry gradually became identified as the Liberal press, espousing, they argued, the same principles as those upheld by the Liberal parties of Ontario and Nova Scotia prior to union. The Conservatives obstructed this identification by arguing that the Ontario Liberals were an Ontario First movement.[20] The Liberals in Halifax were particularly embarrassed by the opposition of the Ontario 'Grits' to the 'better terms' agreement of 1869.[21]

According to the Conservatives, they were the party of national policy in contrast to the Liberals, who were really sectionalists at heart.[22] In replying to this argument the Liberal press in Halifax adopted a very cautious line. Once the Nova Scotian anti-confederates had been forced to accept union, they argued that they had worked to protect the interests of the province by obtaining more money from Ottawa. Now that this was done they had to strive to establish proper constitutional government based on the principles of reform. And in this project they were joined by the Ontario Liberals.[23] No part of the national policy was constitutional, they contended, because it was extravagant, wasteful, and intended primarily to provide John A. Macdonald with the patronage required to corrupt parliament.[24] The duty of protecting parliament and re-establishing purity in government was a duty for all voters, regardless of previous party affiliation.[25] At the same time, the Liberal press also reminded its readers of the terrible damage that they had suffered in 1867 at the hands of such traitors as Tupper, who had used the same methods as John A. Macdonald was now using in 1872.[26]

Although the Liberal press contended that existing political divisions were obsolete, there was no indication that the political balance, in existence since 1869, was about to change. Of the sitting members, only E.M. McDonald of Lunenburg, who was appointed collector of customs in Halifax, decided not to seek re-election. Most of the federal members had been elected in 1867 with the help of the same group which had supported the local members. Since that time several of the federal members had accepted the compromise of 1869 and had become government supporters. If at the same time they had managed to retain the allegiance of their original supporters, then they were relatively immune to attacks from the local ministry. The advantage of retaining local support was graphically shown in the instance of Chipman of Kings, who returned from Ottawa bearing a letter of endorsement from Tupper.[27] Supporters of the local government rejected him as their candidate but he had built up sufficient independent strength in his riding to withstand their opposition and to carry the seat.

There were several federal members whom the local ministry would have liked to see defeated, but there was little they could do to bring it about. In Antigonish, for example, Hugh McDonald, a well-known supporter of Howe, was re-elected by acclamation. And Howe himself, seriously ill in a Boston hospital, was returned by acclamation for the first time in his political career.[28] The general feeling that this was Howe's last campaign, coupled with sympathy for his ill-health, might have made his opponents reluctant to oppose him. His case was unique, but the open support, or the acquiescence in the re-election, of several of the 'compromisers' at the county level, seriously inhibited the Liberal campaign in the province. The degree of support for the Macdonald government by these 'compromisers' was open to question, but if the Conservatives were unable to rely on them, neither could the Liberals. The best solution, from the viewpoint of the local ministry, was for the 'compromisers' to desert the government. All the Liberals had to offer, however, was the cold, barren seats of the opposition. The existing situation was far more pleasant than joining the Liberals, because they enjoyed the benefits of government patronage and yet remained independent of the confederates. One result of this arrangement was that in approximately eight counties the local ministry was unable to rally its own supporters to the cause of the Liberal party. It was thus impossible to bring about a major change in the political balance until this situation was changed.

The inability of the Liberals to mount a full-scale attack in the province did not prevent a number of interesting contests for the seats at stake. Of the twenty-one seats (two more than in the 1867 election), six went by acclamation, as compared with four in 1867. One of them was Digby, where Vail tried to create opposition to A.W. Savary, but the latter was able to have both of his opponents disqualified.[29] In the counties where there were contests, the voter turnout was approximately the same as in 1867, although there had been an increase in the number of registered voters. The bad weather which covered the province, however, probably prevented some people from reaching the polls. For according to one Halifax paper: 'There never was a wetter day, nor a wetter community. No one ever saw so dirty a crowd of highly respectable people.'[30] When the results from the election were totalled, twelve of the seventeen sitting members were returned. Of the five defeated members, three had been identified with the federal Liberal party.

One of the more important contests took place in Halifax where a prominent Liberal, A.G. Jones, and his running-mate, Patrick Power, sought re-election. For some time Power, who had differed with Jones over the Treaty of Washington, had considered supporting the Conservatives, but at the last minute he had been unable to break his political ties.[31] The strength of the Liberal hold over the city had earlier been tacitly recognized by the Conservatives when they had decided against granting a third federal member to Halifax, although it was entitled to another member on the basis of population. The Conservatives were badly divided, and one likely candidate, P.C. Hill, worried about his lack of support from the Roman Catholics, refused to run.[32] When an attempt was made to convince Tupper to contest the city against Jones, his answer, short, curt, and probably intended to alarm the Halifax factions, refused aid to those who had 'destroyed the party by their hostile criticism.'[33] The Halifax Conservatives did finally select Dr W.J. Almon, a lifelong Conservative and a supporter of union, and as his running-mate they endorsed Samuel Tobin, an insurance broker. Tobin, a former mayor of the city, had really wanted to run with Jones,[34] and he preferred to be known as an independent. Although not a very convincing Conservative, he did have the support of Archbishop Connolly, and therefore the support of some Irish Catholics. Much to the surprise of many, Almon and Tobin carried the constituency.[35] The course of the election left little doubt that they had won because of the unpopularity of the Liberal cause.

Elsewhere in the province the Liberals suffered blows both to their strength and to their pride. In Pictou, newly established as a double riding, the leading Liberal, James Carmichael, met his principal opposition from James McDonald, who had resigned from the local assembly in order to contest the seat. Although popular in his own right, Carmichael was handicapped by factious quarrels within party ranks, and both he and his partner went down to defeat. In Cumberland the Liberals lost prestige despite months of work by Annand who toured the county, found a candidate, and apparently financed much of the campaign.[36] Annand tried to gain support on the basis of the projected Spring Hill railway, which the legislature had endorsed in the spring.[37] Tupper, a master of that style of campaigning, replied with a proposal to build a canal across the Isthmus of Chignecto. Tupper won the contest easily and then left to take part in several contests in Ontario.

Whether by an accident or by design it was evident that the Liberals had concentrated their efforts in three or four counties.[38] This in turn enabled the Conservatives to devote their resources to defeating Jones and Carmichael. Although the new members-elect for Lunenburg and Colchester could be regarded as Liberals, the party had obviously lost strength in the election. Jones, bitter at his own loss, was inclined to blame his provincial supporters for a lack of effort.[39] Little fault could be found with the assistance given by some individual members, but the government supporters had seemed to hold back.[40] This laxity obviously caused embarrassment in party ranks.[41] While lethargy was one reason for the Liberal setback, a more likely explanation lay in their turning the provincial party, with its anti-confederation origins, into an arm of a federal party. In view of the fact that the election turnout in 1872 was approximately the same as in 1867, it would seem that a number of voters were uninterested in federal party divisions but were willing to accept any benefits from the federal government. Although the local ministry was able to control the assembly, it did not follow that it would extend its dominance into the federal sphere. In a provincial contest the ministry could promise rewards to the party workers and financial supporters, but such methods were not as effective in a federal contest. The support of the local government for the federal or Liberal party could not overcome the lack of involvement in federal party decisions or the lack of political rewards. What was needed was a more or less distinct organization which was separate from the local government.

The prospect of being able to build a Liberal party in Nova Scotia increased as the election results began to come in from other sections of the country. The upper provinces, unlike Nova Scotia, did not have simultaneous elections, and the daily telegraphic reports slowly spelled out the defeat of such government leaders as Sir Francis Hincks and Sir George Etienne Cartier. Alternative seats were found for the party chieftains, but as the casualty list of Conservative stalwarts grew, the difficulties of the Macdonald government became apparent.[42] The prospect of the Liberals forming a government could quite well influence some of the uncommitted politicians in Nova Scotia.

As a result of the election results elsewhere in Canada, the Liberal press in Halifax renewed its attempts to extend the Liberal party in the province. In its campaign the press advanced the view that the provincial political divisions based on the issue of union were obsolete.[43] A new party should be formed in the province which would unite all Liberals, both supporters and opponents of union, with their natural allies in Ontario.[44] This proposal to reconstruct the Liberal party did have the merit of placing the basis of party on principle rather than on provincialism.[45] At the same time the ministry could not forget that the opponents of union had come from the former Conservative and Liberal parties in the province. Vail and Jones had been Conservatives prior to union and several supporters of the local government continued to regard themselves as such.[46] The affiliation with the federal Liberals thus had repercussions within the provincial party, and prudence indicated that the local ministry should use some care in advocating the Liberal cause.[47]

In supporting the Liberal party the Halifax newspapers adopted a broad view of history in an attempt to relate the familiar problems of provincial politics to federal issues. According to the *Morning Chronicle* the Liberal party was the proper vehicle for the respectable middle class. Without being specific, the Halifax Liberal papers assumed that their party was the instrument of reform and progress. This view amounted to the contention that the middle class, which should dominate society, provided the dynamic force in the march towards progress.[48] Although the respectable elements had a natural desire for reform, some people had a natural inclination to preserve the familiar. It was the proper role of the political parties, according to the *Citizen*, to express the contradictory aims of preservation and change. Since the two parties expressed different goals, the argument continued, party solidarity was a necessity and coalitions must be avoided. Indeed, coalitions had the taint of corruption about them because they went against human nature, and they had to be maintained by improper means.[49]

Applying their doctrine of progress to the Canadian political scene the Liberal press returned to the subjects which they had raised during the election campaign. Particular stress was laid on the necessity of controlling the power of government over parliament.[50] To the Liberal press it was evident that the Conservative, by his very nature, was given to great extravagances and 'sickly artificial grandeur.'[51] The Liberals, by exerting the will of parliament, could reassert frugality as a virtue and take steps to restrict the government's powers by controlling patronage. Macdonald was enthusiastic about building a railway to the west, asserted a Liberal paper, because it would provide him with the steady flow of patronage needed to manipulate parliament.⁵² The creation of a large corporation to build the railway was thus part of the Conservative policy to destroy the independence of parliament. For once such a corporation was formed, it would have sufficient power to control the government. It was the Liberal aim, continued the *Chronicle*, to build the railway without destroying parliament.⁵³ It would be some time before there would be any discernible results of the campaign on the behalf of the Liberals, but a straightforward appeal for party reform and progress was in itself a change from midsummer.

In provincial politics three by-elections were held during the fall to fill vacancies in the local house created by the resignation of men who had run in the federal election. Of the three newly-elected members, two were supporters of the opposition; thus the strength of the two parties in the assembly remained unchanged from the previous assembly.⁵⁴ The one indication of future trouble for the government came during the contest in Pictou. The Liberal candidate in the county was supported by the government press in Halifax⁵⁵ but was rejected by a sizable faction identified with Dr Murray.⁵⁶ Handicapped by a split party organization, the Liberal candidate was beaten by the largest margin ever recorded in the county.⁵⁷ To the extent that the division in Pictou sprang from quarrels between the groups which originally made up the anti-confederate party, it could be regarded as a purely county affair. The difficulty between Dr Murray and the government, however, involved the government's covert courting of the Catholic vote. Since it was doubtful the government would alter its policy, Pictou was likely to continue in opposition to the government. And the ministry could but hope that the Protestant dissatisfaction would not spread to other counties.

Despite the situation in Pictou the local ministry seemed to be in control of provincial politics. This was particularly evident when a by-election occurred in Halifax in February 1873 to fill a vacancy caused by the death of William Garvie. Most of the leading Conservatives in the city decided that they could not carry the seat, particularly now that provincial law deprived them of the votes of federal employees. They were thus receptive to the suggestion of W.S. Fielding of the *Morning Chronicle* that they should support the election of Captain John Taylor, who was an associate of Annand.⁵⁸ While a number of Conservatives accepted their weakness, the prospect of continual defeat no doubt helped prompt a faction to search for a new programme. This group held two public meetings, which were marked by arguments and fights, and finally settled on George Motton, a disbarred lawyer, as their candidate.⁵⁹ Supported by George

Johnson of the *Evening Reporter*, Motton developed a campaign which amounted to a rebuttal of the local government's policy of economic development and of the recent press appeal by the Liberals to the 'respectable' elements of society. The merchants, declared Motton, wanted freedom in order to grind the poor. In order to reduce the power of the merchants, the upper house of the legislature should be abolished. In addition, the method of selecting candidates by caucus, which according to Motton gave too much influence to the financial supporters of the party, should be replaced by public nominations.[60] Attacks on the merchants had been heard before in Halifax, but Motton introduced a new note by insisting that the workingman had interests distinct from the merchants and needed special protection to end privilege and favouritism. The merchants were not used to hearing themselves denounced as agents of privilege and the *Morning Chronicle* declared that Motton's speeches were suitable for a New York mob, but were an insult to a Halifax audience.[61]

The merchants of Halifax were no doubt reassured when Taylor ran up a large majority over Motton.[62] The appeal to the workingman did indicate that the tone and the issues of Nova Scotian politics were undergoing a transformation. In the previous decade various groups had organized co-operatives, building societies, and unions. Such activities seemed to have had little political effect, except possibly to make the merchants more self-conscious of their own position. A more specific result of Motton's campaign was to increase the possibility of a split within the Conservative party. The effectiveness of the organization in Halifax had been reduced by internal disputes over such issues as the 'better terms.' With the passage of time making these quarrels obsolete, the support of controversial social policies by factions within the party might produce defections to the provincial government in the future.

The immediate prospect of any political change appeared slight as both the provincial and the federal forces seemed to maintain their supremacy in their respective areas. The 'compromisers' of 1869 continued to link together the two groupings and to act as an obstacle to any change of party strength. This peculiar political balance had arisen out of a temporary situation which could be easily disturbed in the future. By the beginning of 1873 it was apparent that several developments were possible. Particularly interesting in this regard were the signs of disintegration in the Conservative ranks in Halifax and the attempts to identify familiar political attitudes with federal issues. Continuation of either trend would establish new policies and alignments in the province.

10

The failure of the coalition

The federal election results of 1872 seemed to be a confirmation of the success of the 'better terms' agreement of 1869. Surface appearances could be deceptive, however, and difficulties, obscured for several years, were beginning to surface. The 'better terms,' intended both as a reward for the abandonment of opposition to union and also as inducement for the Nova Scotian federal members to support the Conservative party, had succeeded in its first objective but not in the second. The Nova Scotian members were not interested in the political divisions of the upper provinces, but they were concerned about improving their position with the government. As their political strength increased in Nova Scotia, they began to exploit the deteriorating position of the federal government to bring forward their long-felt grievances.

On 5 March 1873 the federal parliament reconvened. The new parliamentary session would soon prove to be just one more stage in the continuing struggle between the Conservatives and the Liberals. Although the government ministers were confident of success, they expected a fierce attack on their proposal for the construction of the Pacific railway.[1] No exact count of party strength was possible before a division in the Commons, but the obvious gains by the Liberals gave impetus to their attacks. In this contest the politicians from the upper provinces would play a major role, but the anticipated narrow margin between the two parties gave some importance to the actions of the Nova Scotians.

As the Nova Scotian members straggled into Ottawa they were immediately caught up in the frantic canvassing of the two parties. Alexander Mackenzie, who was confirmed as leader of the Liberal party on the opening day of parliament, was hampered by the absence of Carmichael and Jones.[2] There was no denying, however, that the opposition had greatly increased its strength in comparison with the previous legislature. Just how strong was revealed two days after the opening of the session when the Liberals came within sixteen votes of upsetting the government on a question involving the seating of a member from Ontario. The issue was of no direct concern to the Nova Scotians, and it was a shock to the Conservatives to see five Nova Scotians vote with the Liberals and four abstain.[3] The government avoided any further division until 19 March when it carried a vote by a majority of twenty-five. On this occasion only two Nova Scotians voted with the Liberals and three abstained.[4] Although the movement of Nova Scotians into the Liberal party had been stopped, they continued to remain separate from the government. And when they refused to attend government caucuses, the government refrained from appointing a whip.[5]

Although Howe had been aware of some dissatisfaction,[6] the timing and extent of the revolt among the Nova Scotian members convinced him that some of the members were guilty of treachery.[7] A less melodramatic view was that the members were taking advantage of a temporary difficulty to express their discontent over their position in Ottawa. Some members disliked various aspects of government policy, but their power to influence the formation of that policy was slight. As Howe had discovered in 1871, in connection with the Treaty of Washington, a few members objected to the government's custom of handing down decisions to its supporters without explanation or consultation.[8] The complaint was endemic to the cabinet system of government, but the Nova Scotians, with their background in provincial politics, were accustomed to a larger role in policy matters. The problem of the relationship between the member and the cabinet was enhanced, however, because the cabinet ministers were supposed to represent various interests and regions. Yet the members from those regions were not involved in selecting their representatives or in influencing the policy adopted by them. Thus, instead of representing the views of the members from a region, the cabinet minister could use the power of his office to control the members. The complaint of some of the Nova Scotians arose from fear that their cabinet ministers did not really represent them. For those members who objected to the policies being adopted or to the ministers chosen, the most effective solution was not to change their party allegiance but to alter their relationship to the cabinet.

The problem of the cabinet was likely to appear particularly acute to the Nova Scotians in the spring of 1873. Tupper, who had recently been appointed to the patronage-rich office of customs, was clearly improving his political position in Ottawa. His rival, Joseph Howe, remained in the cabinet, but in the fall of 1872 Macdonald had asked Tupper to persuade Howe to resign.[9] Howe was not likely to accept such a suggestion from Tupper, yet in December he did offer to leave the cabinet in disagreement over a proposal concerning the Pacific railway.[10] His resignation was rejected, but it was understood he would be appointed lieutenant-governor of Nova Scotia at the end of Doyle's term in May.[11] Howe took little part in debate during the session, and he made his last brief comment in parliament on 4 April.[12] His retirement was bound to affect the political balance in Nova Scotia, as well as raise again the question of the relationship of the Nova Scotian members to the federal government.

The revolt of the Nova Scotian members of parliament was brought to a close at the end of March. At a gathering of most of the members, which started out at Howe's home and later met with John A. Macdonald, they agreed to re-enter the government caucus.[13] The very noticeable omission of Tupper from the negotiations was obviously intended by the Nova Scotians as a rejection of his leadership.

Within two or three days of their meeting with Macdonald the Nova Scotians were called upon to show their support for the government. The occasion was the long-anticipated attack by the Liberals on the government's railway policy. On 2 April the Liberal member from Shefford, Lucius Huntingdon, charged that the government had granted the charter for the Pacific railway to Sir Hugh Allan in return for a sum of money which had been used in the general election of 1872. Without further explanation Huntingdon proposed that a committee of inquiry be established by the House of Commons. Macdonald offered no defence to the accusations and the resolution was defeated by thirty-one votes. Of the Nova Scotians, only Forbes, Charles Church, and Pearson voted with the Liberals.[14] William Ross and two or three others, however, privately informed one of the ministers that unless the charges were investigated, they would defect to the Liberals.[15] Although Macdonald may have been unaware of this ultimatum, he was quite conscious of the need to provide some answer, and on 3 April he moved for an inquiry. Reassured by this move, Ross and his associates did not bolt, and even Forbes returned to the government fold.

In presenting his charges Huntingdon had made his motion in the name of the supremacy of parliament over the executive. Such an appeal was likely to gratify the several life-long Liberals among the Nova Scotian members but they could not ignore the fact that Huntingdon's charges were supported by a political party in a chamber dominated by its opponents. Unsubstantiated accusations did not constitute reason to leave the government, and it was obvious there would be ample time to reconsider the decision to support the government. There were probably few members who had any grounds for supporting the Liberals rather than the Conservatives. If some government policies were unsatisfactory, so was the attitude of some Liberals. A number of Nova Scotian members believed Tupper when he claimed that Mackenzie felt he had a right to rule Canada because he had a majority from Ontario.[16] Ontario's overbearing attitude was clearly shown by one Liberal when he intimated broadly that no Maritimer had the right to speak on any issue concerning Ontario.[17] Possibly the Maritimers were prepared to accept the status of a junior partner in the new firm, but they were not ready to accept the position of an annexed colony, or merely to act in terms acceptable to Ontario.[18] Thus, although the opposition party embraced a political doctrine familiar and acceptable to several of the Nova Scotians, it also expressed a sectional attitude which could easily keep the Nova Scotians from leaving the government benches.

It was particularly unlikely that the Nova Scotians would desert to the Liberals as a means of blocking construction of the railway to the west; and their return to the government camp at the end of March carried an implicit acceptance of government policy. The Nova Scotians did feel that this particular railway project would impose a long-term obligation on the entire nation although it would be of direct benefit to a limited part of the country. Yet it was likely that Nova Scotia would benefit from the railway by producing iron and steel supplies. Some of the necessary manufacturing facilities existed because Nova Scotian firms were already providing equipment for the Intercolonial Railway,[19] but the most promising development was being promoted by Sir Hugh Allan. In 1872 he acquired the long-established Acadian Iron Charcoal Company in Cumberland county[20] and he was also president of the Vale Coal and Iron Company in Pictou, which began full-scale coal mining in 1872. Some federal members might well have decided that the construction of the railway could promote the development of manufacturing industries based on Nova Scotia's coal resources.

Thus the immediate response of the Nova Scotians to the charges brought by Huntingdon was to continue to support the government. The transformation of nineteen members from professed independents to apparent government supporters raised strong suspicions that the government had made concessions.[21] One suggestion, which appeared in a Conservative paper in Halifax, was that the agreement at the end of

March involved a promise by Macdonald to increase railway construction in Nova Scotia[22] as compensation for the Pacific railway. On the face of it this allegation carried a certain plausibility, particularly since in March a projected railway to Cape Breton had been promoted in Ottawa.[23] Another popular scheme for Halifax members was the completion of a railway into the city through the dockyard.[24] A further project involved Frank Killam, and at the close of the session a company headed by him was granted a lease on the federally-owned Windsor and Annapolis Railway.[25] These were but slight concessions, however, and it was unlikely that any such commitments would, by themselves, keep the loyalty of the Nova Scotians.

Before the session adjourned on 22 May the charges made by Huntingdon were referred to a parliamentary committee of five members, including as one of the three Conservatives James McDonald of Pictou. At the insistence of the Liberals the house passed an act empowering the committee to examine witnesses under oath, and when the members left Ottawa they understood they would meet again on 13 August to receive a report.[26] These arrangements were disrupted when the British law officers decided against the oath bill. The Liberals rejected a proposal that the committee be transformed into a royal commission, and the Conservatives forced an adjournment of the committee, allegedly to seek further guidance from parliament.

The Liberals then adopted a new tactic – the publication of various documents in newspapers in Montreal and Toronto. Macdonald had anticipated this move and had already decided to force Sir Hugh Allan to take sole responsibility for carrying out negotiations with American interests connected with the Northern Pacific Railway. Once Macdonald had cleared himself of as much of the scandal as he could, Huntingdon released a second group of documents which showed that during the federal elections of 1872 Macdonald had received large sums of money for campaign funds from Allan, at the same time that he was negotiating with him for construction of the Pacific railway. Macdonald had been brutally trapped, and he could only hope that there would be no further revelations.[27]

This series of blows to the Macdonald ministry occurred at the same time as important changes were taking place in Nova Scotian politics. The direct cause of these changes was Howe's resignation from the cabinet to become lieutenant-governor on 7 May 1873. Howe welcomed his appointment as the proper ending to a lifetime devoted to his province. His satisfaction was not shared by Annand, who provoked Howe by trying to

The failure of the coalition 153

arrange for the governor's residence to be taken over by the British garrison in Halifax. Howe was determined to live in Government House 'from where,' he said, 'Momma and I were excluded for years and where we so often met black looks and cold shoulders.'[28] Despite such unfriendly skirmishing, Howe was convinced he would observe the constitutional niceties of his new position. And he predicted that his critics within the provincial ministry who doubted this would be 'as mistaken in this as in everything else.'[29] The controversy was senseless and pathetic, for one month after taking office, Howe died.

It was fitting that Howe, the great leader of the Liberal party in Nova Scotia, should be succeeded as governor by the equally eminent Conservative, J.W. Johnston, who had recently retired as judge-in-equity.[30] His appointment would probably have been acceptable to most politicians, but Johnston, who had retired to the southern coast of France, was too ill to return to Nova Scotia.[31] Several people wanted the now vacant position, but Tupper selected A.G. Archibald, who had just been appointed to the Supreme Court of Nova Scotia, as a replacement for Johnston.[32] Although Archibald was a former leader of the Liberal party, he had become a noted supporter of union and was closely identified with the policies of the Macdonald government. His political services included a cabinet position and a tour of duty in Manitoba as lieutenant-governor. Since his return to Nova Scotia he had been appointed as a director of the Canadian Pacific Railway Company,[33] although no one seemed to know where he obtained the money to buy the shares necessary to qualify as director.[34] He was well suited for his new position as governor, but the selection of Johnston, followed by Archibald, suggested that Tupper was abandoning the coalition of 1869.

The problems of the coalition were particularly acute when it came to selecting a cabinet replacement for Howe. The actual choice fell to Hugh McDonald, a lawyer from Antigonish, who wanted to retire from politics and already had been promised he would be the first Roman Catholic appointed to the provincial bench.[35] McDonald had little political support of his own and his appointment could be regarded as a reward for party loyalty which, in the circumstances, meant recognition of Tupper's supremacy. This was particularly unsatisfactory to the rebels of the past spring, who were disinclined to accept Hugh McDonald or Tupper and mistrusted any tightening of party discipline. They were quite right to do so because a number of Conservatives hoped that with Howe dead the coalition with the anti-confederates could be broken. By the summer of 1873 the Conservative supporters were able to argue that the coalition was about to break up anyway, and Tupper should anticipate this development by insisting upon party regularity.[36] The appointments made during the summer did appear to be a move in that direction. While the coalition might be doomed, it also appeared that much of the criticism of it came from a strong belief in the necessity for party organization.

During the early part of the summer it was not altogether evident that the political balance was shifting away from the Conservatives. In Hants county a by-election was held to fill the seat left vacant by Howe. The seat was won by Monson Goudge, who had run against Howe in 1869, but his victory was not clear-cut for the Liberals[37] because he had campaigned in Hants as a professed independent in order to appeal to the former supporters of Howe.[38] After the publication of the second set of documents on the Pacific scandal, however, Mackenzie began to receive assurances of support from several Nova Scotian members. Among the first to reach him were letters from Dr Forbes of Queens and Thomas Coffin of Shelburne,[39] both of whom had anticipated receiving the cabinet position[40] recently given to Hugh Macdonald. It was therefore probable that these defections came about in part because of their personal dissatisfaction with recent developments in Nova Scotia.

Mackenzie, no doubt, would have liked to display his new strength at the session of parliament scheduled for 13 August. Macdonald had originally stipulated that parliament would merely meet to receive a report on Huntingdon's charges, and he was unlikely to allow parliament to issue new instructions. In all probability the session would be short and the trip to Ottawa was a long one for a Nova Scotian to make. Mackenzie finally left it up to each member whether or not he should take the trip.[41] Eight Nova Scotians accepted the invitation, and of these, six signed a petition against any immediate prorogation of parliament.[42] Of these six only Samuel Macdonnell had any claim to be a Conservative. He had already obtained a certain notoriety in 1866 when he had abandoned his opposition to union and seconded Miller's motion to support union in principle. The other defectors to the Liberals were all opponents of union, which was not surprising since most of the federal members had taken this position. It was noticeable, however, that the defectors included men such as Forbes, who had remained aloof from the confederates in their counties. This revealed their own attitude, but it also made it easier for them to change political allegiance. Some of the other members might have wanted to change, but were hindered by the threat of an unfriendly reception from the local government supporters.

The Liberal petition requesting time for a parliamentary debate was finally signed by ninety-two members and taken to the governor general by a delegation which included Forbes. Dufferin, however, had already decided that parliament was not a fit body to investigate the conduct of the government. He accepted Macdonald's plan for the immediate prorogation of parliament and the appointment of a royal commission, consisting of three judges. In addition, he added the proviso that parliament should reconvene within a few weeks, rather than at the usual time in February, in order to receive the report of the commission. With his plea rejected by Dufferin, Mackenzie could only hope that he might be able to move a resolution in the Commons before the summons arrived to wait on the governor general in the Senate chamber. But although he tried his best, he was caught in mid-motion and parliament stood adjourned. The frustrated Liberals then streamed into the railway committee room, where they made angry speeches and passed harsh resolutions.[43]

With parliament prorogued, Mackenzie was able to set out on the tour of the Maritimes, which he had originally planned for July. He stayed a week in Nova Scotia where he devoted part of his time to establishing agencies for the Isolated Risk Fire Insurance Company of which he was president.[44] His trip to the province was badly needed because he was not well known there. He concentrated mainly on Halifax, and his only visit outside the city was to New Glasgow where he spoke to a crowd of 500 people.[45] In order to introduce him to the Halifax business community the ministry arranged a public banquet, but it was scarcely a success because the hall, which could seat 700, was only one-quarter filled. Moreover, all the federal members declined their invitations to attend.[46] Mackenzie might well have deduced that he could not rely on much aid from Nova Scotia if he failed to unseat Macdonald.

Whether or not the Nova Scotians felt themselves fully involved in the affairs of Ottawa, they were kept posted on all aspects of the charges against Macdonald. The newspaper comments, which had declined briefly after the prorogation of parliament, intensified when the royal commission opened its public hearings in Montreal on 1 September. The editorial treatment of the charges was influenced by the testimony firmly establishing that Macdonald had received large sums of money from Allan during the 1872 election campaign. The Conservative newspapers in Halifax concentrated on the issue of bribery, which they contended was endemic to all representative systems. Hence, the resort to bribery was a mark of the venality of the people and was not a reflection on the nature of the Macdonald government.[47] While none of these papers was willing to condone the use of bribery,[48] they did agree that Macdonald should be judged in accordance with his record in office. As prime minister, they contended, he had managed to establish a state which was based on the virtues of honesty and justice. This image of Macdonald as the creator of the state was seriously damaged by the Liberal charges that he had sold the Pacific railway to American interests. The Conservative press not only argued that Macdonald had made no connection with the Americans but insisted upon identifying him with the state, which created a tendency to regard opposition to Macdonald as opposition to good government in Canada. In this context the claim of good government referred not so much to a degree of excellence as to an ethical quality which supported the institutions of the country and controlled political conduct. A violation of these moral imperatives, embedded in the rules controlling respectable behaviour, would pose a threat to the stability of society. The Conservative papers argued that the Liberals represented just such a threat. The manner in which the Liberals obtained their information and then ignored all the proprieties in pressing their case, contended one leading Conservative paper, reflected base motives which sprang from moral turpitude.[49] This argument was pressed to its logical conclusion when the newspaper called for some federal member to be 'patriotic enough to turn the table on these false accusers, and move that they be impeached for high crimes and misdemeanors, in foully and wickedly aspersing the fair character of the country through its representatives.'[50]

Along with the notion that Macdonald was responsible for establishing good government, the Conservative press expressed the idea that society needed protection from ever present dangers. This aspect of the argument was particularly developed by the *Evening Express*, a Catholic lay paper edited by the twenty-seven year old Martin Griffin. The *Express* came close to arguing that the government, in the interests of social stability, had to control the people by any and all available means.[51] In carrying out its responsibilities the government should not be judged by the same code of ethics which applied to an individual. In applying this view to the use of bribery in elections, the *Express* developed a distinction between a private and public act. The acceptance of a bribe, a private act, was reprehensible, but the offer of a bribe for the public good was not subject to the standards guiding personal conduct. When a clergyman in Halifax denounced Macdonald for corruption, this paper ordered him to stick to his duty of bringing the poorer classes to church and teaching them 'to be humble, charitable, pure, sober, honest and penitent.'[52] The *Express* had no hesitation in declaring that such classes needed instruction because they were, by their very nature, corrupt. Obviously the lower classes had to be supervised by the respectable classes of society and care had to be taken that the latter kept their social and political power.

Although the arguments of the government press were shot through with special pleading, these papers did sympathize with the problem of corruption for the politician. In reply, the *Morning Chronicle* offered the flat opinion that a crime for an individual remained a crime even when committed in the name of the state.[53] At the same time the Liberal press admitted that bribery was widespread amongst both parties. However, continued the *Citizen*, this was no reason to ignore corruption, because 'we shall prefer that hypocrisy which pays the tribute of respect, at least, to virtue and honour, to that unblushing coarseness that admits bribery and then asks for a liberal view of its actions.'[54] The Pacific scandal, with all its plots and subplots, was unique in its scope, the Liberal press contended, because it provided a case study of the methods which Macdonald had been using for twenty years. The charge of corruption thus arose not out of specific acts of bribery, but out of the alleged Conservative conspiracy to subvert the moral tone of Canada.[55]

The argument developed by the Liberal press in Halifax was really built around the familiar contention that the will of the people, as expressed in parliament, would foster reform and progress. The press was, thus, interested in curtailing the power of the cabinet to escape from the control of the Commons. In this regard it noted that the disallowance of the oath bill by the British government early in the summer worked to the advantage of the cabinet.[56] Similarly it noted that the use of prerogative by the governor general to prorogue parliament and to establish a royal commission represented a fusion of the powers of the prerogative with the powers of the Cabinet against the rights of the Commons.[57] The Conservative press decided to interpret these various charges as a partisan attack on the governor general and thus a direct attack on the colonial tie with England.[58] Rather than immediately retreating before this charge of disloyalty, the *Citizen* accepted the challenge and replied: 'If the people and Parliament of this country are to find themselves trammelled in the administration of their own affairs by impertinent interferences by the Home Government, they will not be slow to realize the necessity of asserting their entire independence of such authority.'[59] Many Liberals in Halifax were undoubtedly sceptical of various aspects of the tie with England, yet there was little point in developing an argument which would allow the Conservatives to drape the flag even more securely over Macdonald's shoulders. The Liberal press therefore refrained from further comments on the tie with England until the fall of the Macdonald government, when it returned to the subject with the prediction that independence would arrive within the decade.[60]

During the fall of 1873 the Conservative press continued to defend the role of the prerogative as constituting an important restraint on political parties. Parties, according to these papers, would place the country under the tyranny of the people if left unchecked.[61] The discussion of this point emphasized the tendency of the Liberals to interpret parliament as consisting of the Commons, whereas the Conservatives emphasized that parliament was composed of the crown, the Senate, and the Commons. The basic policy of Macdonald, argued one Conservative paper, was to stop 'an arbitrary, intolerant majority' in the Commons from seizing control of the government and destroying all the influence of the crown.[62] Thus, the function of the prerogative was to aid the cabinet in controlling the people. One result of this view was to make the government, rather than parliament, or political parties, the dynamic force in the task of nation building. 'The people need not care much which political party wins or loses,' argued the *Reporter*, because 'political organizations are but the foam on the crest of the waves.' The paper continued: 'we are laying the foundations of a State, and these must be laid in honour, truth and integrity. It is bosh to talk of this parliamentary tradition or that ancient prerogative, in matters of this sort ... Dry technicalities should not be allowed to warp our sense of justice.'[63]

The debate in the Conservative newspapers thus centred on the defence of nation building by a strong executive which, to protect the state, was obliged to use all necessary methods to carry out its role. The Liberals, in their turn, stressed a doctrine of progress, with the Commons acting as the spokesman for the respectable classes. The Liberals in Nova Scotia had long argued about the danger of the cabinet misusing its executive powers, but they had not been seriously concerned with the problem of a major concentration of wealth. The issue of 1873 was clearly tied up with the relationship between the government and the business community. The Liberal press did contend that Macdonald, in return for four more years of power, had sold the railway charter to Allan, who, in addition to receiving the railway, also benefitted from various other government perquisites and subsidies. According to the Liberal press, Allan was the head of a Montreal ring which was tied in with similar rings in Chicago and New York.[64] It was apparent that the Liberal papers were concerned about the danger arising from a large concentration of wealth. The Liberal press might well have been inhibited in its attack by the arguments against corporations advanced by some Conservative papers. These papers had also contended that since corporations in both Canada and the United States had corrupted governments, the government should build the railway to the Pacific coast as a public project rather than create a private company to undertake it.[65] Opposition by Liberals to corporations was to be expected, but they objected even more violently to increasing the power of Macdonald's cabinet.

Although some of the editors may not have fully supported the arguments which they used,[66] the newspapers did express conflicting attitudes on several significant issues. These issues involved attitudes and policies essential to the development of the modern state. In contending that the government was the true representative and guardian of the nation, the Conservatives were reaffirming a basic contention that opinions of representative bodies are binding. On the other hand the cautious attitude of the Liberals towards a strong executive and an emphasis on parliamentary authority was a reaction, in part, to the rise of the corporation. The Conservative's emphasis on the state as the dynamic force in society and their fear of the intolerant majority, however, were not confined to Canada. Policies undertaken by Bismarck on these very subjects became a model for the collectivist theories of government in modern Britain. The debate on the Pacific scandal, therefore, with its examination of cabinet responsibility and parliamentary authority, formed part of the development of modern attitudes towards government and bureaucracy in Canada.[67]

While critical issues were involved in the Pacific scandal, the politicians of the day were caught up in the secondary issue of the shattering of the Conservative government. The Nova Scotian federal members were subjected to a continual barrage of conflicting pressures. During the fall Tupper pursued several members and succeeded in recapturing, for a time, two who had strayed into the Liberal camp.[68] Of the twenty-one Nova Scotian members, Mackenzie eventually won over ten. The chief prize was N.L. McKay who explained to the Commons that although a Conservative and a unionist, he was convinced that Macdonald was destroying the principles of parliament.[69] His course impressed Mackenzie,[70] but it failed to inspire other Conservatives in the Nova Scotian ranks to imitate his action. Tobin of Halifax did drop hints that he would be willing to change parties, but Jones was unlikely to accept him as a colleague and Mackenzie did not even bother talking to him. Of the ten defectors, five had been elected in 1867 as opponents of union, one had been elected first in a by-election in 1869, three had been elected in 1872, and the remaining member had been elected only the previous summer.

Of those who transferred their party allegiance, only McKay was clearly an opponent of the provincial government. Of those who remained with the Conservatives, five had originally been elected as opponents of union. The question of whether a member changed parties in 1873 did not depend so much on whether or not he had opposed union as whether he had good relations, at the county level, with the supporters of the local government.

The number of defections from Nova Scotia, added to those from other provinces, made it impossible for Macdonald's government to continue in office. It was probable that the government had never expected to survive because shortly after the session began it secretly made a number of appointments. One of the fortunate members was Hugh McDonald of Antigonish, who exchanged his place in the cabinet for a position on the bench of the Superior Court of Nova Scotia.[71] During most of the brief session Macdonald provided no leadership, and it was not until 3 November that he made a major speech. Two days later he handed his resignation to the governor general. The resignation, which came before the vote on the motion of non-confidence, spared the members the agony of publicly committing themselves either for or against the Macdonald government.

Immediately following the resignation, Mackenzie was summoned by the governor general to form a new cabinet. The task had to be done quickly and with the material at hand. Although he might have wished to make his choice on the basis of merit, no one doubted that Mackenzie's cabinet, like Macdonald's, would recognize various sectional, ethnic, and religious groups. The Nova Scotian supporters assumed that their province would continue to receive two cabinet positions. The members insisted, however, on the right of nomination in order to make the cabinet members their true representatives. Mackenzie, harassed and short of time, reluctantly agreed to the procedure, although it effectively prevented him from trying to arrange for Jones or some member of the provincial cabinet to enter the cabinet. After meeting in caucus, the Liberal supporters from Nova Scotia endorsed Coffin of Shelburne and William Ross of Victoria as their candidates.[72] Mackenzie would have preferred two other members, but he acquiesced.[73] The demand by the members to select their own representatives in the cabinet was a continuation of the rebellion of the previous March. In many ways they were reacting to Tupper's use of his cabinet position to control the federal members and the province. To insist that a cabinet minister should be picked by his colleagues did lay the ground work for the members to demand the right of dismissal of a minister and to determine, in provincial caucus, the policies of their cabinet ministers.

The selection of Ross and Coffin was apparently made on the simple grounds that they had the longest parliamentary service. Coffin, who took the office of receiver-general, was popular in his own county, although he had not played a conspicuous role in parliament. Ross, who became the minister of militia and defence, seemed to have good relations with the provincial government. His brother was a supporter of the local ministry in the provincial assembly and he himself had been offered a seat in the provincial upper house.[74] Despite these connections with the local government, he had remained a supporter of the Macdonald government. In 1873 Tupper offered him the position as inspector of customs for Nova Scotia.[75] As the difficulties of the Macdonald government increased, his salary demands went higher[76] and he did not finally reject the offer until September 1873.[77] Once in office Ross's lack of judgment quickly became apparent. He, like the other ministers, had to resign his seat in the Commons on his acceptance of a salaried office and seek re-election.[78] Panic-stricken at finding himself opposed by a strong opponent, he immediately asked Mackenzie for campaign funds. Mackenzie was later astonished to learn that Ross had drawn funds from Jones as instructed and had also borrowed $2000 from another government supporter. Mackenzie could only conclude that Ross had pocketed the money or that he would be unseated on grounds of bribery.[79] When Mackenzie heard that Tupper was indeed collecting evidence of bribery against Ross, he immediately summoned him to Ottawa for an explanation. Ross, after some delay, did finally go to Ottawa, but finding Mackenzie absent, slipped back to Cape Breton.[80] It was apparent that he would not remain long in the cabinet.

The selection of Ross by the members as one of their representatives undoubtedly did little to help their demand for increased political power. Their claim for greater participation also met with opposition from the local government, which expected to be rewarded for its support of the federal Liberals. Mackenzie was only in office a month when Annand, accompanied by Vail, arrived in Ottawa with a list of grievances. In Mackenzie's view, 'Annand was much displeased that he was not consulted about local patronage alone and altogether as an Irishman would say.'[81] Annand had to be satisfied with a promise from Mackenzie that he would consult him on appointments to such major positions as judgeships. The demand by Annand for control of all patronage was really a revival of a similar claim which had helped bring about the split with

Howe in 1868. Control of the political organization by the local government would at least prevent a repetition of the troubles faced by the Conservatives since 1869. Annand's demands, however, would not merely have infringed on the political influence of the federal government but would have turned the federal members into mere associates of the local government. In view of their own demands for greater influence, the federal members were likely to resist Annand's pretension to political supremacy in the province. Any conflict between the federal members and the local government was certain to harm the party because the federal Liberals still had no organization of their own and needed the help of the provincial government.

The threat of difficulties within the Liberal camp could not conceal the great changes which had taken place in Nova Scotian politics during 1873. The single most important event was obviously the formation of the Mackenzie government with the support of half of the Nova Scotian delegation. Several of the members, as former Liberals, were likely to be concerned by the charges that the policies of Macdonald threatened reform and progress in Canada. Despite their concern, some members, because they were not particularly involved in the issues between the Canadian political parties, might not have defected to the Liberals had it not become apparent that the Conservatives were about to fall. During 1873, however, they did show an interest in the cabinet. The revolt of the members in the spring, and the selection of the cabinet ministers by caucus, showed that the members were more concerned with their relationship to the government than with party politics. Some Nova Scotians, however, were deeply concerned about the rise of Tupper and the deterioration of the coalition of 1869. All these issues were caught up in the furor over the Pacific scandal, but the scandal, in a fashion, acted as a catalyst. Even without the scandal, Macdonald would have had trouble with his Nova Scotian supporters. As it was, local and federal issues melded together to shatter the Conservatives in Nova Scotia.

11

The winter election

The fall of the Macdonald ministry opened opportunities for the continued adjustment of Nova Scotia to the political structure of confederation. Perhaps the most pressing issue was the manner in which the Nova Scotians would relate to the political parties of the upper provinces, but other questions of prime importance included economic development and federal-provincial relations. Although the debate on these issues throughout 1873 had been extensive, it had often been inconclusive. Whether the provincial supporters of the new Liberal government could provide any more definite proposals would be seen during the impending federal election.

In December 1873 Mackenzie decided to call an election immediately, rather than recall the existing parliament. The political climate seemed suitable since all of his cabinet ministers had been re-elected, seven of them by acclamation. The Nova Scotian Liberals were soon warned by Mackenzie to prepare for an election[1] and parliament was dissolved on 2 January. In calling the election Mackenzie gambled that the resignation of the Macdonald government would have left the Conservatives disorganized and without an effective rebuttal on the Pacific railway issue. The election campaign in general thus seemed to be a referendum on the Pacific scandal, but in Nova Scotia the situation was far too complex to be interpreted in the light of any one issue.

The newspaper editorials seemed scarcely to change in tone as they switched from discussing the resignation of the Macdonald government to dealing with the general election due to take place on 2 February. Although the Liberals wanted to make the Pacific scandal the central issue of the campaign,[2] it had been dealt with at such length in 1873 that there was little left to say. While some Conservatives believed that the entire incident was due to bungling and incompetency by Macdonald, and others felt indignation at the evidence of bribery, they all preferred to ignore the issue. When this was not feasible they tried to salvage what they could by stressing the need for the railway, and dealt at length with Mackenzie's professed intention to proceed most cautiously with construction. Any railway, however, necessitated discussion of government involvement in the project. Although some Conservative papers, such as the *Evening Express*, had proposed the previous fall that the government should build the railway as a public project, a similar proposal from Mackenzie was greeted as a blatant device to corrupt parliament.[3]

The Conservatives presented Mackenzie's equivocal stand on the Pacific railway as an example of the general weakness of the Liberal ministry. The incompetency of the Liberals was so obvious, asserted the Conservative press, and was in such marked contrast with the skill of their predecessors as to constitute a danger to the state.[4] In view of the bungling of the Pacific railway by the Macdonald ministry, this was a startling, if not unexpected, claim. When the Conservative press began citing Hincks, Cartier, and Howe as shining examples of Macdonald's ministers, it was apparent they were at least not referring to that battered cabinet which resigned with Macdonald in 1873. The argument being made by the Conservatives was not likely to be resolved, however, by any comparison of the relative merit of individual members of the two governments. Rather, they were using the question of quality to assert once more the Conservative bias in favour of the central role of government as opposed to the championship of the House of Commons by the Liberals. Although the Conservatives stressed the ideal of national unity being developed by an active government, their view of the cabinet embodied an appeal to sectionalism. They tried to exploit sectionalism by attacking the choice of Ross and Coffin as the provincial representatives in the cabinet. They ignored the role of the Nova Scotian caucus in forcing these two men on Mackenzie and argued instead that Mackenzie, steeped in Ontario sectionalism,[5] had appointed two weak, incompetent members to his ministry as part of his design to ignore Nova Scotia entirely.[6]

The Halifax Liberals were embarrassed by Ross and Coffin but they took the position that for each province to depend on its cabinet ministers for defence of its interests would be, in itself, unhealthy. They also insisted that Macdonald's practice of recognizing different ethnic, religious, and sectional interests was mere pandering to disruptive forces that would tear apart, rather than create, a nation.[7] They retreated from this position, however, by contending that in this case Mackenzie must follow what Macdonald had initiated, even though Mackenzie had the eventual goal of creating a cabinet which would truly express national unity rather than sectional interests.[8] As the descendants of the anti-confederation movement they were unlikely to ignore the problems of sectionalism. At the same time, however, they conceived that government should be founded on principles accepted by the people. The Conservatives, on the other hand, thought the function of the government was to create the nation by imposing unity on disparate factions. Although it did the Conservatives little good at this time, their argument appealed more directly to sectionalism than did the Liberal argument. Whatever difficulties the Liberals may have had in expressing sectionalism in terms of political ideas, their claim to be the defenders of the province against union was a matter of record. As the political divisions of 1867 broke down, however, and the Liberals tried to win the support of the confederates, their past role became of less immediate value.

The election campaign demonstrated that the position of the Nova Scotian Conservatives in federal politics had been damaged by the events of 1873. The Pacific scandal and the loss of office compounded the strains which had already existed within party ranks. Tupper's promise to avoid coalitions in future and to reward party regulars came too late and was insufficient to save the Conservatives in 1874. Nevertheless their strength did not disappear entirely because they only allowed four counties to go by acclamation in 1874, which was three less than the Liberals allowed to go unchallenged in the previous federal election. One sign of weakness, however, was their inability to field a full slate in two of the three double ridings in the province. Most of the sitting members ran again, the exceptions being the two Halifax Conservative members and Isaac LeVesconte, also a Conservative, from Richmond County.

Morale sagged among the Conservatives because it was difficult not to conclude that the Liberals were going to be in office for some time.[9] Rather than oppose the Liberals openly, several of the Conservative candidates began to argue that they would work with the Liberal government and give it fair support. In Kings County Samuel Chipman tried to convince the local Liberals that although he had remained loyal to Macdonald, he would now support Mackenzie. But this ploy failed when Tupper said that he wanted Chipman re-elected. The Liberals then promptly nominated Dr (later Sir) Frederick Borden,[10] who went on to win the seat. Even Tupper, recovering from an attack of diphtheria, insisted that he would continue to have access to the new government, particularly in matters of patronage. The statement was ridiculous, but

Annand was sufficiently alarmed at the gullibility of the voters to request a denial from Mackenzie.[11] In Hants county one Conservative, William Allison, who resigned from the local house in order to contest the federal seat, issued a carefully worded letter in which he claimed that he had always been able to work with the Liberals.[12] This refusal of candidates to stand openly as Conservatives blurred party allegiances and made party designations, particularly for new candidates, somewhat difficult. Seven of the Conservative candidates, however, were sitting members who had remained loyal to Macdonald. As for the new candidates, two weeks before the election a Liberal paper classified five of them as Conservatives. This list included Allison, as well as William Kidston. The latter, a onetime rebel in the local legislature, had offered his support to Mackenzie in 1873 but had been rejected by the Nova Scotian members.[13] There were, therefore, some half-dozen seats that were not being contested by Conservative candidates.

Pre-election disputes concerning the candidates' political allegiance were due in part to the lack of a provincial party organization which could accredit the candidates. Any organization that did exist was essentially decentralized and was significant chiefly at the local level. The county organizations usually consisted of various factions which combined to select candidates and to decide on campaign policy. During 1873 this practice had given rise in Halifax to the complaint that the political rights of the citizen were being ignored by small cliques. There were a few signs that existing practices might change, especially when the Liberals in Halifax established a Reform League in November 1873. This society was ostensibly modelled on new societies being established at that time in Ontario.[14] The Halifax society, however, seemed similar to the old Repeal League, established in 1868, which in turn developed from the anti-confederation association formed by Howe in 1866. The duties of the new body were the traditional ones of raising funds and canvassing for candidates in Halifax county. The league, however, had little impact on the province because it had only one branch, in Pugwash, outside of the city,[15] and the city branch did not appear to be particularly active.

It was typical of the mood of provincial politics that the Reform League, at its first meeting in Halifax, protested against the failure of the Mackenzie government to dismiss Conservatives from the civil service.[16] Although the Liberals were much concerned about patronage, it posed a critical problem for the Conservative party, particularly since it went into opposition. The belief that political support should be rewarded by the government sprang from the same type of paternalism that dictated that property owners should protect their employees and servants. Political rewards, however, could be a challenge to economic power and in the 1850s many Conservatives had seen political patronage as a challenge to their own position in society. There was no reason for the Conservatives to remain permanently opposed to patronage because it could be used to supplement the position of the respectable elements of society. While patronage might have levelling tendencies, it could also support élitism and, as a means of disciplining the members of parliament, it appealed particularly to the Conservatives with their tendency to emphasize the role of government. The Conservatives were, thus, likely to support an extra-parliamentary party organization that would partly compete with the elected members. The Liberals were opposed, not only because they were now in office but because they concentrated on the position of the member in parliament. Although changes in party organization were developing, the emphasis on having patronage dispensed through the member of parliament inhibited the development of a provincial party organization. This affected the role of Nova Scotia in federal politics because it placed a premium on good relations with the government and gave a definite edge to the Liberals in the election campaign.

The change in fortune of the two national parties made the task of popularizing the Liberals much easier for the provincial government. Individual members of the government were active, as they had been in 1872, but this time there were fewer local members aiding supporters of John A. Macdonald[17] However only two members, one from each party, resigned their seats in order to contest federal seats. Perhaps those members with ambitions in federal politics had already been drawn off in 1872. By 1874 provincial politics may have seemed much more tranquil and less hazardous than federal politics.

The federal scene did have a definite attraction for Vail who spent some time considering whether he should remain in provincial politics. Mackenzie appealed to Vail's vanity by arguing that he was the only man capable of defeating Savary, the sitting member.[18] Vail made arrangements to contest the seat in Digby, but three weeks before the election he suddenly withdrew.[19] One of Vail's supporters, E.R. Oakes, was hurriedly pressed into service[20] and he went on to defeat Savary. Vail's indecision was perhaps caused by his failure to secure a firm promise that he would replace either Ross or Coffin in the cabinet. He might also have been concerned over a breakdown in negotiations to find a new house leader and provincial secretary in the local ministry. The proposed arrangement would have seen P.C. Hill desert the Conservatives and take over Vail's position. The local house was due to meet shortly after the federal election and there was little time to find Hill a seat. The change from Vail to Hill may simply have been too complex to carry out in the time available.[21]

The loss of Hill was a severe blow to the Conservatives in Halifax. Hill, a lawyer, former mayor of the city, director of several firms, and president of the Halifax Banking Company, was one of the richest men in the province. During his political career he had helped form the short-lived confederate government in July 1867 and in 1870 had won a by-election giving him a seat in the provincial house. Although he had been Tupper's agent for patronage since 1867, he had apparently become dissatisfied with his party, perhaps because Tupper had not selected him as lieutenant-governor in 1873 and had not promoted his brother in the civil service.[22] Although he did not publicly declare himself a Liberal during the federal campaign of 1874, he gave no aid to the Conservatives and they were well aware of his negotiations with the Liberals.[23] For practical purposes, therefore, the Conservatives had lost one of their most influential supporters.

Hill's defection was only one of the difficulties facing the Conservatives in Halifax. Neither of the two sitting members would run again and the party could not find replacements. Probably their main hope was that Jones, who was thinking of retiring from politics for business reasons, would not run again; then the Conservatives might avoid a contest by making some arrangement to split the riding. Jones, however, did stand and as nomination day came closer it appeared that Jones and Power would be returned by acclamation. Some Conservatives, unwilling to permit defeat, determined to find a candidate. Even a token opposition would force the Liberals to spend time and money in Halifax that otherwise would be used on their candidates in the rest of the province. George Johnson of the *Evening Reporter* took advantage of the situation to urge the type of campaign waged by Motton in the Halifax by-election the previous winter. His choice of candidate fell on Donald Robb, a master plasterer who had lived in the United States. Robb was well known to the working men of the city[24] and he had done some canvassing for the Conservatives.[25]

The first major step in Robb's campaign came with the publication of an unsigned petition calling on all working men to attend a meeting at Temperance Hall on 27 January to consider selecting a candidate. Fifteen hundred men turned out in eighteen below zero weather to attend. Finally a member of the typographical union presented a petition, signed by the executives of five unions, protesting they had not been consulted about the meeting.²⁶ Some unionists objected to any third party movement aimed at working men because they should not take an independent role in politics nor did they, as working men, have specific interests which bound them together politically. While this view may have represented the craft unions, others in the audience set up a chant for Robb, but when he appeared he declared he would not run.²⁷ Despite the disclaimer, he settled the details of his campaign the following day at a meeting with some leading Conservatives, among whom were Johnston, Alpin Grant of the *British Colonist*, and Dr Wickwire, a former partner of Tupper. Robb agreed to run as a workingman's candidate favouring a protective tariff in return for $3000 from the Conservatives to offset his election expenses.²⁸

In advancing Robb's candidacy the *Evening Reporter* stressed an organic view of society which assumed that its welfare depended upon the rights and interests of each of the various classes. This summation broke with the prevailing attitude that the interests of society had to be left to the care of the respectable elements, who had proved their fitness to lead. It declared that its own policies were above politics because they were concerned with the welfare of society.²⁹ Society, according to this paper, consisted of the farmer, the worker, and the manufacturer.³⁰ Each had its own legitimate interest, but in the past the farmer had received more than his share of political preference. Notably absent in this analysis of society was a mention of the merchants, particularly the West Indies commission merchants who played a major role in the economic and political life of the city. Dr Almon, a former federal member for the city, went further than the *Reporter* when he asked by what right the cod-fish aristocrats, who only engaged in truckage, sneered at the artisans.³¹

The demand for an active, independent role in politics for the working man was new in Nova Scotian politics.³² Until this election, working men had not played a conspicuous role in politics and had certainly not made any effort to form a third party. Although some interest was expressed by a number of workmen in the proposal, it was obvious that the chief initiative in 1874 was coming from the Conservatives. The campaign in support of Robb might have been made partly to embarrass the Liberals, but it did indicate a Conservative bias against the pre-eminence of the merchants even though many Conservatives who were lawyers, doctors, and journalists shared the notion that economic success was one criterion of leadership. Some Conservatives, therefore, objected to the claims for equality inherent in the demand for a working man's candidate. The Conservative *Evening Express* declared that the election of a working man would degrade public life, and openly campaigned for Jones and

Power.³³ P.C. Hill, who had once supported benefit and self-help societies, also came out against a movement which he declared could end with social unrest and disorder. It was no light thing, he declared '... to set class against class and to foster the idea that there is some privileged class who lives at the expense of the working man.'³⁴ He did not bother denying that there were class distinctions; he merely assumed that they were not fit subjects for political discussion. It was interesting that Hill's support for Jones and Power was based on the premise that Robb was a threat to decency and order and that he made no reference to the Pacific scandal. Although Robb's campaign began after Hill had negotiated with the Liberals, several of the issues raised by Robb were similar to those discussed by Motton and the *Evening Reporter* a year before. It was therefore quite possible that Hill was disturbed at the trends of certain factions within the Halifax Conservative party.

For the *Morning Chronicle* the mere nomination of Robb was a sign that communism and anarchy might soon reach the shores of Halifax. The owner of the paper and many other Liberals were, if anything, even more indignant with Robb because of his support of a high tariff policy. A protective tariff to aid manufacturing was, of course, opposed by many merchants, although they were quite prepared to defend the incidental tariff protection which they received. Moreover, the merchants had a decided impact in Halifax because they controlled seventeen of the nineteen private firms estimated by Bradstreet to be worth over $100,000.³⁵ Both Jones and his chief fund raiser, James Duffus, were merchants with firms worth in excess of $150,000. Jones condemned any suggestion of a workingman's movement, but he refused even to mention the subject of a protective tariff. He had no objection to a high tariff on individual items such as sugar, but he did not believe that there was sufficient harmony of interests in the country as a whole to support a comprehensive protective system. Robb's juxtaposition of the interest of the worker with a strong industrial economy was probably an attempt to appeal to the several small and medium sized industries which existed in the Halifax area. Workers might well accept high tariffs on pragmatic grounds, and their support for tariffs provided a possible ground for co-operation with those who resented the supremacy of the merchants. Thus, the support of a tariff policy came not because of the strength of the manufacturers but rather as a reaction to the merchants. The introduction of the issue into local politics at that time was a matter of expediency, but the issue was too deeply rooted to be swept away by any failure of Robb's campaign in 1874.

The actual outcome of the elections was never in doubt. Robb began his campaign only a week before the election and even with an efficient organization he would probably not have been able to overcome the lead of his opponents. Although he did receive some aid from trade unionists, he was mainly dependent on the Conservatives, and this made him vulnerable to the charge of being their pawn. Robb suffered a further blow two days before the election when a blizzard swept across the province, blocking the roads with twelve-foot drifts and making campaigning impossible.[36] He was not only soundly defeated but some of his campaign workers actually voted against him.[37] Although Robb could be dismissed with impunity, he did have the support of some influential Conservatives, particularly George Johnston of the *Evening Reporter*. Rather than helping the Conservative party out of a difficult position, its support of Robb merely deepened the split within the party. Those Conservatives who voted for Jones and Power at least demonstrated that the party lines drawn around the issue of union were obsolete. The successful burying of the old anti-confederation party was achieved partly at the expense of the Conservatives. The campaign probably did little immediate good for the working man since it crystallized a growing opposition to the workers within the city. The attitude was summed up by the *Evening Express* when it wrote: '... there must be always working men, men to work with their hands, to be poor, to be industrious, to be unfortunate, to suffer; it is the will of God and the destiny of the race. That will and that destiny are not to be counteracted by public meeting, by agitations, by the speeches of demagogues, by public orations, or other foolish means.'[38] Labour agitation, similar to that which had broken out in London and New York, now seemed to be a distinct possibility for Halifax.

The blizzard which disrupted the campaign in Halifax raged elsewhere in the province as well.[39] County roads were blocked, and many voters were prevented from reaching the polls. Yet the total vote in 1874 was virtually the same as in 1872. Of the fourteen counties holding an election, one-half had a turnout equal to or slightly higher than that in the previous federal election. Some interesting comments on campaign methods and attitudes were recorded by Vernon Smith, chief engineer for the Yarmouth railway, who campaigned for Frank Killam, president of the railway company and member for Yarmouth. The people he encountered were, he wrote in his diary: '... Puritanical, hypocritical factious democrats who have no God but the Dollar, no religion but self, no politics but personal aggrandizement. I filled my sleigh with small handy bottles of whiskey – convenient flat flasks, and surrounded myself with twenty old men of the W.A.R. [Windsor Annapolis Railway]. I do not condescend to talk to the people about any question of morality or politics. I went sharply for the dollars and gave the whiskey. There was two million dollars to spend on this railway, and through this county if Frank was elected. Nothing if he was not ... The low hypocritical humbugs, how I hated them all.'[40] This degree of scorn was unusual but the methods were not and his comments provided an insight into some of the reaction against Robb in Halifax.

Of the members who had supported John A. Macdonald, only Tupper and W. McDonald of Cape Breton County were re-elected. Even the latter's credentials were suspect because he was a self-professed supporter of the new government. Of the successful candidates all but Tupper were pledged to support Mackenzie.[41] The election results of 1874 formed an interesting contrast with those of 1872. In both cases almost all the elected candidates expressed some sort of support for the government of the day. The rapid turnover in support was indicative of a belief that government services and political rewards were closely allied to party allegiance. This emphasis on patronage also served to magnify the role of government in political affairs. The defeat of all but two of Macdonald's supporters was due, at least partially, to viewing political allegiance in terms of its relation to the source of power. Conservatives and Liberals differed as to whether this source was the Commons or the cabinet, but on a practical level there was broad agreement that political rewards followed allegiance to the government. Support of the Mackenzie government in 1874 thus confirmed an existing orientation of thought about the nature of politics, and the rapid change in political support in Nova Scotia was due to the success of the Liberals in gaining office rather than to any specific acceptance of their programme or policies. Easy as it was to look on the election as a virtual referendum on the Pacific scandal, it was apparent that the voters were influenced by more than moral indignation.[42]

Although the election did not change the nature of the political tie between the province and the federal parties, it did help break down the old alignments within the province. This was achieved not by the disintegration of the old anti-confederate party but through the collapse of the Conservatives, especially in Halifax where the various factions within the Conservative party fell apart and new issues developed because of the chaos. It was open to question whether the Liberals could simply add defectors from the Conservatives to their party without themselves undergoing some form of internal dissolution.

12

New ways and old conflicts

The success of the Liberals in the federal general election was in many ways a victory for the local ministry. They, in conjunction with such supporters as Jones and Carmichael, had managed to overcome the disunity of the anti-confederate party elected in 1867 and become identified as part of a Canadian party. They had also managed to circumvent Macdonald's strategy of 1868 and 1869 to form a coalition around Tupper which would be inalienably tied to the Conservative government. Their very success in ensuring strong political allies outside the province, however, created new problems. If the local ministry could now expect a more co-operative attitude from Ottawa, they would have to bear responsibility for federal policies which might be decidedly unpopular in the province. The period of harmony thus did not remove all conflicts between the two levels of government; it merely ensured that the politicians would experiment with new ways of resolving old conflicts.

Questions about the proper role of the local ministry in federal affairs arose as soon as the legislature met on 12 March. Some members of the opposition supported a policy of harmony between the two levels of government in the name of national unity,[1] but a majority of their number accepted the politically attractive argument that such a policy would lead to the supremacy of the Ontario Grits to the ultimate disadvantage of Nova Scotia. The contention that protecting the interests of Nova Scotia required perpetual hostility to Ottawa was a return to a theme often exploited by Tupper both before and after confederation. No one in the assembly at this time seemed particularly interested in the view that provincial affairs were different from federal affairs and should therefore be organized differently. Instead, the role of the federal government and the problem of provincialism were pushed into prominence.

During the session, concerns relating to Ottawa arose at different times and in different ways. The policy favoured by the Conservatives, and Tupper especially, was clearly demonstrated by the confusion over the federal subsidy due to the province under an act readjusting the allowance for all provinces. When the auditor-general made out the provincial accounts in September 1873 he decided that the new subsidy for Nova Scotia should be based on the original terms enacted in 1867 and not on the revised terms granted to the province in 1869. S.L. Tilley, the finance minister, did not learn of this decision until the day before he was to resign from office, when it was too late to act. Although he agreed that the statute was poorly phrased, he thought that in all justice the Nova Scotian debt allowance should be based on the 1869 revision. Tupper was not only aware of the difficulty but had exploited it: at one point during passage of the bill he had assured the New Brunswick members that the revision of 1873 would not be based on the terms of 1869, but later had assured the Nova Scotian members that it would. Tupper had seen no advantage in clarifying the measure and the statute had been duly enacted in a defective form. It was not until November 1873 that the provincial government discovered that its federal subsidy was $60,000 less than had been anticipated. Mackenzie agreed with the local government that Nova Scotia should receive the money in dispute, but the Liberal minister of justice did not feel he could authorize payment of the money without an amendment to the act.[2] The Conservatives capitalized on the consequent delay by alleging that the Liberals were once more trying to deny justice to Nova Scotia.[3] Although Tilley refused to support Tupper's claim that the difficulty had been manufactured by the Liberals,[4] the Conservatives continued with their charges.

The exploitation of sectional animosities for party advantage illustrated the sensitivity of the relations between the federal and provincial governments. The importance of the subject gave weight to the question of whether or not federal-provincial relations should be conducted exclusively by the two cabinets or by the two legislatures. In raising the federal subsidy issue in the local house, the Conservatives proposed that the assembly itself should inform the federal government that the province had a right to the larger subsidy.[5] Vail countered with the opinion that the matter would be settled more satisfactorily if it were left to the two governments.[6] This problem of the role of individual members was not primarily one of federal-provincial relations, for it pertained to the general dominance of the cabinet in the assembly. Throughout the session of 1874 Vail was increasing party control within the house and thereby enhancing the influence of the cabinet. On one occasion he stated distinctly that any member who voted against the government would receive neither grants nor patronage.[7] Not only did he try to keep firm control over his followers but he used his position in the assembly to choke off the opposition whenever possible.[8]

The growth of cabinet power through party control deeply concerned Hiram Blanchard, leader of the opposition. In 1874, as in 1873, Blanchard routinely flaunted the most elementary rules of party conduct in the assembly.[9] He was well aware that party control was a by-product of executive power. To curb one, the other had to be restricted or at least not allowed to expand. He realized the potential impact on the position of the cabinet if it secured complete control of communications with Ottawa. This attempt to involve the assembly in federal-provincial affairs reflected his assertion of the independence of the assembly over the cabinet. His efforts were too late since J.W. Johnston and his supporters had tried a similar move in the early 1850s with respect to relations between the assembly and the British government. In terms which echoed the Liberals of the 1850s, Vail asserted the logic of the cabinet system and rejected Blanchard's feeble gestures for the independence of the assembly.

Owing to substantial reductions in the powers and resources of the local government, the issue of relations with the superior government was probably more critical to Vail in the 1870s than it had been to Howe in 1850. The situation had been changed further by the creation of federal members, two of whom sat in the federal government, who could also speak for the province. Questions of the relations between the local ministry and the federal members had arisen almost as soon as the election of 1867 had been completed. The federal members were a very real danger to the local ministry but they were also a threat to the assembly. During the 1874 session the opposition tried to establish that the assembly could instruct the federal members. On one occasion Blanchard moved that the federal members be requested by the assembly to act as a bloc in opposing proposed tariff increases on materials for ship building.[10] Simon Holmes, another member of the opposition, made a similar suggestion when he proposed that the federal members be instructed to seek a tariff on coal.[11] These attempts by two confederates to turn the federal members into delegates of the assembly received no support from the local ministry. In rejecting the two proposals the Nova Scotian government explicitly acknowledged the constitutional division of powers and denied that the assembly had become the sole protector of provincial interests.[12] Public recognition of the role of the federal members was emphasized when the Liberal newspapers credited them with persuading the federal government to modify its tariff proposals.[13]

As far as direct statements were concerned, the local government observed the constitutional niceties. Some pronouncements did conflict with arguments advanced earlier, but since 1871 the government had held that it should adhere to the constitutional division of powers. In fact, however, it was not too scrupulous when its own political interests were involved. One area of disagreement between the federal members and the local government involved plans for railway development. The most controversial concerned the plan of the local ministry in 1874 to grant the line from Truro to Pictou as a subsidy to any promoter who would build a railway running from Pictou to the Gut of Canso; the premier, Annand, had come to the conclusion that a railway could not be extended across Cape Breton Island as had been first proposed. Although the local members from the island accepted this decision there was no assurance that the federal members would prove so manageable.

During the session one of the few important measures approved by the legislature was a county court bill, which the attorney-general had wanted passed in 1872. This bill established district courts, but, in order not to offend the sensitivities of the members, did not affect such existing bodies as the court of probate. Although the measure was useful, it did not provide for the thorough overhaul of the provincial court system that was really needed.[14] The bill passed but it could not be implemented until the federal government allotted money for the salaries of the new judges.

The general policy of inaction was demonstrated by the government's approach to a growing anti-Catholic movement in the province. Nova Scotia was no stranger to the rhetoric of religious bigotry and many people in the province did not want to undergo another religious battle. Both New Brunswick and Prince Edward Island, however, were embroiled in religious struggles and there was a definite danger that these quarrels would stir a controversy, begun in Antigonish the previous summer, into a province-wide movement. This difficulty had begun when some Presbyterian ministers invited Charles Chiniquy, a former Roman Catholic priest who had visited Halifax in 1869, to come to Antigonish, a predominantly Catholic area, to speak of his work as a Presbyterian missionary in Illinois. When he began to denounce the Catholic church, a mob of three hundred Catholics gathered and the Protestants promptly broke for cover. The Protestants in Antigonish were too intimidated to do much about the riot that ensued but the Presbyterian synod in Pictou pressed for a government inquiry. Once the federal election was over the government established a commission of inquiry which absolved the magistrates of Antigonish of any responsibility for not suppressing the riot on the grounds that they had not had a police force to call out.[15] The results of the inquiry, which the government probably expected the Presbyterian synod to reject, were indeed valid but the government made no attempt to remedy the situation by providing for a police force.[16]

One of the dangers of the agitation in the eastern counties was the possibility of escalating the controversy over the Halifax schools, which had begun after the federal election. In part the dispute sprang from the contention that the public school system should meet the needs of the public and be responsible to it. The call for civil rights echoed certain aspects of the Robb campaign, and it was noticeable that the *Evening Reporter* was an active supporter of the proposed changes, one of which demanded that the separation of church and state be observed by preventing the appointment of Roman Catholic priests to the school board. A public meeting was organized by the proponents of the reforms which were declared to be the opening step in the battle between 'ignorance, and half-hearted loyalty on the one hand and whole-hearted loyalty on the other.'[17] This call to arms heralded the formation of the Halifax School Association, which was intended to be a 'patriotic' society with the function of overseeing the school board.[18] When this association asked the legislature to amend the school act, Vail quickly buried the issue.[19] His efforts to pacify the Catholics were helped by the fear, fortunately shared by members of the association, that the school issue could develop into a general religious dispute.[20]

Clearly, the local government was not likely to innovate or adopt any radical measures. Rather, it adopted a mild form of pragmatism intended to accept and protect the position of the respectable elements of society. With reference to union, the government was interested in justifying its dominance in the local political structure within confederation. It therefore seemed out of character when Vail, at the end of the session, and seconded by Blanchard, moved a resolution authorizing the ministry to discuss the subject of Maritime union with New Brunswick. The initiative for this motion, however, had come from New Brunswick and no one in the Nova Scotian house was much interested in the proposal. After a desultory debate, the assembly was summoned to hear the governor prorogue the legislature without a vote being taken on the Maritime union resolution.[21] The lack of interest on the part of Vail and the other members of the assembly indicated that they were not prepared to take any steps that might upset the political system of 1867. They were certainly not willing to exchange their own legislature and cabinet in establishing a sectional bloc against the upper provinces.[22]

The government ended the session apparently in full control of the province. Yet, the agitation in Halifax in favour of the 'rights of the people' was a potential danger to some of its policies, as was the religious quarrel in the eastern counties. To some extent the appearance of strength was a façade, for there was a good deal of dissension and dissatisfaction within the local government. At the centre of the difficulty was William Annand, who, at sixty-eight, had been active in politics for thirty-eight years. His brusque, dictatorial methods led some people to encourage his known inclination to retire from politics. Relations between Annand and Vail in particular were strained to the point where, by the spring of 1874, Vail was determined to leave provincial politics, even if it meant accepting the position of customs collector for Halifax. In addition to dealing with tension within the cabinet, Vail had endured a particularly tumultuous legislative session.

Any reorganization of the provincial cabinet was likely to affect the federal cabinet, as A.G. Jones wanted Vail in Ottawa as a replacement for the unsatisfactory Ross. Tupper and Mackenzie were both convinced Ross was vulnerable to attack, if not over his handling of his campaign in the general election[23] then because of the election which had preceded it.[24] The replacement of Ross was complicated, however, by the fact that both he and Coffin had been nominated by the Nova Scotian federal caucus. The federal members were unlikely to appreciate having one of their own choosing thrust aside in favour of Vail. When, early in June, Mackenzie explored the possibility of bringing Vail into the cabinet, he became alarmed at the threat of dissension.[25] He failed to appreciate Jones' concern for Vail, and offered Annand the position of customs collector for Halifax. Jones was not disposed to consider Mackenzie's political problems and pressed Mackenzie to appoint Vail to the cabinet as he was the only man capable of controlling the federal members.[26] Since the county members would still have one representative, Mackenzie had little choice but to accept the representative of the Halifax faction of the party. He could perhaps comfort himself with the thought that whatever temporary trouble might arise, he would be securing the services of an experienced politician.

Ross had been aware of the manœuvring which had been going on during the summer, but he made no attempt to rally support from his Nova Scotian colleagues until he received Mackenzie's request to resign.[27] He complained bitterly, but sent in his resignation. Then, after receiving letters from some friends, he declared he could not be removed without the consent of those who had put him in the cabinet. He openly challenged the prime minister by informing him that 'as many Nova Scotian members have complained to me about your position as ever could complain that I was not fit for mine.'[28] Ross was an unlikely candidate to head a palace revolt, however, and after being rebuffed by Mackenzie, he meekly applied for the post of customs collector for Halifax.[29]

Vail finally entered the cabinet as minister of militia, but his method of entry did little to ensure tranquillity amongst the Nova Scotian members. A principal difficulty was that neither of the original nominees had represented the influential party supporters of Halifax. Mackenzie could probably have removed Ross more easily if he had worked through the caucus, but he had decided to discipline the members instead. Yet, in view of the need to dispose of Ross and because of Jones's stand on the selection of Vail, Mackenzie had very little choice. The decision to accept nominations by caucus, which had really been unavoidable, was proving to be a hindrance and would continue to complicate future changes in cabinet personnel from the province.

The departure of Vail for Ottawa had been anticipated by the Conservatives since early summer. They had concluded that the ensuing reorganization of the local government would precipitate a provincial election. They were in poor condition to face an election, however, as they had been badly buffetted by the federal contest in February and the Halifax section of the party was particularly rent by dissension. The one-time party organizer for Halifax, P.C. Hill, had left the party and had no wish to return.[30] The *Evening Reporter* was another source of trouble and for the past year it had been irritating the *Evening Express* with its support of Robb and the Halifax School Association. The *Express* became so dissatisfied that it began to attack Blanchard and seemed to be preparing to join the Liberal party. The possibility of such a wholesale defection of the Roman Catholics seriously bothered Tupper, who was convinced that electoral success in the city depended on keeping 'some of our friends out of a snarl with the Catholics on the school question.'[31] The critical role assigned to the Catholics by Tupper meant that the *Reporter* was a liability to the Conservatives and a new policy, more acceptable to the *Evening Express*, would have to be developed.

In an attempt to solve their problems, the Conservatives decided to form a Liberal Conservative Association, which, they hoped, would give the party leaders more control over the party and prevent the type of bickering which had developed in Halifax. The new organization was modelled after Liberal Conservative Associations being formed in Montreal and Ontario. The association was expected to have branches in every polling district in the province which would supervise voter registration and select, with the approval of a committee in Halifax, an official party candidate. It was doubtful, however, that the new organization could actually handle the mechanics of an election better than did the old election committees. Increased control by the party leaders over county politics would help reduce some of the confusion consequent upon having several competing candidates, all claiming to be of the same party and all advocating different policies. It was also unlikely that the party leaders expected the branches to play a major role or to influence party policy to any extent. Rather, the chief role of the branches between elections would be to work at keeping up the morale of the party faithful.[32]

A measure of party control by the leadership was no doubt attractive to some Conservatives after the confusion of the past year in Halifax, even though much of the difficulty in the city was caused by disputes over policy rather than by faulty organization. The need for a new policy was recognized in July at the first public meeting of the Liberal Conservative Association held in Halifax. Supported by such party notables as Sir Edward Kenny and James McDonald, a platform was put forward and adopted without amendment. For those of an innovating turn of mind the platform advocated an income franchise and the establishment of municipal institutions. For those disturbed by this appeal to urban voters there was a traditional call for honest, economical government. Not only could the platform be read in different ways, but it also avoided any reference to controversial subjects of federal-provincial relations and the dangerous topic of the school system.[33] Just what policy the party would adopt would depend to a large extent on who was in control. In this respect it was noticeable that the editor of the *Evening Express* was involved in the association but the editor of the *Evening Reporter* was not.[34] It was therefore likely that any serious possibility of reform would be put aside in favour of party unity.

The party platform was intended primarily for provincial politics and did not contain any reference to a federal economic policy. During the summer, however, the problem of economic policy received more attention than the party platform because of the proposed trade agreement with the United States. Many defenders of Nova Scotia's commercially-oriented economy regarded trade in various staple goods with the United States as a necessity for the economic health of the province. During the struggle for confederation Tupper had argued that union would promote manufacturing in the province and thereby provide an alternative course for economic development. He had also contended that political union would strengthen the British North American provinces so they would be in a better position to renegotiate the Reciprocity Treaty. Following union Tupper had spoken out on occasion in favour of selected tariff increases which would augment the trade ties of his province with other Canadian provinces. Manufacturing had received further support during the federal election of 1874 when Robb had endorsed a high tariff policy. After the election a group, which included a number of well-known Conservatives, established the Nova Scotian Association for the Encouragement of Industrial Interests[35] which favoured the adoption of a protective tariff. This society and the announcement of the terms of the proposed treaty with the United States allowed the Conservatives to test the popularity of a tariff programme without giving it specific endorsement.

The most immediate benefit to Nova Scotia in the proposed arrangement lay in the suggestion to allow American registry of Canadian-built vessels. Although shipbuilding was on the verge of a permanent decline, Nova Scotian shipyards continued to expand, more vessels being built in 1874 than in any previous year, Nova Scotians saw no pressing need to find new markets.[36] The treaty, moreover, did not seem to offer any particular advantage to exports of other Nova Scotian products, particularly since free trade in fish was already provided under the terms of the Treaty of Washington.[37] During the preceding four or five years the Nova Scotians had experienced prosperity that had made them feel less dependent upon trade with the United States. It was perhaps not surprising to find a marked coolness towards the proposed treaty, and the comments in the Liberal press ranged from outright opposition[38] to rather hesitant approval.[39] This lack of firm support from the Liberals could only encourage the Conservatives in their attacks.

In dealing with the treaty, the Conservatives emphasized the harm which could come from the suggested tariff reductions on manufactured goods.[40] They did not say that the existing custom duties should be increased, but they insisted that the incidental protection provided by the existing tariff structure should be maintained. The Conservative newspapers played up public opposition to the treaty, particularly that coming from various boards of trade and chambers of commerce throughout the country.[41] The debate over the proposed treaty marked a further stage in the larger debate concerning the proper nature of the Nova Scotian economy. It was particularly apparent that the Conservatives were stressing the need to develop manufacturing[42] as a means of counteracting the Liberal belief in the need for a limited form of economic continentalism.[43]

As the fall of 1874 progressed the papers gradually ignored the proposed treaty in favour of speculation about developments in provincial politics. Interest heightened when, at the end of October, Annand returned from a two-month holiday in England and at once plunged into negotiations involving the reorganization of the ministry. A new provincial secretary had to be appointed and a replacement found for Smith, who, in spite of opposition within the party, wanted an appointment to the Supreme Court.[44] Adding importance to the selection of the new ministers was the likelihood that Annand would finally retire. A possible position was created for him in November when a conference on immigration in Ottawa decided that the Maritime provinces should be represented by an agent in London. Annand may have even promised his party supporters that he would resign before the election,[45] although he did not do so. In view of the cabinet changes, it might have been difficult for him to leave at that time but his imminent departure from the government was frequently predicted.[46]

The extent of the changes in the ministry caused heightened interest over Vail's successor as leader of the government in the assembly. One possible candidate was W.A. Henry, who had served as attorney-general under Tupper. Henry had never accepted the coalition with Howe in 1869, but he had not supported the Liberals publicly until after the fall of the Macdonald administration. With thirty-five years' experience in politics Henry might well have been more interested in a seat on the bench than in the government. Nor would his appointment have been entirely satisfactory since there was strong opposition to him from within the party.[47] By early November, therefore, it was decided that P.C. Hill, who was backed by Jones, would enter the government.[48] He was sworn in as provincial secretary on 1 December and election writs were issued for 17 December.

The entry of Hill into the government was cheered by the *Evening Reporter*, which finally acknowledged its break with the Conservatives.[49] The support of the new provincial government by the paper was qualified, however, because it continued to attack Mackenzie and the federal Liberal party. It sought to explain its position by denying the need for political parties at the provincial level. According to the paper, party organization should spring from significant differences in ideology but at the provincial level the local ministry dealt only with administrative questions. Rather than trying to impose federal political divisions in the provincial arena, the paper contended that the electors should select the most capable men regardless of their stand in federal politics.[50] Although these comments were tailored to fit the existing political situation, they were similar to those about political parties that the paper had made during the previous federal election.

According to the *Evening Reporter* one immediate result to be obtained from forming a provincial government without regard for federal party divisions would be a separation of all federal and provincial issues. This was in direct contrast to the argument, advanced by the local government for the past year, that the interests of the province could best be served if the local ministry had close ties with the government making the administrative decisions which affected the province in so many ways. The *Evening Reporter* believed that administrative questions did not properly belong in the political field, and also contended that political ties between the federal and provincial governments could negate the constitutional division of powers. The federal government might intervene in provincial affairs, argued the paper, and the provincial ministry could be so enmeshed in federal politics that it would be unable to protect provincial interests. Only if there were complete neutrality between federal and provincial parties could the constitutional division of powers function properly.[51] This view of federal-provincial relations was strongly influenced by the paper's attitude towards the nature of politics. In questioning what others took for granted, the paper did emphasize the many-faceted nature of federal-provincial relations.

This view of the proper basis for a federal-provincial system was completely rejected by the government press.[52] By advocating the need for a political tie between the two levels of government, the Liberal press in Halifax also became involved in supporting the existing constitutional structure. It contended that the interests of the province would be met by co-operation with Ottawa, rather than through an attempt to expand the constitutional powers of the local ministry. Neither was the local government press interested in adopting new policies which might enhance the political bargaining power of the province. They particularly disliked the proposal, put forward earlier in the year by New Brunswick, that the Maritime provinces consider a form of union. The government, and its supporters among the newspapers, were not interested in a political change which might reduce the status of the local government, even if it might increase the influence of the region.[53]

One advantage of the policy of co-operation was that it allowed the local ministry to participate in subjects affecting the province. Even if the local ministry was not a full partner with the federal government, it was at least involved with it. The value of the tie with Ottawa lay primarily in matters of joint concern to the two governments. According to the Liberals, co-operation on administrative matters was possible because of a prior agreement on political principles. In effect, though, the policy of co-operation was an attempt to create a political philosophy out of administrative questions. One difficulty was that the local ministry was far weaker than the federal government but it regarded its own interests as paramount to those of the federal ministry. In addition, the federal government did not seem to be very popular with a number of Liberals in the province. This may have been due to a dislike for Mackenzie and a preference for Blake, who had been in the province during August.[54]

The problems inherent in the policy of co-operation were fully revealed during the election campaign. One of the more difficult questions facing the two governments involved the integration of the Nova Scotian railways into a national system. This integration had been begun by Macdonald over the violent protests of the Maritimes. Nevertheless, Mackenzie decided to carry on the policy, and in the spring of 1874 he entrusted the project to C.J. Brydges, formerly of the Grand Trunk Railway. As part of his duties Brydges prepared a report, which was issued a few weeks prior to the provincial election. In it he criticized the past management of the railway, referring particularly to some dubious transactions involving a hardware store in Halifax which was partly owned by the editor of the Conservative *British Colonist*.[55] The Liberals enjoyed uncovering this evidence against their opponents, but they were far less satisfied with Brydges' policy of operating the railways as a commercial venture; the canals of Ontario, after all, were run as a public service and were not expected to make a profit. To a large extent, however, the Nova Scotians were unduly sensitive because the railway operations did need reorganizing; the lines were over-staffed and the rates were lower than in the rest of Canada. Some Liberals, despite their public comments to the contrary,[56] seemed to expect the Canadian government to continue to meet the mounting deficit of the provincial railways. A basic difficulty was that neither the Nova Scotians nor the Liberal government looked on railways as part of an integrated transportation system. Changes in one region of the country or in one type of transportation were seen in isolation from each other and from the total economy.

The Liberals were particularly upset at the prospect of an increase in the rate structure of the railway. An increase had been proposed early in 1874, but Jones had managed to have part of it postponed. Late in the fall

Brydges decided to implement the postponed increases in the middle of the provincial election. Jones stormed at Mackenzie for ignoring his advice on railways and declared he would write no more letters. His criticism, however, was quite unwarranted as he had not sent information requested by Mackenzie. Despite the lack of co-operation from Jones, Mackenzie offered to compromise on the increases and on patronage, even though this might set off a reaction in the other provinces.[57]

The response of the Liberals to Mackenzie's policies was intensified by charges from the Conservatives that the increases were possible because the federal government had complete power over the local ministry.[58] This was an irresponsible charge, for Mackenzie was merely following a policy initiated by Macdonald. Nonetheless, the Conservatives used the issue of the railway increases to justify their claim that the provincial government should be in political opposition to the federal government.[59] In the long run this would result in the Nova Scotian provincial parties having only tenuous ties with any party outside of the province. Such a policy was much more isolationist in tone that the policy of the *Evening Reporter*. The latter began its argument with certain premises about the nature of politics; the point about potential federal interference was a secondary argument. The Conservatives were much more direct about exploiting the notion that there were separate provincial interests which required protection from Ottawa.

A question involving federal relations arose again over Annand's attempts to have a railway built from Pictou to the Gut of Canso. He had been trying for some time to arrange for construction of this railway and had found two contractors, C. Schreiber and E.R. Burpee, who were willing to build the line if the federal government would turn the Truro-Pictou railway over to them. The chief opposition to this demand was likely to come from Cape Breton, which wanted the railway extended across the island.[60] In the spring of 1874 Annand had been able to persuade his supporters in the assembly and the federal members to agree to the transfer.[61] The Cape Breton members remained hesitant, however, and they were encouraged by D.V. Kennely, a promoter of a Cape Breton coal company that had been trying to build a railway on the island for some time.

Mackenzie was worried about the federal members from Cape Breton and tried to persuade Annand to deal with Kennely,[62] but Annand was determined to carry out his own scheme. He made no attempt to win over the federal members and curtly informed the prime minister that the only railway which could be built was the one to Canso: 'this can be done only by your government co-operating with ours.'⁶³ A delay followed, and then a federal official wired Annand to proceed with his project. But before a contract could be signed, Mackenzie suddenly ordered a delay. He was not prepared to run counter to the federal members who had 'strong feelings' against the transfer of the Pictou railway.⁶⁴ Mackenzie, who had already bowed to a Halifax faction over the appointment of Vail, could not afford a further concession which might have serious repercussions among the federal members.

Annand was quite willing to benefit from his ties with the federal government, but he showed no willingness to consider Mackenzie's position. Had Annand been more conciliatory towards the federal members he might have arranged for the construction of a railway. In dealing with Ottawa Annand acted as if he had the stronger hand, but in fact he was quite dependent upon the co-operation of the federal government. The incident also indicated that the policy of co-operation between the two levels of government disregarded the position of the federal members. In practice, Annand acted as if his government represented the province and the federal government had to deal with him. The policy of co-operation was far removed from the programme of repeal adopted in 1867, but it nonetheless contained elements of provincialism.

The problem of federal-provincial relations emerged in one form or another as the most important issue in a rather murky election campaign. The Conservatives, who had spent the summer preparing for the election, were unable to overcome their internal disputes. Their province-wide association, announced with such fanfare in July, did not live up to its expectations.⁶⁵ In Halifax, the Conservatives did manage to appease the Catholics by accepting Martin J. Griffin, editor of the Catholic *Evening Express*, as one of the three party candidates for the city, but in so doing offended both their supporters who had concurred in the attacks on the school system and those interested in political reform who had consistently been opposed by Griffin's paper. Although the party platform of July was revived, most attention was paid to the call for retrenchment in provincial expenditures.⁶⁶

A potentially serious question during the election was the simmering anti-Catholic movement. In Halifax the school association met several times in an attempt to formulate some policy, and it finally issued a moderate list of proposed reforms.⁶⁷ The Wesleyan ministers in Halifax delivered a more trenchant statement which provoked mumblings from the *Evening Express*. Some 'schoolmen' did side with the government,⁶⁸ but the government press did not try to win them over. Without taking any action at all, the Liberals could benefit from the resentment of some Conservatives towards Griffin and at the same time assure the Catholics that the government would be far better able to help them than would the opposition.[69] The religious issue also helped disrupt party allegiances elsewhere in the province. In Pictou the Presbyterians took a strong stand against the Catholics and the government;[70] this action may have been one of the reasons why the Conservatives took the three county seats by acclamation. In the neighbouring county of Colchester the Orange Association pledged its support to any candidate who opposed separate schools. The two successful candidates, who did take such a stand,[71] were first classified by a government paper as belonging to the opposition.[72] After the election, however, the same paper classified them as government supporters.[73] Such manœuvrings prevented the religious issue from becoming polarized along political lines, but it did not enable the Liberals to contain the incompatible cliques that were bound to cause trouble in the future.

The results of the election at first seemed unsatisfactory to the government. Eighteen of the successful candidates, or one-half of the assembly, had sat in the previous house. Eight former members seeking re-election were defeated, but one of them was the victim of an obvious case of ballot stuffing[74] and was later declared elected. The most important loss to the government came with the defeat of John Fergusson, who had been minister without portfolio since 1867, in his county of Cape Breton. Initial returns indicated that the government had been returned by a narrow margin, but much depended on what the new members might do.[75]

Some new members could perhaps be won over by a skilful distribution of favours, but only at the expense of the ambitions of the older members. It would be too hard, said one member who had made demands of his own, if the government bought up the 'independents' and gave them all the offices.[76] The need for as many supporters as possible, however, forced the government to accept whoever they could find, regardless of their stand on such controversial issues as separate schools. Finding some policy acceptable to the various supporters of the government would have to wait. After several weeks of negotiation Hill cheerfully wrote: 'we have a larger majority than we thought.'[77]

The task of reorganizing the executive was particularly delicate, but with the legislative session due to begin in March it could not be delayed. The first task was to ease Annand out of the government, which began with the appointment of Stayley Brown, president of the Legislative Council, as treasurer. Annand remained as premier but the first move, said Hill, 'appears to give general satisfaction and I have no doubt will command the confidence of the people.'[78] Several other executive positions were filled but the only surprise came with the appointment of Colin Campbell, a staunch confederate who had been claimed by the opposition, as minister without portfolio.[79]

Campbell was the only prominent confederate in the assembly who followed Hill into the ranks of government, but it was apparent that the party divisions formed around the issue of confederation had broken down. The *Evening Reporter* still called for a further reorganization on a non-party basis,[80] but within a week of the election it was 'authorized' to state that it did not represent Hill.[81] The success of the government in quietening unrest among its supporters and winning over new members was due in part to the power of holding office. The opposition offered promises but the government gave positions. Any dissatisfaction which existed within government ranks was not sufficient to drive the members into the risky venture of creating a new government.

Conclusion

The years from 1864 to 1874 were momentous ones for Nova Scotia. The political fabric of the province had been torn apart and its political institutions reshaped, yet there remained a continuity to provincial politics as many of the substantive issues remained constant. At the same time the issues were altered in shape and tone.

One of the most significant problems for many Nova Scotians concerned Great Britain. British determination to withdraw from purely North American affairs had precipitated changes which provided a major justification for Nova Scotia to enter colonial union, and thus Britain played a significant role in bringing Nova Scotia into confederation. British policy on colonial issues, particularly on such Nova Scotian issues as the fisheries, was made explicit in the years 1864–7. The continuation of these policies in 1871 during the negotiations over the Treaty of Washington merely confirmed for some Nova Scotians, such as Howe, that they were now living in a new period and would have to develop policies of their own.

Just what new policies would be found in the coming years was uncertain. Many of the professions of loyalty, both before and after 1864, had been suspect because the Nova Scotians, like colonials elsewhere, tended to identify the ties of empire with their own special interests. The consciousness of being Nova Scotian predated 1864 and was encouraged by events after that date. This fostered a critical attitude towards the link with Great Britain and by 1874 public predictions of imminent independence were not uncommon, although still shrouded with bravado or cloaked in bathos. Other Nova Scotians, suspicious of independence, were encouraged to adopt some form of imperial union. Whether Nova Scotians adopted one or the other of these options, or neither of them, the British tie had been altered and some new focus for it had to be found.

In the early 1860s Nova Scotia had relied on British power to balance ever increasing economic ties with the United States. Forced to face American power after 1867 with only the dubious support of the upper provinces, many Nova Scotians foresaw their complete domination, economically and politically, by the United States. This analysis of their position was not borne out by the Treaty of Washington, as some of those who were most critical in 1867 found the economic terms of the treaty quite palatable. While their fears, especially with respect to the policies of the Upper Canadians, were not without foundation, there was no sudden shift in Nova Scotia's position vis-à-vis the United States. Economic prosperity in the years following Confederation made the province less dependent on American markets; even shipbuilders and merchants by 1874 were not as ready as they once were to adopt any means of increasing exports and were critical of the projected trade treaty with the United States. While few in Nova Scotia were prepared to admit it, their fears about change in relations with the United States were exaggerated, not to say hysterical.

The most apparent difference in the status of Nova Scotia was in relation to Upper Canada. The extent and nature of Canadian control over Nova Scotian internal affairs was new, but in actual fact the upper provinces had established a dominance over Nova Scotian affairs involving the United States and Great Britain long before 1867. Indeed, as Tupper frequently asserted, confederation was an attempt to ameliorate the subordinate position of Nova Scotia in British North America. His view that Nova Scotia would have less control of its own affairs outside of colonial union than in was also used to justify the adoption of the federal system of government. The confederates contended, in brief, that historical differences and conflicting interests among the provinces could only be reconciled through federalism.

These arguments for union and the federal system were valid, perhaps even compelling, but many Nova Scotians found their negative tone chilling and depressing. To embark on a new venture surely required some more positive goal, perhaps similar to the Upper Canadian talk of a new nation. No really plausible positive goal was devised, so some Nova Scotians rejected the scheme because of its inadequacies.

The confederates did try, it was true, to present union as a blueprint by which they could design the future. Tupper, in particular, was emphatic that through confederation the colony could foster its manufacturing and heavy industry and become the economic core of a new nation. The notion of progress through technology was persuasive, perhaps, but it confused the nature of the provincial economy to contend that industrial interests were necessarily in competition with the needs of the mercantile economy. The dichotomy was oversharp since both tended to develop simultaneously, often promoted by the same men and, to an extent, in the same regions of the province.

The prospect that union would be a spur to the economy discounted the numerous proposals made by Maritimers for co-operation with the upper provinces which had been rebuffed by the Canadians. The confederates asserted that the situation would change with union, and there was indeed some improvement, such as the investment by Montreal financiers in provincial coal mines. But the federal government was little more willing to extend economic concessions after 1867 than the Province of Canada had been before. Both in the extension of the Canadian tariff system to the Maritimes in 1867 and in the negotiations over the Treaty of Washington, the Canadian government was indifferent to Maritime interests in general. In their search for support for their own economic objectives, some Nova Scotians showed by the early 1870s that they were prepared to accept a measure of tariff protection for Upper Canadian goods if reciprocal duties were applied on some of their products. These overtures were not to bear results until 1879. The earlier proposals had indicated that the acceptance of protection marked less a revolution in thought in Nova Scotia than it did a shift in the attitudes of Upper Canadians.

Although the politicians discussed economic issues, they were naturally preoccupied with the new political institutions. Before 1867 many commentators had explored the possible ramifications of the scheme. Some, and especially the Liberals, paid particular attention to the confusion which could develop from the retention of provincial legislatures. In agreeing to the 'better terms' of 1869, Howe adopted Macdonald's notion that the federal government was supreme over the provinces and would be the creator of the state. When he entered the cabinet he supported the view that the dynamic role of the federal government could only be achieved through the appeal to sectionalism implied by the regional composition of that body. This approach was not a system of federal-provincial relations as much as a means of providing for the adjustment and survival of provincial interests.

There were several possible alternatives to Macdonald's method of governing Canada. One of them which was investigated during the 1870s by Liberals in both Ottawa and Nova Scotia was to allow the provincial governments to speak for purely sectional interests and to limit the scope of federal government policies so as not to provoke sectional animosities. This approach, asserted the Liberals, would remove the need for a strong cabinet and allow the Commons to become the dominant force of national unity. In this system the realities of regionalism were dealt with in terms of traditional Liberal thought. What attracted Nova Scotian politicians most in this Liberal scheme was the position given to the provincial legislature as the only true protector of the province. Some tentative moves were made in this direction in the period under consideration, but more commonly sectionalism was promoted by means of provincial representation in the federal cabinet. It was possible for Howe to feel with sincerity that his province could not be protected unless he entered the federal government. In this respect Howe was following Tupper who, both before and after confederation, always balanced his arguments for a national policy with appeals to provincial interests. Thus the provincial government could not establish itself as the sole protector of the province because the confederation argument was ambiguous.

At the same time some Nova Scotians began to develop the argument, which later became identified with the Liberal party, that provincial interests would be best protected by the provincial government. This approach doubtless appealed to the provincial ministry, particularly since the Macdonald view made no room for provincial governments. Although his system allowed for the adjustment and survival of regional and provincial interests, it was not really a theory of federal-provincial relations. The Liberal theory had attraction for those who saw some point in preserving the provincial governments. Yet the Liberal approach was not really an appeal to provincialism, as it had only a limited role for provincial governments. The federal parliament would become the centre for expressing the will of the people and the cabinet would express national unity. The disagreement between the Liberals and the Conservatives was thus not over whether or not to recognize provincialism, but merely over the best means of giving expression to it. Any attempt to enhance the existing powers of the provincial government was also inhibited by the fact that the powers allotted to the province had been designed to suit Quebec's particular needs. The constitutional duties assigned to the province thus had no political appeal and could not be used to justify an increase in the powers of the provincial government.

The Liberal theory of parliament did make an appeal to the old pre-confederation Liberal tradition in Nova Scotia that maintained that the

Conclusion 193

assembly expressed the will of the people. This idea, which in the 1860s had been an important reason for the opposition to union, in the 1870s helped to set the opponents of union to work within the new political structure. The contest between the Liberal and Conservative theories became obvious in Nova Scotia when the Mackenzie government was formed. However, the idea of national unity remained weak and the Liberal theory of federal-provincial relations did not adequately provide for appeals to sectionalism. Thus, the Nova Scotian Liberals, although successful in both the federal and provincial general elections of 1874, were not really able to answer the sectionalism contained in Tupper's attacks on the Mackenzie administration. The immediate defect with the Liberal programme was not that it was overly sectional but rather that it was too idealistic in tone. Ironically, the sectionalism inherent in the anti-confederation campaign was exploited by the Conservatives' emphasis on the central role of the federal cabinet.

Included among the policies of the Liberal party was a belief in the basic authority of parliament. The amount of concern was illustrated during the debate over the Pacific scandal, which had examined the relationship between the Commons, the cabinet, and corporations. Similar themes had constituted an integral part of the discussion over confederation from 1864 to 1867. This debate had emphasized that there was also a belief in the need for a strong executive authority and Howe himself openly subscribed to that doctrine in joining the Macdonald cabinet in 1869. It was part of the concern over cabinet responsibility which led the Conservative party in particular to attempt to establish a party organization which would be separate from parliament. Indeed, this debate is confused when it is presented as an issue of federal-provincial relations. Much of the actual debate, whether over the revision of the terms of union in 1868 or relations with Mackenzie in 1874, involved the power of the executive, both in its relation to other components of parliament and to other sources of power such as corporations.

The Nova Scotian adjustment to confederation was made easier by the realization that union was not accompanied by the sudden destruction of the provincial economy. Many Nova Scotians continued to suspect Canadian motives, but the general recovery of the provincial economy, beginning in 1870, and the Treaty of Washington which restored economic ties with the United States convinced them they could survive within union. Concern over the proper development of the province was thus quieted, but the important question of continentalism, as opposed to a national policy, had in no way been resolved. The developing campaign for a protective tariff in Halifax during 1874 and the growing depression indicated that economic issues remained as controversial as ever.

Although the debate as to Nova Scotia's place in confederation would continue, it would, on the whole, be cast in the framework of union. The belief that England was leaving its colonies to a North American fate forced many Nova Scotians, however belatedly, to accept the fact of union. These Nova Scotians, disgruntled at their treatment by Great Britain, found that their loyalty had markedly diminished. The more they considered taking over the responsibility for their own affairs from England, however, the greater trust they had to place in confederation. Thus, the very sentiments which helped create opposition to union later helped smooth away that opposition and bring the Nova Scotians to accept the fact of confederation.

Notes

CHAPTER 1: THE INTRODUCTION OF CONFEDERATION

1 Nova Scotia [NS], House of Assembly 1864, *Debates*, 28 March 1864, 180–6
2 Public Archives of Nova Scotia [PANS], Lieutenant-Governor's Office, Despatches and Memoranda, Monck to MacDonnell, 30 June 1864
3 Public Archives of Canada [PAC], CO 217/234, 281–8, MacDonnell to Cardwell, 18 July 1864
4 CO 217/235, 70–6, MacDonnell to Cardwell, 15 Sept. 1864, confidential
5 *Morning Chronicle* (Halifax), 16 Aug. 1864
6 CO 217/234, 281–8, MacDonnell to Cardwell, 18 July 1864
7 Speech of Charles Tupper, 31 Dec. 1864, *Novascotian* (Halifax), 9 Jan. 1865
8 W.I. Smith, ed., 'Charles Tupper's Minutes of the Charlottetown Conference,' *Canadian Historical Review* [CHR], XLVIII, 2, June 1967, 102–11
9 J.S. Martell, 'Intercolonial Communications, 1840–1867,' Canadian Historical Association [CHA], *Report*, 1938, 41–61
10 *British Colonist* (Halifax), 20 Sept. 1864
11 P.B. Waite, *The Life and Times of Confederation* (Toronto 1962), 104–16
12 D.G. Creighton, *The Road to Confederation* (Toronto 1964), 143–6
13 J.T. Saywell, *The Office of Lieutenant Governor* (Toronto 1957), 3–30
14 J. Pope, ed., *Confederation* (Toronto 1895), 75–6
15 *Morning Chronicle*, 27 Dec. 1864. For one discussion of the role of the upper house see K.G. Pryke, 'Nova Scotia and Prince Edward Island Consider an Effective Legislative Council,' *Dalhousie Review*, L, 3, autumn 1970, 330–43.
16 Chester Martin, *Foundations of Canadian Nationhood* (Toronto 1955), 337
17 D.G. Creighton, *The British North American Colonies at Confederation* (Ottawa 1939), 72

18 NS, House of Assembly 1865, *Journals*, App. 7, Tupper to James McDonald, 5 Oct. 1864
19 A.G. Doughty, ed., 'Notes on the Quebec Conference,' CHR, I, 1, March 1920, 33
20 NS, House of Assembly 1865, *Journals*, App. 3, Dickey to MacDonnell, 11 Feb. 1865
21 New Brunswick Museum [NBM], Tilley Papers, Tupper to Tilley, 4 Dec. 1864
22 CO 217/235, 226–9, MacDonnell to Cardwell, 24 Nov. 1864, confidential
23 CO 217/235, 230, Cardwell to MacDonnell, 8 Dec. 1864, confidential
24 *Tribune* (Yarmouth), 5 Oct. 1864
25 *Morning Chronicle*, 6 Dec. 1864
26 PAC, Macdonald Papers, LI, 36–7, John A. Macdonald to Tupper, 14 Nov. 1864
27 PAC, Tupper Papers, no 25, Tupper to John A. Macdonald, 4 Jan. 1864
28 P.B. Waite, 'A Chapter in the History of the Intercolonial Railway,' CHR, XXXII, 4, Dec. 1951, 363
29 *Morning Chronicle*, 4 Jan. 1865
30 *Halifax Herald*, 23 July 1901
31 Union was also opposed by the *Sun* (Halifax), which had only a small circulation, and by the *Bulldog* (Halifax). The latter was edited by two British officers, who reversed their position on union before ceasing to publish in 1865.
32 These were the *Evening Express*, *Evening Reporter*, *British Colonist*, and the *Morning Chronicle* (all published in Halifax).
33 Tupper Papers, no 25, Tupper to John A. Macdonald, 4 Jan. 1865
34 Harriet Irving Library, University of New Brunswick [UNB], Stanmore Papers, MacDonnell to Gordon, 15 Jan. 1865
35 *Morning Chronicle*, 22 Feb. 1864
36 J.M. Beck, *Joseph Howe: Anti-Confederate*, CHA Booklet 17 (Ottawa 1965)
37 D.G. Whidden, *The History of the Town of Antigonish* (Wolfville 1934), 102
38 Archives de la Province de Québec [APQ], Chapais Collection, W.A. Henry to A.T. Galt, 24 March 1865
39 *Report of the Board of Trustees of the Public Archives of Nova Scotia*, 1948 (Halifax 1949), 35–8, Howe to William Garvie, 14 Aug. 1868
40 *British Colonist*, 17 Nov. 1864
41 *Morning Chronicle*, 17 Jan. 1865; R.W. Winks, *Canada and the United States: The Civil War Years* (Baltimore 1960), 235
42 *Halifax Evening Reporter*, 31 Dec. 1864
43 NS, House of Assembly 1865, *Debates*, 11 April 1865, 203–17
44 *Morning Chronicle*, 18 Jan., 31 March 1865
45 *Evening Express*, 23 Jan. 1865

46 Ibid., 3 March 1865
47 *Halifax Evening Reporter*, 3, 10 Dec. 1864; *Morning Chronicle*, 5 Dec. 1864
48 NS, House of Assembly 1865, *Debates*, 12 April 1865, 233-4
49 For one analysis of this view see Irene Hecht, 'Israel D. Andrews and the Reciprocity Treaty of 1854: A Reappraisal,' CHR, XLIV, 4, Dec. 1963, 313-29.
50 P.B. Waite, 'Halifax Newspapers and the Federal Principle,' *Dalhousie Review*, XXXVII. Spring 1957, 72-84
51 *Morning Chronicle*, 27 Dec. 1864
52 Ibid., 29 March 1865
53 Ibid., 19 Nov. 1864; *Halifax Evening Reporter*, 27 Dec. 1864
54 *Halifax Citizen*, 19 Nov. 1864
55 *Morning Chronicle*, 6 Jan. 1865
56 Tupper to Galt, 15 Dec. 1864, in W.G. Ormsby, ed., 'Letters to Galt Concerning the Maritime Provinces and Confederation,' CHR, XXXVI, 2, June 1953, 166-7
57 CO 217/235, 289-301, MacDonnell to Cardwell, 16 March 1865, confidential
58 Tupper Papers, no 28, John McKinnon to Tupper, 18 March 1865
59 CO 217/235, 289-301, MacDonnell to Cardwell, 15 Feb. 1865, confidential
60 Ibid., 226-9, 24 Nov. 1864, confidential
61 'Botheration Scheme No. 8,' *Morning Chronicle*, 1 Feb. 1865
62 Beck, *Howe*, 17-18
63 Lieutenant-Governor's Office, Miscellaneous Despatches, 51, MacDonnell to Monck, 9 Jan. 1865, confidential
64 CO 217/235, 289-301, MacDonnell to Cardwell, 16 March 1865, confidential
65 *Morning Chronicle*, 4 Feb. 1865
66 R.H. Campbell, 'Confederation in Nova Scotia' (unpublished MA dissertation, Dalhousie University, 1939), 238-43
67 NS, House of Assembly 1865, *Debates*, 22 March 1865, 115
68 Ibid., 10 April 1865, 203
69 Ibid., 21 April 1865, 297-8
70 PAC, CO Cardwell Papers, box 6, file 40, 69-70, Cardwell to Gordon, 1 April 1865, private (microfilm)
71 CO 217/237, 303, Cardwell to MacDonnell, 1 April 1865
72 CO 217/237, 551-4, MacDonnell to Cardwell, 7 June 1865, confidential
73 NS, House of Assembly 1865, *Debates*, 17 April 1865, 265-8

CHAPTER 2: APPROVAL OF UNION IN PRINCIPLE

1 Public Archives of Nova Scotia [PANS], Lieutenant-Governor's Office, Miscellaneous, no 121, MacDonnell to Tupper, 2 May 1865

2 Lieutenant-Governor's Correspondence, unbound volumes, 1865, Tupper to MacDonnell, 10 May 1865
3 Nova Scotia [NS], House of Assembly 1866, *Journals*, App. 4, Tupper to Baring Bros. and Co, 11 Aug. 1865. In order to secure financing for this section of the Intercolonial, Tupper had to agree to the issuing of short-term financing until Confederation. If construction had begun and union not followed, the province would, therefore, have been in serious financial difficulty. As it happened, however, no construction took place.
4 Ibid. 1865, *Journals*, App. 4, Agreement between the Chief Commissioners of Railways of Nova Scotia and the International Contract Company, 15 Aug. 1865
5 Lieutenant-Governor's Correspondence, unbound volumes, 1865, Monck to MacDonnell, 9 Sept. 1865
6 NS, House of Assembly 1866, *Journals*, App. 7, Monck to MacDonnell, 15 July 1865. Lieutenant-Governor's Correspondence, Miscellaneous Despatches, no 129, MacDonnell to Monck, 29 July 1865
7 Lieutenant-Governor's Correspondence, CIX, 212, Cardwell to MacDonnell, 8 July 1865
8 NS, House of Assembly 1866, *Journals*, App. 7, Cardwell to Monck, 22 July 1865
9 *British Colonist* (Halifax), 14 Sept. 1865
10 NS, House of Assembly 1866, *Journals*, App. 4
11 Ibid. 1865, *Debates*, 10 April 1865, 211
12 Ibid. 1866, *Journals*, App. 10, Cardwell to MacDonnell, 24 June 1865
13 New Brunswick Museum [NBM], Allison Notebooks, no N, Cardwell to Williams, 26 Sept. 1865
14 *Morning Chronicle* (Halifax), 15 Nov. 1865
15 D.G. Creighton, *The Road to Confederation* (Toronto 1964), 322–8
16 NS, House of Assembly 1866, *Debates*, 13 April 1866, 236–7
17 *Evening Express* (Halifax), 8 Jan. 1866
18 *British Colonist*, 2 Jan. 1866
19 *Morning Chronicle*, 24 Jan. 1866
20 NS, House of Assembly 1866, *Debates*, 1 May 1866, 311. See also *Morning Chronicle*, 23 March 1869.
21 NBM, Williams Papers, Monck to Williams, 26 Feb. 1866, private
22 Lieutenant-Governor's Correspondence, 1866, Williams to Monck, 27 Feb. 1866, telegram
23 E.M. McDonald to –, 18 March 1866, *Halifax Citizen*, 25 Feb. 1869
24 NS, House of Assembly 1866, *Debates*, 5 April 1866, 197
25 P.B. Waite, *The Life and Times of Confederation* (Toronto 1962), 222–8

Notes to pages 24-8 199

26 Major T.J. Egan, *History of the Halifax Volunteer Battalion and Volunteer Companies, 1859-1887* (Halifax 1888), 25-6
27 Public Archives of Canada [PAC], CO 217/239, 145, Williams to Cardwell, 26 Feb. 1866, confidential
28 PAC, RG 7, G1, CLXIV, Cardwell to Monck, 3 March 1866, confidential
29 PAC, RG 13, II, Monck to Williams, 19 March 1866, telegram
30 Williams Papers, Monck to Williams, 4 April 1866, private and confidential
31 Archives de la Province de Québec [APQ] Chapais Collection, A.T. Galt to Cartier, 17 Jan. 1866
32 NS, House of Assembly 1866, *Debates*, 3 April 1866, 185
33 Charles Tupper, 'An Incident of Confederation,' *Canadian Magazine*, XXXII, 3, Jan. 1909, 216-18. I am indebted to Professor P.B. Waite for drawing this article to my attention.
34 NS, House of Assembly 1866, *Journals*, App. 6, Contract between the government of Nova Scotia and S. Fleming, 10 Jan. 1866
35 *Eastern Chronicle* (New Glasgow), 1, 8 March 1866
36 PAC, RG 13, II, Williams to Monck, 26 March 1866, telegram
37 E.J. Chambers, 'A Crisis of Confederation: Senator Miller's Reminiscence of How the Cause of Union Narrowly Escaped Shipwreck in Nova Scotia,' *Canadian Magazine*, XXXI, 5, Sept. 1908, 424-8. Miller, in 1892, told of this incident to support a request for a knighthood. See PAC, Miller Papers. According to Miller, McDonald returned to Halifax on Saturday, 24 March, but he actually arrived at 2 AM, 28 March. See *Evening Express*, 28 March 1866.
38 PAC Tupper Papers, 1426-7, Miller to Tupper, 10 May 1870
39 They were Miller, Caleb Bill (King's County), and John Bourinot (Cape Breton County). Howe, Speech at Dartmouth, June 1867, J.A. Chisholm, ed., *The Speeches and Public Letters of Joseph Howe* (Halifax 1909), II, 518
40 PAC CO Cardwell Papers, box 6, file 40, Williams to Cardwell, 21 June 1866, private
41 NBM, Tilley Papers, McCully to Tilley, 8 June 1868
42 PAC, Macdonald Papers, CXVI, 201-4, McCully to John A. Macdonald, 28 April 1868
43 NS, House of Assembly 1866, *Debates*, 10 April 1866, 211-22
44 Tupper Papers, no 41, Bishop C.F. McKinnon to Tupper, 12 April 1866
45 Tilley Papers, McCully to Tilley, 8 June 1866
46 NS, House of Assembly 1866, *Debates*, 17 April 1866, 295
47 Williams Papers, Cardwell to Williams, 3 Feb. 1866
48 Absent supporters of union were Ezra Churchill (Hants) and James McDonald (Pictou East). Absent opponents were Isaac Le Vesconte (Richmond) and Thomas Caldwell (Cape Breton). The Liberal supporters of

union were A.G. Archibald and F.R. Parker, both of whom represented Colchester South, W.O. Heffernan (Guysborough), and H. Blanchard (Inverness), the law partner of J. McCully.

49 Harvard University, Houghton Library, Howe Papers, Howe to Susan Ann Howe, 12 March 1866
50 PAC, Howe Papers, IX, 22–31, Howe to Cardwell, 12 April 1866, private
51 NS, House of Assembly 1866, *Journals*, App. 10
52 PAC, Howe Papers, XXX, 'League of the Maritime Provinces,' 25 April 1866
53 *Acadian Recorder* (Halifax), 11 May 1866
54 For an excellent discussion of the survival of English political traditions in the pre-revolutionary American colonies see J.P. Green, 'Political Nemesis: A consideration of the Historical and Cultural Roots of Legislative Behaviour in the British Colonies in the Eighteenth Century,' *American Historical Review*, LXXV, 2, Dec. 1969, 337–60
55 *Tribune* (Yarmouth), 2 May 1866
56 Harvard University, Howe Papers, Howe to Susan Ann Howe, 25 May 1866
57 *Halifax Citizen*, 5 May 1866
58 *Eastern Chronicle*, 10 May 1866
59 Tilley Papers, McCully to Tilley, 21 April 1866
60 NS, House of Assembly 1866, *Debates*, 17 April 1866, 267–9
61 *Evening Express*, 7 May 1866
62 NS, House of Assembly 1867, *Journals*, App. 18, Cardwell to Williams, 25 April 1866, confidential
63 Ibid., 26 May 1866
64 NS, Executive Council, Minutes, 9 May 1866
65 Ibid., 21 June 1866
66 *British Colonist*, 23 June 1866
67 *Sun and Advertiser* (Halifax), 27 June 1866; *Halifax Citizen*, 30 June 1866
68 Tupper Papers, no 46, Tupper to Macdonald, 17 June 1866
69 Williams Papers, Monck to Williams, 10 July 1866, private
70 CO 217/240, 108–9, Williams to Cardwell, 5 July 1866, confidential

CHAPTER 3: PASSAGE OF THE ACT OF UNION

1 Public Archives of Canada [PAC], CO 217/240, 123–6, Williams to Carnarvon, 19 July 1866, separate
2 PAC, CO Cardwell Papers, box 6, file 40, 35–6, Carnarvon to Cardwell, 19 July 1866; 88–91, Cardwell to Carnarvon, 27 July 1866
3 Nova Scotia [NS], Executive Council, Minutes, 4 July 1866

4 Harvard University, Houghton Library, Howe Papers, Howe to Susan Ann Howe, 18 Aug. 1866
5 Public Archives of Nova Scotia [PANS], Vernon Smith, Diary, 3 Dec. 1866
6 New Brunswick Museum [NBM], Williams Papers, Cardwell to Williams, 1 Sept. 1866
7 Ibid., Carnarvon to Williams, 15 Sept. 1866, private
8 PAC, Howe Papers, XXX, Howe to W.J. Stairs, 23 Nov. 1866
9 Ibid., IX, 182-9, Howe to Lord Stanley, 14 Nov. 1866
10 Harvard University, Howe Papers, Howe to Susan Ann Howe, 29 Sept. 1866
11 Sir Charles Tupper, *Recollections of Sixty Years in Canada* (Toronto 1916), 44-51
12 J. Pope, ed., *Confederation* (Toronto 1895), 95
13 PAC, Tupper Papers, no 46, Tupper to John A. Macdonald, 17 June 1866
14 Chester Martin, *Foundations of Canadian Nationhood* (Toronto 1955), 387
15 Archives de la Province de Québec [APQ], Chapais Collection, Sir Hector Langevin to Justine T. Langevin, 27 Nov. 1866
16 NS, 28 Vic., c 29
17 NS, House of Assembly 1865, *Debates*, 29 March 1865, 161-3
18 Archbishop Connolly to Tupper, 1865, in E.M. Saunders, ed., *The Life and Letters of the Rt. Hon. Sir Charles Tupper* (London 1916), I, 115
19 Chapais Collection, H. Langevin to Edmond Langevin, 19 Nov. 1866
20 Archdiocese of Toronto, Chancery Office, box 1, holder H, document 3, Archbishop Connolly to Archbishop Lynch, 1 Feb. 1866
21 Chapais Collection, Archbishop Connolly to Langevin, 15 Dec. 1866, and Saturday 5 PM [Dec. 1866]
22 PAC Macdonald Papers, LI, 383-6, Henry to John A. Macdonald, 26 Dec. 1866
23 PAC, Howe Papers, XXX, Howe to Stairs, 5 Jan. 1867
24 Ibid., Howe to Stairs, 15 Feb. 1867
25 *Acadian Recorder*, 13 March 1867; PAC, Howe Papers, XXVI, pt 1, 228-46, 'The Speech That Was Never Spoken,' undated draft
26 PAC, Howe Papers, XXX, Howe to Stairs, 2 Feb. 1867
27 Ibid., X, 180-3, Howe to John Bright, 8 March [1867]
28 Harvard University, Howe Papers, Stairs to Howe, 28 Feb. 1867
29 G. Rawlyk, 'Nova Scotian Regional Protest, 1867-1967,' *Queen's Quarterly*, LXXV, 1968, 105-23
30 PAC, Howe Papers, XXX, Howe to Stairs, 29 March 1867
31 Howe to Stairs, 12 April 1867, *Morning Chronicle* (Halifax), 29 May 1867
32 NS, House of Assembly 1867, *Debates*, 19 March 1867, 54
33 Ibid., 64-5
34 NS, 13 Vic., c 1

35 NS, House of Assembly 1867, *Journals*, App. 1
36 Ibid. 1868, *Journals*, App. 18
37 Vernon Smith, Diary, 23 April 1867
38 NS, 15 Vic., c 4
39 Tupper Papers, no 77, Tupper to Macdonald, 26 May 1868
40 CO 217/242, 108, Williams to the Duke of Buckingham and Chandos, 27 June 1867
41 W.H. Townshend, speech on Declaration Day, 25 Sept. 1867, *Herald* (Yarmouth), 26 Sept. 1867
42 Tupper, *Recollections*, 52–3
43 Macdonald Papers, CXVI, 262–5, R.B. Dickey to John A. Macdonald, 11 July 1867
44 The flag was not to appear over the governor's residence on 1 July again until 1901.
45 *Eastern Chronicle* (New Glasgow), 3 July 1867

CHAPTER 4: THE FEDERAL AND PROVINCIAL ELECTIONS OF 1867

1 Howe, speech at Dartmouth, 22 May 1867, in J.A. Chisholm, ed., *The Speeches and Public Letters of Joseph Howe* (Halifax 1909), II, 508–20
2 Public Archives of Canada [PAC], Howe Papers, IX, 366–8, Howe to John Young, 11 May 1867
3 Howe to the People of Canada, 18 June 1867, *Halifax Citizen*, 18 June 1867. See also Chisholm, ed., *Speeches and Public Letters of Howe*, II, 521–4.
4 Howe, speech at Truro, 4 June 1867, *Morning Chronicle* (Halifax), 7 June 1867
5 *Halifax Citizen*, 27 June 1867
6 PAC, Macdonald Papers, CXVI, 497, E.M. McDonald to the Electors of the County of Lunenburg, Feb. 1869
7 *Herald* (Yarmouth), 18 July 1867
8 Martin I. Wilkins, *Confederation Examined in the Light of Reason and Common Sense and the British North American Act Shown to be Unconstitutional* (Halifax 1867)
9 *Colonial Standard* (Pictou), 14 May 1867
10 *Eastern Chronicle* (New Glasgow), 22 June 1867
11 W.B. Vail to the Electors of Digby, 20 May 1867, *Herald*, 30 May 1867
12 Howe to the People of Nova Scotia, 2 May 1871, *British Colonist* (Halifax), 9 May 1871
13 *Acadian Recorder* (Halifax), 29 May 1867
14 James W. King to the Electors of the County of Hants, 12 June 1867, *British Colonist*, 25 June 1867

15 *Herald*, 18 July 1867
16 *Tribune* (Yarmouth), 18 Sept. 1867
17 *Evening Express* (Halifax), 23 Aug. 1867
18 McCully to D.B. Hill, 28 Jan. 1868, *Halifax Citizen*, 17 March 1868. McCully, who held a mortgage for Hill, wrote to him after the election: 'It was at the very urgent insistence of my friend Hon. A.C. Archibald, that you obtained the loan, and now that you have succeeded in helping him out of the county, I will thank you to repay me my money ...'
19 *Eastern Chronicle*, 8 June 1867.
20 PAC, Howe Papers, IV, 309–12, W. Garvie to Howe, 25 May 1867
21 *British Colonist*, 13 Aug. 1867
22 Nova Scotia [NS], House of Assembly 1868, *Journals*, App. 12
23 *Morning Chronicle*, 9 Aug. 1867
24 Letter to the editor, *Evening Express*, 12 June 1867
25 *Herald*, 15 Aug. 1867
26 Public Archives of Nova Scotia [PANS], Vernon Smith, Diary, 31 May 1867
27 *Evening Express*, 12 Aug. 1867
28 *Colonial Standard*, 19 Feb. 1867
29 PAC, Tupper Papers, no 45, Archibishop Connolly to Tupper, 9 PM Wednesday 1867
30 *Acadian Recorder*, 14 Jan. 1867
31 *Evening Express*, 13 May 1867
32 *Eastern Chronicle*, 9 Feb. 1867
33 *Evening Express*, 3 April 1867
34 W.H. Townshend to the Electors of Yarmouth, 10 July 1867, *Herald*, 10 July 1867
35 Harvard University, Houghton Library, Howe Papers, Archbishop Connolly to Howe, 22 May 1867
36 Ibid., Howe to Archbishop Connolly, 23 May 1867
37 Macdonald Papers, CCLXXXI, no 13, Tupper to John A. Macdonald, 10 May 1867
38 PANS Lieutenant-Governor's Office, Despatches from the Secretary of State, CX, Duke of Buckingham and Chandos to Williams, 6 July 1867, separate
39 Tupper Papers, no 68, Tupper to Duke of Buckingham and Chandos, 9 April 1868
40 Macdonald Papers, CXVI, 262–5, R.B. Dickey to John A. Macdonald, 11 July 1867
41 Ibid., 17–9, Edward Kenny to John A. Macdonald, 11 Aug. 1867. Letter should be dated Sept. because it was written on Nomination Day.
42 *Evening Express*, 13 Sept. 1867

43 Macdonald Papers, CXVI, 28–31, P.C. Hill to John A. Macdonald, 23 Sept. 1867, private
44 Ibid., 34–41, Archbishop Connolly to John A. Macdonald, 25 Sept. 1868. The letter should be dated 1867.
45 Ibid., 7–10, 17 June 1867
46 Archbishop Connolly to the Roman Catholic Inhabitants of the City and County of Halifax, 13 Sept. 1867, *British Colonist*, 17 Sept. 1867
47 *Evening Express*, 30 Oct. 1867
48 Macdonald Papers, CXVI, 31–41, Archbishop Connolly to John A. Macdonald, 25 Sept. 1868
49 Ibid., 20–7, McCully to John A. Macdonald, 20 Sept. 1867
50 Archives de la Province de Québec [APQ], Chapais Collection, Archbishop Connolly to H. Langevin, 27 Oct. 1867. However, see also ibid., Archibald to G.E. Cartier, 4 Nov. 1867.
51 D. A. Muise, 'The Federal Election of 1867 in Nova Scotia,' *Nova Scotia Historical Society Collections*, XXXVIII, 1968, 327–51
52 *British Colonist*, 29 Aug. 1867; *Evening Express*, 16 Sept. 1867
53 PAC, Howe Papers, IX, 390–3, Howe to Sir Frederick Rogers, 26 Sept. 1867
54 Ibid., 374–89, Howe to Lord Stanley, 25 Sept. 1867, private
55 *Tribune*, 18 Sept. 1867
56 Information derived from the Nova Scotian newspapers. See also PANS, *A Directory of the Members of the Legislative Assembly of Nova Scotia: 1759–1958* (Halifax 1958).

CHAPTER 5: THE REPEAL MOVEMENT

1 *Morning Chronicle* (Halifax) 9 Oct. 1867
2 *Herald* (Yarmouth) 3 Oct. 1867; *Acadian Recorder* (Halifax), 18 Oct. 1867; *Eastern Chronicle* (New Glasgow), 19 Oct. 1867
3 Public Archives of Canada [PAC], Howe Papers, IX, 394–8, Howe to Doyle, 5 Oct. 1867
4 Ibid., IV, 361, W.J. Stairs to Howe, 19 Oct. 1867
5 PAC, Mackenzie Papers, 140–3, Brown to Mackenzie, 3 Oct. 1867 (microfilm)
6 W.F. Williams to the administration, 30 Sept. 1867, *Acadian Recorder*, 4 Oct. 1867
7 PAC, Macdonald Papers, CXIV, 34–7, John A. Macdonald to P.C. Hill, 7 Oct. 1867, private
8 PAC, Howe Papers, XXXVII, Howe to Doyle, 15 Jan. 1868, private
9 PAC, CO 217/242, 125, Colonial Office to Williams, 3 Oct. 1867, telegram
10 *Report of the Board of Trustees of the Public Archives of Nova Scotia*, 1948 (Halifax 1949), 38–43, Howe to William Garvie, 31 Dec. 1868

11 Declaration of the convention of the House of Assembly, 7 Nov. 1867, in *Morning Chronicle*, 9 Nov. 1867
12 Harvard University, Houghton Library, Howe Papers, Howe to [Susan Ann Howe?], 18 Nov. 1867, typescript
13 Wilkins, speech on Nomination Day, 5 Dec. 1867, *Colonial Standard* (Pictou), 10 Dec. 1867
14 *Acadian Recorder*, 18 Nov. 1867; *Halifax Citizen*, 30 Nov. 1867; *Morning Chronicle*, 3 Dec. 1867
15 Canada, Parliament, House of Commons 1867–8, *Debates* (Ottawa 1967), 8 Nov. 1867, 10–3
16 Macdonald Papers, CXIV, 243, John A. Macdonald to P.C. Hill, 11 Nov. 1867, private
17 Mackenzie Papers, 144–7, Mackenzie to Brown, 8 Nov. 1867
18 Harvard University, Howe Papers, Howe to [Susan Ann Howe?], 1 Dec. 1867
19 Canada, House of Commons 1867–8, *Debates*, 12 Dec. 1867, 268–9
20 *Tribune* (Yarmouth), 11 Dec. 1867
21 *Halifax Citizen*, 24 Dec. 1867
22 Macdonald Papers, CXI, 331–4, John A. Macdonald to McCully, 2 Jan. 1868
23 *Morning Chronicle*, 23 Dec. 1867
24 Macdonald Papers, CXVI, 91–4, McCully to John A. Macdonald, 28 Dec. 1867
25 *Morning Chronicle*, 18 Jan. 1868. See also J.A. Chisholm, ed., *The Speeches and Public Letters of Joseph Howe* (Halifax 1909), II, 528–33.
26 Macdonald Papers, CXIV, 6–12, Doyle to John A. Macdonald, 31 Dec. 1867
27 PAC, Howe Papers, XXXVII, Howe to Doyle, 13 Jan. 1868
28 Nova Scotia [NS], House of Assembly 1871, *Debates*, 3 April 1871, 328–30
29 Meeting at Bridgeville, East River, Pictou County, 20 Jan. 1868, *Halifax Citizen*, 25 Jan. 1868
30 Macdonald Papers, CXVI, 111–14, Archbishop Connolly to John A. Macdonald, 15 Jan. 1868
31 Ibid., 127–42, McCully to John A. Macdonald, 3 Feb. 1868
32 *Halifax Citizen*, 6 Feb. 1868
33 PAC, RG 7, G24B, I, Doyle to Monck, 13 Feb. 1868, confidential
34 PAC, Tupper Papers, no 65, Tupper to John A. Macdonald, 14 March 1868. See also Sir Charles Tupper, *Recollections of Sixty Years in Canada* (Toronto 1916), 71
35 NS, House of Assembly 1866, *Debates*, 5 Feb. 1868, 34–5
36 Ibid., 21 Feb. 1868, 162
37 Ibid., 10 Feb. 1868, 39–44
38 Macdonald Papers, CCLXXXII, 53–60, Tupper to John A. Macdonald, 2 May 1866
39 San Marino, California, Huntington Library, Duke of Buckingham and

Chandos Papers, ST, 46, I, 5–6, Duke of Buckingham and Chandos to Doyle, 11 March 1868
40 Archives de la Province de Québec [APQ], Chapais Collection, no 8, G. Brown to Cartier, 17 Feb. 1868
41 Macdonald Papers, CXV, 613–14, John A. Macdonald to Tupper, 23 March 1868
42 Harvard University, Howe Papers, Howe to – 9 April 1868, typescript
43 Tupper Papers, no 69, Tupper to John A. Macdonald, 9 April 1868. See also Tupper, *Recollections*, 77–9.
44 Macdonald Papers, CCLXXXII, 42–5, Tupper to John A. Macdonald, 25 April 1868
45 Harvard University, Howe Papers, Susan Ann Howe, Diary, 2 May 1868
46 Ibid., 20 May 1868
47 Ibid., 30 May 1868
48 PAC, Howe Papers, IX, 424–7, Howe to C.B. Adderly, 13 June 1868
49 Duke of Buckingham and Chandos Papers, ST 46, II, f 106, Duke of Buckingham and Chandos to Monck, 21 Aug. 1868
50 PAC, RG 7, G24 B, I, 4 June 1868
51 PAC, Howe Papers, XXVI, pt 2, 363–77, Howe, Annand, Troop, and Smith to Vail, 18 June 1868
52 Macdonald Papers, CCLXXXII, 74–81, Tupper to John A. Macdonald, 20 June 1868. See also Tupper, *Recollections*, 99.
53 Macdonald Papers, CXIV, 693–7, John A. Macdonald to Tupper, 30 April 1868
54 Canada, House of Commons 1867–8, *Debates*, 27 March 1868, 410–11
55 Ottawa, Parliamentery Library, Senate 1867–8, Scrapbook Debates, 15 May 1868, 252
56 *Acadian Record*, 23 March 1868
57 Canada, Senate 1867–8, Scrapbook Debates, 26 March 1868, 141–2
58 *Report of the Board of Trustees*, 1948, 35–8, Howe to Garvie, 14 Aug. 1868
59 Canada, House of Commons 1867–8, *Debates*, 29 April 1868, 583–5
60 PAC, Howe Papers, XXXVII, Howe to Doyle, 1 Jan. 1868
61 Macdonald Papers, CCLXXXII, 74–81, Tupper to John A. Macdonald, 20 June 1868
62 Ibid., CXIV, 986–90, John A. Macdonald to Tupper, 4 July 1868, private
63 Ibid., CXV, 5–35, S.L. Tilley to John A. Macdonald, 17 July 1868, private and confidential
64 *Herald*, 30 July 1868
65 This newspaper was published by James B. Cossett, who, with his father, John A. Cossett, had published the Digby *Weekly Courier* until it had closed on 31 Dec. 1867.

Notes to pages 71–5   207

66 Macdonald Papers, CXVI, 303–8, Archbishop Connolly to John A. Macdonald, 16 Sept. 1868
67 PAC, Howe Papers, IV, A.W. Savary to Howe, 20 July 1868
68 *Morning Chronicle*, 29 June 1868; *Halifax Citizen*, 18 July 1868
69 Howe to the editor, 30 July 1868, *Morning Chronicle*, 30 July 1868
70 Macdonald Papers, CXV, 69–82, John A. Macdonald to Monck, 4 Sept. 1868, confidential
71 *Report of the Board of Trustees*, 1948, 35–8, Howe to Garvie, 14 Aug. 1868
72 Ibid., 44–52, E.M. McDonald to Garvie, 25 Dec. 1868
73 NS, House of Assembly 1869, *Debates*, 24 May 1869, 104
74 Macdonald Papers, CXV, 264–7, John A. Macdonald to Howe, 20 Dec. 1868, confidential
75 Ibid., 69–82, John A. Macdonald to Monck, 4 Sept. 1868, confidential
76 PAC, Howe Papers, XXVI, pt 2, 520–3, Resolution of the Committee, 6 Aug. 1868
77 Ibid., IV, 451–6, A.W. McLelan to Howe, 21 Aug. 1868; *Report of the Board of Trustees*, 1948, 35–8, Howe to Garvie, 14 Aug. 1868
78 *Report of the Board of Trustees*, 1948, 44–52, E.M. McDonald to Garvie, 23 Dec. 1868
79 Macdonald Papers, DXV, 90–7, Howe to John A. Macdonald, 15 Sept. 1868, confidential
80 Ibid., CXV, John A. Macdonald to Howe, 15 Sept. 1868, private and confidential
81 Ibid., CXVI, 293, McCully to John A. Macdonald, 8 Sept. 1868
82 NS, House of Assembly 1868, *Debates*, 10 Aug. 1868, 169
83 Ibid., 14 Aug. 1868, 171–6
84 Macdonald Papers, DXV, 144–7, John A. Macdonald to Tupper, 20 Nov. 1868, confidential
85 Ibid., CXVI, 293, McCully to John A. Macdonald, 8 Sept. 1868
86 NS, House of Assembly 1868, *Debates*, 3 Sept. 1868, 276
87 Correspondence published in *Evening Express* (Halifax), 7 Sept. 1868
88 NS, Lieutenant-Governor's Correspondence, unbound volumes, 1868, memorandum of Doyle to the Executive Council, 9 Sept. 1868
89 Harry Moody, Jr, 'Political Experiences in Nova Scotia, 1867–1869,' *Dalhousie Review*, XIV, April 1934, 71
90 PAC, Howe Papers, XXXVIII, Nova Scotian delegation to Vail, 8 May 1868
91 NS, House of Assembly 1869, *Debates*, 17 Aug. 1868, 176
92 PAC, Howe Papers, IX, 471–4, Howe to Annand, 19 Aug. 1868
93 NS, House of Assembly 1868, *Debates*, 4 Sept. 1868, 277–81
94 PAC, Howe Papers, XXXVIII, Howe to Wilkins, 14 Sept. 1868
95 *Evening Express*, 14 Sept. 1868

208 Notes to pages 75–8

96 NS, Lieutenant-Governor's Correspondence, unbound volumes, 1868, Martin I. Wilkins, 19 Sept. 1868, second opinion
97 NS, House of Assembly 1868, *Debates*, 14 Sept. 1868, 296
98 Ibid., 18 Sept. 1868, 305
99 *British Colonist*, 22 Sept. 1868
100 Macdonald Papers, CXVI, 291, Blanchard to John A. Macdonald, 7 Sept. 1868, telegram
101 Ibid., 325–31, McCully to John A. Macdonald, 12 Oct. 1868
102 Tupper Papers, no 83, Tupper to John A. Macdonald, 14 Oct. 1868
103 Macdonald Papers, CXII, 51–3, John A. Macdonald to Archibald, 27 Oct. 1868, confidential
104 *Halifax Citizen*, 10 Nov. 1868
105 E.M. McDonald to Robert Boak, Jr, 13 Oct. 1868, in F. Patterson, *More Studies in Nova Scotian History* (Halifax 1941), 109
106 Macdonald Papers, CXV, 130–8, Howe to John A. Macdonald, 29 Oct. 1868, private
107 Ibid., CXVI, 363, McCully to John A. Macdonald, 12 Nov. 1868
108 PAC, Howe Papers, IV, 481–9, John A. Macdonald to Howe, 6 Oct. 1868, private
109 Ibid., IX, 508–16, Howe to Robert Boak, Jr, 26 Sept. 1868
110 Ibid., IV, 491–4, A.G. Jones to Howe, 19 Oct. 1868
111 Howe to the editor, *Eastern Chronicle*, 24 Oct. 1868
112 PAC, Howe Papers, XXXVIII, Howe to Ross, 7 Dec. 1868
113 John G. Marshall to the editor, *Morning Chronicle*, 4 Nov. 1868
114 PAC, Howe Papers, IV, 508–11, A.G. Jones to Howe, 4 Nov. 1868
115 Ibid., 523–33, A.W. McLelan to Howe, 7 Nov. 1868
116 Howe to the editor, 6 Nov. 1868, *Morning Chronicle*, 7 Nov. 1868
117 Macdonald Papers, CLXXXVII, 53–5, Archibald to John A. Macdonald, 23 Nov. 1868, private
118 *Acadian Recorder*, 7 Dec. 1868
119 J.C. Troop to the electors of Annapolis, 1 Dec. 1868, *Morning Chronicle*, 7 Dec. 1868
120 PAC, Howe Papers, IX, 596–618, Howe to John A. Macdonald, 16 Nov. 1868, confidential
121 Ibid., 466–79, Howe to Livingstone, 12 Aug. 1868
122 Macdonald Papers, CXVII, 363, McCully to John A. Macdonald, 12 Nov. 1868
123 Ibid., CXIV, 58–65, Doyle to John A. Macdonald, 18 Nov. 1868
124 PAC, Howe Papers, IV, 479–80, John A. Macdonald to Howe, 6 Oct. 1868, confidential
125 Ibid., 592–7, John A. Macdonald to Howe, 23 Dec. 1868, confidential

Notes to pages 78-87 209

126 Macdonald Papers, CXVII, 296-9, John A. Macdonald to A.W. McLelan, 26 Dec. 1868, confidential
127 *Report of the Board of Trustees*, 1948, 52-6, E.M. McDonald to Garvie, 11 March 1869

CHAPTER 6: HOWE AND THE FEDERAL GOVERNMENT

1 Nova Scotia [NS], House of Assembly 1868, *Journals*, App. 38
2 Ibid. 1869, *Journals*, App. 1, Report of the Auditor-General
3 Public Archives of Canada [PAC], Howe Papers, XVI, pt 1, 129-36, memorandum of Howe to A.W. McLelan, Dec. 1868
4 NS, House of Assembly 1869, *Journals*, App. 1, Report of the Finance Minister
5 Ibid., Report of the Committee of the Honourable Privy Council, 25 Jan. 1869
6 *Halifax Citizen*, 2 Feb. 1869
7 PAC, Macdonald Papers, CCLXXXII, 134-7, Tupper to John A. Macdonald, 25 Jan. 1869
8 Ibid., CXV, 485-90, John A. Macdonald to Tupper, 28 Jan. 1869, confidential
9 Canada, House of Commons 1869, *Debates*, 16 June 1869, 134-5
10 *Report of the Board of Trustees of the Public Archives of Nova Scotia*, 1948 (Halifax 1949), 52-6, E.M. McDonald to William Garvie, 11 March 1869
11 PAC, Howe Papers, CXV, 191, Howe to John A. Macdonald, 5 Feb. 1869, telegram
12 NS, House of Assembly 1869, *Debates*, 20 May 1869, 66-9
13 J. Northup to L.G. Power, secretary of the Repeal League, 3 Feb. 1869, *Evening Express* (Halifax), 5 Feb. 1869
14 *Herald* (Yarmouth), 18 March 1869; *Morning Chronicle* (Halifax), 23 March 1869
15 *Morning Chronicle*, 6 Feb. 1869
16 Macdonald Papers, CXV, 566-8, John A. Macdonald to Tupper, 15 Feb. 1869
17 Ibid., CXVI, 205-28, Doyle to John A. Macdonald, 25 Feb. 1869, private
18 Ibid., 169-72, Doyle to John A. Macdonald, 9 Feb. 1869
19 Ibid., CXIV, 189-99, Doyle to John A. Macdonald, 12 Feb. 1869, private
20 Ibid., CCLXXXII, 149-52, Tupper to John A. Macdonald, 8 Feb. 1869
21 Ibid., CXVI, 489-96, H.A.N. Kaulback to Tupper, 8 March 1869; Ibid., CXIV, 189-99, Doyle to John A. Macdonald, 12 Feb. 1869, private
22 Ibid., CXVI, 293, McCully to John A. Macdonald, 8 Sept. 1868
23 NS, Lieutenant-Governor's Correspondence, unbound volumes, 1869, Annand to Doyle, 5 March 1869
24 Macdonald Papers, CCLXXXII, 149-52, Tupper to John A. Macdonald, 8 Feb. 1869
25 Ibid., CXVI, 427-37, S. Campbell to John A. Macdonald, 20 Jan. 1869

26 *Unionist and Halifax Journal*, 15 Feb. 1869
27 Macdonald Papers, CCLXXXII, 176–9, Tupper to John A. Macdonald, 23 March 1869
28 *Evening Express*, 15 Feb. 1869
29 PAC, Howe Papers, LXXI, Archbishop Connolly to Doyle, p.m. [3 April] 1869
30 'A merchant' to the editor, *Acadian Recorder* (Halifax), 19 Feb. 1869
31 *Evening Express*, 15 Feb. 1869
32 PAC, Tupper Papers, no 89, Tupper to John A. Macdonald, 16 Feb. 1869. See also Sir Charles Tupper, *Recollections of Sixty Years in Canada* (Toronto 1916), 87.
33 Harvard University, Houghton Library, Howe Papers, Howe to –, 2 March 1869, typescript
34 *Evening Mail* (Halifax), 8 June 1909
35 Macdonald Papers, CCLXXXII, 176–9, Tupper to John A. Macdonald, 23 March 1869
36 Ibid., CXVI, 415–18, N.K. Clements to John A. Macdonald, 12 Jan. 1869
37 Ibid., DXV, 485–90, John A. Macdonald to Tupper, 28 Jan. 1869, confidential
38 Ibid., CXII, 471–2, John A. Macdonald to N.K. Clements, 25 Jan. 1869, private
39 Ibid., CXVI, 442–5, W.J.H. Rowley to Meagher, 20 Jan. 1869
40 Ibid., 508–15, C.T. Schreiber to John A. Macdonald, 9 March 1869
41 Ibid., 499–506, J.A. McLellan to John A. Macdonald, 9 March 1869
42 Ibid., 368–475, J.A. McLellan to John A. Macdonald, 23 Feb. 1869
43 F. Killam, speech at Hartford, 19 March 1869, *Herald*, 25 March 1869
44 *Herald*, 8 April 1869
45 NS, Lieutenant-Governor's Correspondence, unbound volumes, 1869, Wilkins to H. Moody, 24 Feb. 1869
46 Macdonald Papers, CCLXXXII, 172–5, Tupper to John A. Macdonald, 15 March 1869
47 Ibid., CXVI, 508–15, C. Schreiber to John A. Macdonald, 9 March 1869
48 Wilkins to the editor, *Acadian Recorder*, 15 March 1869
49 According to the census of 1861 there were 6965 French, 4902 Scots, and 1347 Irish out of a total population of 14,268. In religion there were 10,243 Roman Catholics and 3188 Presbyterians.
50 Macdonald Papers, CCLXXXII, 176–9, Tupper to John A. Macdonald, 23 March 1869
51 *Evening Express*, 15 March 1869
52 Macdonald Papers, CXVI, 524–31, William Miller to Tupper, 17 March 1869
53 PAC, Howe Papers, XXXVIII, Howe to John A. Macdonald, 20 March 1869
54 Canada, House of Commons 1869, *Debates*, 16 June 1869, 134–5

55 Macdonald Papers, CXVI, 260–3, Doyle to John A. Macdonald, 23 March 1869
56 *Halifax Citizen*, 22 April 1869
57 NS, House of Assembly 1869, *Debates*, 7 June 1869, 147–9
58 PAC, Howe Papers, XXXVIII, Howe to John A. Macdonald, 20 March 1869
59 Ibid., IV, 680–3, Rose to Howe, 2 April 1869
60 Macdonald Papers, CXXXIX, 186, cheque stub nos 12, 13, and 14
61 *Report of the Board of Trustees*, 1952, 15–16, Alexander Mackenzie to A.G. Jones, 10 May 1869
62 PAC, Howe Papers, LXXI, S.L. Tilley to Howe, 25 March 1869
63 Macdonald Papers, CXIV, 241–8, Doyle to John A. Macdonald, 5 March 1869, private
64 *Halifax Citizen*, 24 April 1869
65 Macdonald Papers, CXVI, 520–3, James W. Allison to Tupper, 16 March 1869
66 PAC, Howe Papers, XL, 109–10, Howe to Elderkin, 17 March 1870
67 *Evening Express*, 26 April 1869. In 1867, with 3070 voters registered, Howe received 1530 votes and his opponent, James King, 956
68 Frank Killam polled 1220 votes to 598 for Clements. In 1867 Thomas Killam won by 1225 to 666 for George Brown
69 With 1232 registered voters in the county, Le Vesconte received 560 votes to 333 for Henry. In 1867 Croke had received 545 and his opponent 279
70 PAC, Howe Papers, XXXVIII, Howe to Morse, 25 April 1869
71 Ibid., LXXII, Howe to Doyle, 4 April 1869, private
72 Ibid., Doyle to Howe, 5 April 1869, private
73 Macdonald Papers, CXIV, 268–79, Doyle to John A. Macdonald, 25 June 1869
74 NS, House of Assembly 1869, *Journals*, 2–3, Speech from the Throne, 29 April 1869
75 *Halifax Citizen*, 18 May 1869
76 NS, House of Assembly 1869, *Journals*, 12 May 1869, 28–9
77 Ibid., 1869, *Debates*, 20 May 1869, 66–9
78 Ibid., 21 May 1869, 78–82
79 Ibid., 18 May 1869, 57–9
80 Ibid., 20 May 1869, 72–7
81 Ibid., 1867, *Journals*, 25 May 1869, 56
82 Ibid., 1869, *Debates*, 28 May 1869, 121–2
83 Ibid., 7 June 1869, 147
84 Ibid., 11 June 1869, 178–89
85 Ibid., 1869, *Journals*, 12 June 1869, 98
86 Ibid., 1869, *Debates*, 7 May 1869, 15
87 Ibid., 10 June 1869, 173–4
88 Ibid., 1 June 1869, 132

89 Ibid., 4 June 1869, 143
90 Ibid., 24 May 1869, 96–7
91 PANS, Provincial Secretary Papers, 1872–3, no 1811, John Fergusson to Vail, 3 June 1872

CHAPTER 7: A TIME FOR REASSESSMENT

1 Canada, House of Commons 1869, *Journals*, 4 June 1869, 190
2 Ibid., 1869, Scrapbook Debates, 16 June 1869, 133
3 Ibid., 12 June 1869, 123
4 Ibid., 1869, *Journals*, 16 June 1869, 261
5 Ibid., 11 June 1869, 231–2
6 Public Archives of Canada [PAC], Howe Papers, XXXIX, 61–4, Howe to A.W. McLelan, 10 July 1869
7 Ibid., 57–8, Howe to F.W. Fishwick, 22 June 1869
8 Ibid., 150–3, Howe to W.H. Chipman, 20 Dec. 1869
9 PAC, Macdonald Papers, CCLXXXII, 197–212, Tupper to John A. Macdonald, 2 Aug. 1869
10 Ibid., 229–32, Tupper to John A. Macdonald, 20 Nov. 1869
11 Ibid., CXIV, 604–7, A.W. McLelan to John A. Macdonald, 1 July 1869, private
12 Nova Scotia [NS], Provincial Secretary Papers, unbound volumes, 1869, no 1038, Thomas Morrison to Vail, 18 Sept. 1869
13 *Halifax Citizen*, 31 July 1869
14 Macdonald Papers, CLXXXVII, 86–94, Archibald to John A. Macdonald, 4 Aug. 1869, private and confidential
15 Ibid., CXVI, 104–5, John A. Macdonald to Tupper, 16 Aug. 1869, private
16 Ibid., CLXXXVII, 101–5, Archibald to John A. Macdonald, 16 Aug. 1869; CCLXXXII, 233–4, Tupper to John A. Macdonald, 30 Sept. 1869
17 PAC, Canada, Privy Council, Orders-in-Council, Minutes, no 762, 23 Oct. 1869
18 Macdonald Papers, CLXXXII, 111–14, Archibald to John A. Macdonald, 14 Sept. 1869, private
19 Ibid., CLXXXVII, 122–6, Archibald to Tupper, 25 Sept. 1869
20 *Morning Chronicle* (Halifax), 11 Aug. 1869
21 Ibid., 18 Aug. 1869
22 *British Colonist* (Halifax), 12 Aug. 1869
23 NS, Lieutenant-Governor's Correspondence, unbound volumes, 1869, John A. Macdonald to Doyle, 3 Sept. 1869, telegram. Macdonald Papers, CXIV, 280–6, Doyle to John A. Macdonald, 26 Oct. 1869
24 Ibid., Doyle to Annand, 4 Oct. 1869
25 Ibid., Annand to Doyle, 5 Oct. 1869, telegram

Notes to pages 104–9 213

26 *Evening Express* (Halifax), 11 Oct. 1869
27 NS, Executive Council, Minutes, 15 Oct. 1869, 137–45
28 Macdonald Papers, CXIII, 299–300, John A. Macdonald to Vail, 27 Dec. 1869, private
29 Ibid., 22 Oct. 1871, 37, A.W. McLelan to Vail, 3 Jan. 1870
30 *Halifax Citizen*, 25 March 1870
31 Macdonald Papers, DXIV, 709–12, Vail to John A. Macdonald, 25 Jan. 1870, private
32 *Morning Chronicle*, 16 and 18 June 1869
33 Ibid., 28 April 1869
34 D. Warner, *The Idea of Continental Union* (Lexington 1958), 81
35 *Acadian Recorder* (Halifax), 7 March 1870
36 *Eastern Chronicle* (New Glasgow), 7 July 1869
37 Warner, *Continental Union*, 82. Warner refers to the existence of thousands of unemployed miners in Pictou county, but in 1866 there were only 3043 miners in the entire province and this number had declined to only 2458 in 1869. In addition, he refers to appalling poverty in the county, but cites a Boston newspaper as his authority
38 J.S. Martell, 'Early Coal Mining in Nova Scotia,' *Dalhousie Review*, XXV, July 1945, 156–72
39 NS, House of Assembly 1870, *Journals*, App. 15
40 K.G. Pryke, 'Labour and Politics: Nova Scotia at Confederation,' *Histoire Sociale/Social History*, no 6, Nov. 1970, 44
41 *Herald* (Yarmouth), 10 and 24, Feb., 14 April, 5 May 1870
42 *Acadian Recorder*, 20 and 21 Sept. 1889
43 'Bright' to the editor, *Halifax Citizen*, 8 May 1869
44 *Halifax Citizen*, 5 June 1869
45 NS, Executive Council, Minutes, 21 Dec. 1869, 152–8
46 NS, House of Assembly 1870, *Debates*, 8 April 1870, 244–9
47 F. Patterson, *Studies in Nova Scotian History* (Halifax 1940), 119, Stairs to Robert Boak, Jr, 15 March 1870
48 George T. Denison, *The Struggle for Imperial Unity* (Toronto) 1904, 10
49 Macdonald Papers, CXVI, 698–704, R.G. Haliburton to John A. Macdonald, 24 Dec. 1869
50 *British Colonist*, 12 Jan. 1870; *Halifax Citizen*, 13 Jan. 1870
51 PAC, Howe Papers, XL, 1–5, Howe to Doyle, 19 Jan. 1870
52 *Morning Chronicle*, 26 Jan. 1870; *Halifax Citizen*, 25 Jan. 1870
53 Macdonald Papers, CXIV, 709–12, Vail to John A. Macdonald, 25 Jan. 1870
54 Ibid.; DXIII, 1043, John A. Macdonald to Vail, 11 Feb. 1870, private
55 NS, House of Assembly 1870, *Debates*, 14 March 1870, 139–42

56 Ibid., 28 Feb. 1870, 29
57 *Halifax Citizen*, 25 and 27 Nov. 1869
58 NS, House of Assembly 1870, *Debates*, 21 Feb. 1870, 9
59 Ibid., 1871, *Debates*, 7 Feb. 1871, 19–26
60 NS, Executive Council, Minutes, 27 July 1870, 24, Vail to John A. Macdonald, 21 and 25 March 1870
61 NS, Lieutenant-Governor's Correspondence, Doyle to Governor General Young, 26 March 1870, telegram
62 NS, House of Assembly 1870, *Debates*, 9 April 1870, 254–8
63 Ibid., 23 March 1870, 186–7
64 Ibid., 16 April 1870, 286–9
65 Macdonald Papers, CXIV, 329–36, Doyle to John A. Macdonald, 8 Feb. 1870
66 NS, House of Assembly 1870, *Debates*, 12 April 1870, 265–6
67 Macdonald Papers, CXIV, 368–71, Doyle to John A. Macdonald, 18 April 1870
68 NS, House of Assembly 1870, *Journals*, 9 March 1870, 31
69 Ibid., *Debates*, 14 April 1870, 274–9
70 Macdonald Papers, CLXXXVII, 127–30, Archibald to John A. Macdonald, 16 Nov. 1869
71 Ibid., CXIV, 291–8, Doyle to John A. Macdonald, 23 Nov. 1869, private
72 Ibid., 337–48, 5 March 1870
73 NS, House of Assembly 1870, *Debates*, 13 April 1870, 270–1
74 Canada, House of Commons 1870, *Debates*, 18 March 1870, 546
75 Macdonald Papers, CCLXXXII, 229–32, Tupper to John A. Macdonald, 20 Nov. 1869; CLXXXVII, 131–7, Archibald to John A. Macdonald, 24 Nov. 1869
76 PAC, Howe Papers, XL, 98–105, Howe to Cathcart Thompson, 14 March 1870
77 *Halifax Citizen*, 11 May 1870
78 Canada, House of Commons 1870, *Debates*, 18 Feb. 1870, 105–8
79 D.P. Gagan, 'The Relevance of Canada First,' *Journal of Canadian Studies*, V, 4, Nov. 1970, 36–43
80 *Report of the Board of Trustees of the Public Archives of Nova Scotia*, 1952 (Halifax 1953), 16–18, Mackenzie to Jones, 3 March 1870
81 Ibid., 18–19, 12 April 1870
82 PAC, Howe Papers, XL, 21–2, Howe to A. Campbell, 29 Jan. 1870
83 PAC, Tupper Papers, no 105, A. McFarlane to Tupper, 30 April 1870
84 *British Colonist*, 21 July 1870
85 *Morning Chronicle*, 17 Sept. 1870
86 *Acadian Recorder*, 27 Oct. 1870
87 NS, Provincial Secretary Papers, unbound volumes, 1870, no 548, F.M. Pearson to Vail, 30 Nov. 1870

88 NS, House of Assembly 1871, *Debates*, 16 March 1871, 223; 18 March 1871, 243; 31 March 1871, 304–6
89 Dale Thomson, *Alexander Mackenzie, Clear Grit* (Toronto 1960), 119
90 *Morning Chronicle*, 17 Oct. 1870
91 Ibid., 5 Nov. 1870
92 Ibid., 7 Nov. 1870
93 PAC, Howe Papers, XXXIX, 298, Howe to Power, 17 Nov. 1870
94 Ibid., XL, 229–30, Howe to Northup, 19 Oct. 1870
95 *Halifax Citizen*, 7 Nov. 1870
96 *Evening Express*, 21 Nov. 1870

CHAPTER 8: THE TREATY OF WASHINGTON, CONFEDERATION, AND NOVA SCOTIA

1 *Report of the Board of Trustees of the Public Archives of Nova Scotia*, 1952 (Halifax 1953), 21–3, Mackenzie to Jones, 31 Dec. 1871
2 Nova Scotia [NS], House of Assembly 1871, *Debates*, 7 Feb. 1871, 19–26
3 Canada, House of Commons 1871, *Debates*, 29 March 1871, cols. 686–7
4 Hill was unseated on 20 March 1871 by an election committee of the assembly on the grounds of undue electoral influence
5 NS, House of Assembly 1871, *Debates*, 25 March 1871, 272–3
6 Dickie had resigned from the council in 1866 in protest against Confederation
7 Tupper to Dr N.W. Wickwire, 31 March 1871, *Acadian Recorder*, 3 April 1871. Dr Wickwire was the medical partner of Tupper
8 NS, House of Assembly 1871, *Debates*, 22 March 1871, 251–7
9 NS, Legislative Council 1871, *Journals*, 28 March 1871, 66–7
10 NS, House of Assembly 1871, *Debates*, 24 March 1871, 262–9
11 Ibid., 3 April 1871, 328–30
12 *British Colonist* (Halifax), 9 March 1871
13 NS, House of Assembly 1871, *Debates*, 20 March 1871, 245–9
14 NS, Legislative Council 1871, *Journals*, 4 April 1871, 97–8
15 NS, Lieutenant-Governor's Correspondence, 1870, Vail to Harry Moody, Jr, 18 April 1870
16 NS, House of Assembly 1871, *Debates*, 14 Feb. 1871, 51–2
17 Allan Nevins, *Hamilton Fish: The Inner History of the Grant Administration* (New York rev. ed. 1957), I, 424
18 Ibid., II, 475–6
19 Smith, *Treaty of Washington*, 63
20 Ibid., 70–1
21 Ibid., 79

22 Public Archives of Canada [PAC], Macdonald Papers, CLXXXVII, 131–7, Archibald to John A. Macdonald, 24 Nov. 1869
23 Ibid., CXIV, 398–404, Doyle to John A. Macdonald, 24 April 1871
24 *Acadian Recorder*, 4 March 1871
25 *Halifax Citizen*, 21 April 1871. The new owners included W.B. Vail.
26 *Morning Chronicle* (Halifax), 3 and 25 April, 9 May 1871
27 Ibid., 1 May 1871
28 *Evening Express* (Halifax), 10 May 1871
29 *Acadian Recorder* (Halifax), 13 May 1871; *Morning Chronicle*, 11 May 1871
30 *Morning Chronicle*, 16 May 1871
31 These letters can be found in J.A. Chisholm, ed., *The Speeches and Public Letters of Joseph Howe* (Halifax 1909), II, 599–619
32 PAC, Howe Papers, XXIX, 674–6, Howe to Edward Roach, 22 May 1871
33 Ibid., XXXIX, 629–32, Howe to Sydenham Howe, 6 May 1871. The Conservative, W.H. Allison, subsequently won the seat
34 Howe to the People of Nova Scotia, 26 April 1871, in *British Colonist*, 2 May 1871
35 PAC, Tupper Papers, no 116, W. Ross to Tupper, 20 May 1871
36 PAC, Howe Papers, XXXIX, 706–7, Howe to John Campbell, *et al.*, 8 June 1871
37 PAC, Tupper Papers, new additions, Doyle to Tupper, 27 April 1871, private
38 Archives de la Province de Québec [APQ], Chapais Collection, XIX, 1919, Tupper to Langevin, 30 April 1871
39 PAC, Tupper Papers, new additions, Tupper to Dr Parker, 14 Feb. 1871
40 Ibid., T. Rand to Tupper, 21 March 1871
41 Ibid., Archbishop Connolly to Tupper, 8 May 1871
42 *Morning Chronicle*, 6 May 1871
43 NS, Executive Council, Minutes, 6 June 1871, 74–6
44 PAC, Howe Papers, IV, 753–6, E.M. McDonald to Howe, 13 June 1871
45 Ibid., XLI, 88–9, Howe to Northup, 24 Nov. 1871
46 *Halifax Citizen*, 18 Nov. 1871
47 *Evening Express*, 19 and 24 May 1871; *British Colonist*, 27 May 1871
48 *Halifax Citizen*, 27 May 1871; *Morning Chronicle*, 30 May 1871
49 *British Colonist*, 17 June 1871
50 Ibid., 9 Dec. 1871
51 PAC, Howe Papers, IX, 729–45, Howe to Archibald, 4 Nov. 1871, private
52 *Tribune* (Yarmouth), 21 June 1871
53 PAC, Howe Papers, XXXIX, 833–5, Howe to Sir John Rose, 26 June 1871
54 Ibid., IX, 725–8, Howe to Governor General Lorne, 22 Aug. 1871, private
55 Ibid., XXXIX, 945–6, Howe to – (circular)
56 Ibid., IV, 780–6, Savary to Howe, 27 Aug. 1871, private

57 Ibid., 787–9, Le Vesconte to Howe, 30 Aug. 1871
58 Ibid., 808–10, Killam to Howe, 1 Dec. 1871
59 Ibid., 794–8, H. McDonald to Howe, 7 Sept. 1871, private
60 Ibid., 799–802, J.F. Forbes to Howe, 15 Sept. 1871
61 Ibid., 787–9, Le Vesconte to Howe, 30 Aug. 1871
62 Ibid., 791–2, Coffin to Howe, 2 Sept. 1871, private
63 Chisholm, ed., *Speeches and Public Letters of Howe*, II, 631–42
64 PAC, Howe Papers, XLI, 364–5, Howe to Donald Ross, 25 March 1872
65 *Evening Express*, 15 March 1872
66 *Morning Chronicle*, 5 March 1872
67 Ibid., 18 March 1872
68 *Acadian Recorder*, 20 and 26 Jan. 1872; *Morning Chronicle*, 17 Feb. 1872
69 *Morning Chronicle*, 8 and 13 Jan. 1872; *Halifax Citizen*, 20 Jan. 1872
70 Canada, House of Commons 1872, *Debates*, 17 April 1872, cols. 53–5
71 Ibid., 10 May 1872, cols. 483–6

CHAPTER 9: MAINTAINING THE STATUS QUO

1 Nova Scotia [NS], House of Assembly 1872, *Debates*, 23 Feb. 1872, 7
2 Ibid., 6 March 1872, 104
3 *Morning Chronicle* (Halifax), 28 Feb. 1872
4 NS, House of Assembly 1872, *Debates*, 18 April 1872, 275–81
5 Ibid., 17 April 1872, 270–2
6 Ibid., 25 March 1872, 147–8
7 NS, House of Assembly 1872, *Debates*, 12 April 1872, 231–3
8 Ibid., 15 April 1872, 237. The attorney general voted for the bill on third reading but he was absent from the house during the other votes on the bill.
9 Ibid., 29 Feb. 1872, 63–71
10 Ibid., 21 March 1872, 137–43
11 Public Archives of Canada [PAC], Macdonald Papers, CXIV, 424–31, Doyle to John A. Macdonald, 20 April 1872
12 PAC, Howe Papers, XLI, 308–13, Howe to George S. Brown, 8 Feb. 1872
13 NS, House of Assembly 1872, *Debates*, 8 April 1872, 216–17
14 PAC, Tupper Papers, new additions, C.H.M. Black to Tupper, 18 Dec. 1871
15 *Eastern Chronicle* (New Glasgow), 25 April 1872
16 *Acadian Recorder* (Halifax), 18 April 1872
17 *Morning Chronicle*, 24 April 1872
18 Macdonald Papers, CXVI, 734–7, W.H. Howland to John A. Macdonald, 1 July 1872
19 *Halifax Citizen*, 23 July 1872

20 *Evening Express* (Halifax), 17 July 1872
21 *Acadian Recorder*, 20 July 1872
22 *Evening Express*, 10 July 1872; *British Colonist* (Halifax), 25 July 1872
23 *Halifax Citizen*, 30 May 1872
24 *Morning Chronicle*, 12 June 1872; *Acadian Recorder*, 2 July 1872
25 *Acadian Recorder*, 27 June 1872
26 *Morning Chronicle*, 15 July 1872
27 Ibid., 17 July 1872
28 New Brunswick Museum [NBM], Tilley Papers, McCully to Tilley, 9 Aug. 1872
29 PAC, Macdonald Papers, CXVI, 738–48, Savary to John A. Macdonald, 12 Oct. 1872, private
30 *Evening Express*, 16 Aug. 1872
31 Tupper Papers, pp 1826–7, Rev. Dr M.J. Hannon to Tupper, 7 Aug. 1872
32 Ibid., 1839–40, Hill to Tupper, 21 Aug. 1872
33 Ibid., new additions, Tupper to Alpin Grant, 15 June 1872
34 *Morning Chronicle*, 19 Aug. 1872
35 Macdonald Papers, CXVI, 757–64, Archibishop Connolly to John A. Macdonald, 6 Jan. 1873
36 *British Colonist*, 24 Aug. 1872
37 PAC, Macdonald Papers, CCLXXXII, 252–5, Tupper to John A. Macdonald, 4 July 1872
38 *British Colonist*, 24 Aug. 1872
39 *Report of the Board of Trustees of the Public Archives of Nova Scotia*, 1952 (Halifax 1953), 25–6, Mackenzie to Jones, 26 Aug. 1872
40 *Acadian Recorder*, 16 Aug. 1872
41 *Halifax Citizen*, 20 Aug. 1872; *Morning Chronicle*, 23 Aug. 1872
42 *Morning Chronicle*, 9 Set. 1872
43 *Halifax Citizen*, 27 Aug. 1872; *Morning Chronicle*, 8 Oct. 1872
44 *Morning Chronicle*, 9 Oct. 1872
45 *Halifax Citizen*, 26 Sept. 1872
46 *British Colonist*, 9 Nov. 1872
47 *Morning Chronicle*, 15 Nov. 1872
48 Ibid., 7 Sept. 1872
49 *Halifax Citizen*, 14 Sept. 1872
50 *Morning Chronicle*, 9 Sept. 1872
51 Ibid., 20 Sept. 1872
52 Ibid.
53 Ibid., 18 Oct., 19 Dec. 1872
54 Ibid., 17 Oct. 1872
55 Ibid., 1 Oct. 1872
56 *Colonial Standard* (Pictou), 1 Oct. 1872; *Eastern Chronicle*, 3 Oct. 1872

57 *Colonial Standard*, 22 Oct. 1872
58 *Halifax Citizen*, 11 Feb. 1873; *British Colonist*, 28 Jan. 1873
59 *Morning Chronicle*, 8 Feb. 1873
60 *Halifax Citizen*, 11 Feb. 1873
61 *Morning Chronicle*, 11 Feb. 1873
62 *Halifax Citizen*, 20 Feb. 1873

CHAPTER 10: THE FAILURE OF THE COALITION

1 Public Archives of Canada [PAC], Tupper Papers, IV, 132, John A. Macdonald to Tupper, Sunday, 1873
2 *Report of the Board of Trustees of the Public Archives of Nova Scotia*, 1952 (Halifax 1953), 29, Mackenzie to Jones, 11 March 1873, confidential
3 Canada, House of Commons, 1873, *Journals*, 7 March 1873, 7
4 Ibid., 19 March 1873, 37–8
5 *Evening Express* (Halifax), 5 April 1873
6 PAC, Howe Papers, XLII, 75–7, Howe to Coffin, 15 Feb. 1873
7 Ibid., XL, 124–9, Howe to Sydenham Howe, 15 March 1873
8 Ibid., IV, 787–9, I. Le Vesconte to Howe, 30 Aug. 1871
9 Tupper Papers, no 130, John A. Macdonald to Tupper, 9 Oct. 1872, private
10 PAC, Macdonald Papers, CXV, 279–81, Howe to John A. Macdonald, 6 Dec. 1872
11 Harvard University, Houghton Library, Howe Papers, Howe to Doyle, 15 Jan. 1873, typescript
12 Canada, House of Commons 1873, Scrapbook Debates, 4 April 1873, 63
13 *Evening Express*, 7 April 1873
14 Canada, House of Commons 1873, *Journals*, 2 April 1873, 116–17
15 Canada, House of Commons 1873, Scrapbook Debates, 3 Nov. 1873, 38
16 Ibid., 19 May 1873, 196
17 Ibid., 18 March 1873, 24
18 Ibid., 28 April 1873, 109
19 PAC, Tupper Papers, pp 1734–5, C.H.M. Black to Tupper, 18 Dec. 1871
20 Ibid., pp 1878–83, T.E. Kenney to Tupper, 15 Dec. 1872, private
21 *Morning Freeman* (Saint John), 12 April 1872
22 *Evening Express*, 7 April 1873
23 NS, Provincial Secretary Papers, Miscellaneous File, F.N. Gisborne to Vail, 14 March 1873; Canada, House of Commons 1873, Scrapbook Debates, 9 April 1873, 69; 28 April 1873, 110
24 Canada, House of Commons 1873, Scrapbook Debates, 12 May 1873, 169
25 Ibid., 23 May 1873, 205

26 Ibid.
27 D.G. Creighton, *John A. Macdonald: The Old Chieftain* (Toronto 1952-5), II, 159-63
28 PAC, Howe Papers, XL, 104-11, Howe to Sydenham Howe, 3 March 1873
29 Ibid., XLII, 55-7, Howe to A.W. Longley, 30 Jan. 1873
30 *Halifax Citizen*, 17 June 1873
31 *Evening Express*, 3 July 1873
32 *Halifax Citizen*, 26 June 1873
33 *Morning Chronicle* (Halifax), 20 Feb. 1873
34 *Halifax Citizen*, 22 July 1873
35 PAC, Howe Papers, LXI, 301-3, Howe to Hugh McDonald, 15 Feb. 1872
36 Tupper Papers, IV, 137, Archbishop Connolly to Tupper, 22 June 1873
37 PAC, Mackenzie Papers, Letterbooks, MG 1, B 2, I, 72-3, A. Mackenzie to T.W. Anglin, 29 July 1873, private
38 *Morning Chronicle*, 27 June 1873; *Halifax Evening Reporter*, 20 June 1873
39 PAC, Mackenzie Papers, Letterbooks, MG 1, B 2, I, 75-6, Mackenzie to Charles E. Church, 21 July 1873, confidential
40 *Morning Chronicle*, 28 May 1873
41 PAC, Mackenzie Papers, Letterbooks, MG 1, B 2, I, 84, Mackenzie to Forbes, 1 Aug. 1873
42 *Morning Chronicle*, 15 and 19 Aug. 1873
43 Dale C. Thomson, *Alexander Mackenzie: Clear Grit* (Toronto 1960), 156-60
44 PAC, Mackenzie Papers, Letterbooks, MG 26, B 2, I, 66, Mackenzie to P.R. Goodfellow, 19 July 1873; *Morning Chronicle*, 21 Aug. 1873
45 *Eastern Chronicle* (New Glasgow), 28 Aug. 1873
46 *Halifax Citizen*, 21 Aug. 1873
47 *British Colonist* (Halifax), 23 Sept. 1873; 28 Oct. 1873
48 *Halifax Evening Reporter*, 23 Sept. 1873
49 *British Colonist*, 23 Sept., 14 Oct. 1873
50 Ibid., 21 Oct. 1873
51 *Evening Express*, 20 and 30 Sept. 1873
52 Ibid., 22 July 1873
53 *Morning Chronicle*, 23 Sept. 1873
54 *Halifax Citizen*, 2 Oct. 1873
55 *Morning Chronicle*, 30 Sept., 11 Oct. 1873
56 *Halifax Citizen*, 2 Sept. 1873; *Morning Chronicle*, 1 Sept. 1873
57 *Halifax Citizen*, 2 Aug. 1873; *Morning Chronicle*, 16 Aug. 1873
58 *Evening Express*, 26 Aug. 1873
59 *Halifax Citizen*, 2 Sept. 1873
60 *Morning Chronicle*, 5 Dec. 1873; *Halifax Citizen*, 9 Dec. 1873

61 *Evening Express*, 15 Aug. 1873
62 *Halifax Evening Reporter*, 3 and 5 Nov. 1873
63 Ibid., 3 Sept. 1873
64 *Morning Chronicle*, 22 and 25 Sept. 1873
65 *Evening Express*, 18 Oct. 1873; *Halifax Evening Reporter*, 14 and 21 Oct. 1873
66 *Evening Express*, 15 Dec. 1873
67 I am indebted to Professor R. Walton of Wayne State University for his assistance on this point
68 *Report of the Board of Trustees*, 1952, 32–3, Mackenzie to Jones, 6 Oct. 1873, private
69 Canada, House of Commons 1873, Scrapbook Debates, 30 Oct. 1873
70 *Report of the Board of Trustees*, 1952, 40, Mackenzie to Jones, 15 Jan. 1874
71 Canada, Privy Council, Minutes, RG 2, I, LXXXVI, no 1366, 21 Oct. 1873
72 *Morning Chronicle*, 15 Nov. 1873
73 *Report of the Board of Trustees*, 1952, 33–4, Mackenzie to Jones, 10 Nov. 1873, private and confidential
74 NS, Provincial Secretary Papers, no 1807, Ross to Vail, 26 April 1873
75 *Morning Chronicle*, 25 June 1873
76 *British Colonist*, 2 Dec. 1873
77 PAC, Mackenzie Papers, Letterbooks, MG 26, B 2, I, 91–2, Mackenzie to A. Smith, 20 Sept. 1873, private
78 *Morning Chronicle*, 27 Nov. 1873
79 *Report of the Board of Trustees*, 1952, 34–5, Mackenzie to Jones, 19 Nov. 1873, private
80 Ibid., 40–1, Mackenzie to Jones, 21 Jan. 1874, confidential
81 Ibid., 36–8, Mackenzie to Jones, 20 Dec. 1873

CHAPTER 11: THE WINTER ELECTION

1 *Report of the Board of Trustees of the Public Archives of Nova Scotia*, 1952 (Halifax 1953), 36–8, Mackenzie to Jones, 20 Dec. 1873
2 *Morning Chronicle* (Halifax), 3 Jan. 1874
3 *Evening Express* (Halifax), 15 and 24 Jan. 1874
4 Ibid., 7 Jan. 1874; *British Colonist* (Halifax), 13 Jan. 1874
5 *British Colonist*, 15 Jan. 1874
6 *Halifax Evening Reporter*, 3 Jan. 1874
7 *Morning Chronicle*, 10, 12, and 31 Dec. 1873
8 *Halifax Citizen*, 3 Jan. 1874
9 Public Archives of Canada [PAC], Tupper Papers, IV, 140, Sanford Fleming to Tupper, 15 Jan. 1874

10 *Halifax Citizen*, 17, 20, 22 Jan. 1874
11 *Report of the Board of Trustees*, 1952, 40–1, Mackenzie to Jones, 21 Jan. 1874, confidential
12 W.H. Allison to the Electors of the County of Hants, *British Colonist*, 17 Jan. 1874
13 *Report of the Board of Trustees*, 1952, 30–1, Mackenzie to Jones, 9 July 1873, private
14 *Evening Express*, 28, 29 Nov. 1873
15 *Halifax Citizen*, 3 Jan. 1874
16 *Morning Chronicle*, 2 Dec. 1873
17 *Halifax Evening Reporter*, 13 March 1874
18 *Herald* (Yarmouth), 22 Jan. 1874
19 *Halifax Citizen*, 24 Jan. 1874
20 *Report of the Board of Trustees*, 1952, 39, Mackenzie to Jones, 6 Jan. 1874, confidential
20 *Halifax Citizen*, 17 Jan. 1874
22 *Halifax Evening Reporter*, 20 Nov. 1874
23 *British Colonist*, 3 Feb. 1874
24 Ibid., 27 Jan. 1874
25 *Halifax Evening Reporter*, 3 Feb. 1874
26 *Halifax Citizen*, 27 Jan. 1874
27 *Evening Express*, 27 Jan. 1874; *Halifax Evening Reporter*, 27 Jan. 1874
28 *Halifax Citizen*, 31 Jan. 1874, 3 Feb. 1874
29 *Halifax Evening Reporter*, 28 Jan. 1874, 2 Feb. 1874
30 Ibid., 28 Jan. 1874
31 *British Colonist*, 31 Jan. 1874
32 See K.G. Pryke, 'Labour and Politics: Nova Scotia at Confederation,' *Histoire Sociale/Social History*, no 6, Nov. 1970, 33–55
33 *Evening Express*, 26 Jan. 1874
34 Hill to the editor, *Evening Express*, 2 Feb. 1874
35 *Bradstreet's Reports of the Dominion of Canada*, 1 Feb. 1876 (New York 1876), 838–47
36 *Halifax Evening Reporter*, 4 Feb. 1874
37 *Halifax Citizen*, 14 Feb. 1874
38 *Evening Express*, 5 Feb. 1874
39 *Sun* (Truro), 7 Feb. 1874; *Herald*, 12 Feb. 1874
40 Public Archives of Nova Scotia, Vernon Smith, Diary, 5 Feb. 1874
41 *Halifax Citizen*, 7 Feb. 1874
42 Ibid., 8 Jan. 1874

CHAPTER 12: NEW WAYS AND OLD CONFLICTS

1 *Evening Express* (Halifax), 14 March, 8 May 1874
2 *Morning Chronicle* (Halifax), 24 March 1874
3 *Halifax Evening Reporter*, 24 March 1874
4 Public Archives of Canada [PAC], Tupper Papers, new additions, Tilley to Tupper, 27 March 1874, strictly confidential
5 Nova Scotia [NS], House of Assembly 1874, *Debates*, 18 March 1874, 24–6
6 Ibid., 20 March 1874, 27–30
7 Ibid., 17 March 1874, 19–22
8 Ibid., 49
9 Ibid., 17 March 1874, 19–20; 10 April 1874, 129–30
10 Ibid., 15 April 1874, 137–8
11 Ibid., 2 May 1874, 247
12 Ibid., 15 April 1874, 138–9
13 *Halifax Citizen*, 2 May 1874; *Morning Chronicle*, 1 June 1874
14 NS, House of Assembly 1874, *Debates*, 10 April 1874, 125–30
15 Ibid., 1874, *Journals*, App. 14, Report of J.W. Johnston, March 1874
16 *Statement and Correspondence of the Pictou Presbytery, P.C.L.P., Respecting the Antigonish Riot* (Pictou 1874)
17 *Halifax Evening Reporter*, 14 Feb. 1874
18 Reverend George Grant to the editor, *Morning Chronicle*, 24 Feb. 1874
19 NS, House of Assembly 1874, *Debates*, 4 May 1874, 249–53
20 *Halifax Evening Reporter*, 28 April 1874
21 NS, House of Assembly, 1874, *Debates*, 7 May 1874, 276–7
22 *Halifax Evening Reporter*, 14 Sept. 1874; *Evening Express*, 17 Sept. 1874
23 PAC, Macdonald Papers, CXVIII, Tupper to John A. Macdonald, 25 May 1874, telegram
24 PAC, Mackenzie Papers, 625–9, Ross to Mackenzie, 25 May 1874
25 *Report of the Board of Trustees of the Public Archives of Nova Scotia, 1952* (Halifax 1953), 43, Mackenzie to Jones, 6 June 1874
26 Mackenzie Papers, 555–6, Jones to Mackenzie, 17 June 1874, private
27 Ibid., 625–9, Ross to Mackenzie, 19 Sept. 1874
28 Ibid., 633–4, 25 Sept. 1874
29 Ibid., 636, Ross to Coffin, 28 Sept. 1874
30 *Halifax Evening Reporter*, 28 Nov. 1874
31 Macdonald Papers, CXVIII, 19–22, Tupper to John A. Macdonald, 22 July 1874
32 Tupper Papers, new additions, James McDonald to Tupper, 11 Aug. 1874

33 *British Colonist* (Halifax), 11 July 1874
34 *Halifax Evening Reporter*, 27 Nov. 1874
35 *Morning Chronicle*, 10 April 1874
36 *Evening Express*, 25 June 1874
37 Ibid., 31 June 1874
38 *Acadian Recorder* (Halifax), 14 Sept. 1874
39 *Halifax Citizen*, 1 and 13 Aug. 1874
40 *Evening Express*, 15 July 1874
41 *Halifax Evening Reporter*, 23 July 1874; *British Colonist*, 1 Sept. 1874
42 *Halifax Evening Reporter*, 28 July 1874
43 *Morning Chronicle*, 6 Aug. 1874
44 Public Archives of Nova Scotia [PANS], Carmichael Papers, Jones to Carmichael, 9 Nov. 1874
45 *Halifax Evening Reporter*, 24 Dec. 1874
46 *Evening Express*, 9 Nov. 1874; *Halifax Evening Reporter*, 2 Dec. 1874
47 Carmichael Papers, Jones to Carmichael, 9 Nov. 1874
48 Ibid., 11 Nov. 1874
49 *Halifax Evening Reporter*, 2 Nov. 1874
50 Ibid., 30 Oct., 26 and 28 Nov. 1874
51 Ibid., 2 and 4 Dec. 1874
52 *Acadian Recorder*, 27 Oct. 1874
53 *Morning Chronicle*, 28 Sept. 1874
54 *Halifax Citizen*, 11 Aug. 1874
55 *Acadian Recorder*, 6 Oct. 1874; *Halifax Citizen*, 10 Oct. 1874
56 *Acadian Recorder*, 1 Dec. 1874
57 *Report of the Board of Trustees*, 1952, 46–7, Mackenzie to Jones, 27 Nov. 1874, confidential
58 *Evening Express*, 25 Nov., 1 Dec. 1874
59 Ibid., 9 Dec. 1874
60 *Morning Chronicle*, 8 May 1874
61 NS, House of Assembly 1875, *Journals*, App. 16, Annand to Mackenzie, 7 Dec. 1874
62 Ibid., Mackenzie to Annand, 11 Nov. 1874
63 PANS, Railway Papers, Eastern Extension, 19 Nov. 1874
64 Mackenzie Papers, Letterbooks, MG 26, B 2, I, 235–46, Mackenzie to Annand, 2 Dec. 1874
65 *Colonial Standard* (Pictou), 15 Dec. 1874
66 *Evening Express*, 3 Dec. 1874
67 *Morning Chronicle*, 7 Dec. 1874
68 *Evening Express*, 21 Dec. 1874

69 Ibid., 18 Dec. 1874
70 Educational Committee of the Synod of the Presbyterian Church of the Lower Provinces to the editor, *Morning Chronicle*, 3 Dec. 1874
71 *Sun* (Truro), 2 and 9 Dec. 1874
72 *Morning Chronicle*, 11 Dec. 1874
73 Ibid., 19 Dec. 1874
74 *Evening Express*, 30 Dec. 1874
75 PANS, Smyth Papers, Annand to Peter Smyth, 18 Dec. 1874, confidential
76 Acadia University, Crockett Papers, W.H. Wylde to A.G. Crockett, 30 Dec. 1874
77 NS, Provincial Secretary Papers, Letterbooks, 1875, 328–9, Hill to Colin Campbell, 30 Jan. 1875
78 Ibid., 324–7, Hill to John A. Fraser, 25 Jan. 1875, private and confidential
79 *Colonial Standard*, 22 Dec. 1874
80 *Halifax Evening Reporter*, 14 and 18 Dec. 1874
81 Ibid., 21 Dec. 1874

Note on sources

Several works have appeared in the past few years which contain comprehensive listings of material on the confederation period. Those interested would do well to consult P.B. Waite, *The Life and Times of Confederation 1864–1867* (Toronto 1962), and D.G. Creighton, *The Road to Confederation: The Emergence of Canada: 1863–1867* (Toronto 1964). A work which covers the general political development for a longer time period is W.L. Morton, *The Critical Years: The Union of British North America, 1857–1873* (Toronto 1964). A particularly useful inventory of manuscript sources, government publications, and other printed sources is included in *Dictionary of Canadian Biography*, x: 1871–1880, edited by M. La Terreur (Toronto 1972). This volume contains many entries, all of which contain bibliographies, on such secondary figures of the confederation period as Hiram Blanchard, Isaac Le Vesconte, and James McKeagney, and has useful biographies of more prominent figures, such as Joseph Howe, J.W. Johnston, and Archbishop Connolly.

The most valuable source of primary material for the pre-confederation period proved to be the dispatches between the Colonial Office and the Nova Scotian lieutenant-governors. Copies of these dispatches may be consulted at the Public Archives of Nova Scotia. It would be more useful, however, to consult the dispatches received by the Colonial Office because they bear the comments of various officials and often contain rough drafts of replies sent to the colonial governors. Copies of these records are on microfilm at the Public Archives of Canada. Some insight into the nature of intercolonial relations can also be gained through the correspondence of the lieutenant-governors in the Public Archives of Nova Scotia, the Stanmore Papers at the University of New Brunswick, and the Williams Papers at the New Brunswick Museum in St

John. The latter depository also possesses the Allison Notebooks which contain copies of Williams' correspondence, some of which are not found in the main file.

One of the more significant sources of primary material, and crucial for the period from 1867 until 1869, is the Macdonald Papers at the Public Archives of Canada. Not only did Macdonald play a prominent role in the events of this period but many Nova Scotians, such as Archbishop Connolly, who left no collections of their own, corresponded more or less regularly with Macdonald. Other significant sources are the Howe Papers (both at the Public Archives of Canada and the Houghton Library, Harvard University) and the Tupper Papers, particularly since the additions of 1967. Some information can frequently be gained on individual events or periods from papers of such people as Edward Cardwell, George Brown, and Alexander Mackenzie. These papers are deposited on microfilm in the Public Archives of Canada. Other useful collections include those of Thomas Chapais at Archives de la Province de Québec and S.L. Tilley in the New Brunswick Museum. The Public Archives of Nova Scotia has some of the papers of William Carmichael and Peter Smyth, as well as the diaries of P.S. Hamilton and Vernon Smith. The papers of D.W. Crockett at Acadia University illustrate, in a most marked form, the complex interconnection between politics, business, and religion.

This study was heavily dependent on government publications and particularly on the published debates of parliament. Unfortunately the record of debates in the Canadian federal parliament from 1867 to 1875 is in a variety of forms. Although plans have been made for the publication of a comprehensive record, in so far as is now possible, to date only one volume, covering the session of 1867–8 and edited by P.B. Waite, has appeared. For the sessions of 1870, 1871, and 1872 résumés of the debates were published. The remaining years are covered only by the 'Scrapbook Debates,' available on microfilm, which were compiled from clippings from Upper Canadian newspapers. Since these newspapers had only a spasmodic interest in Maritime issues and politicians, it is frequently necessary to consult the summary of parliamentary affairs which T. Anglin prepared for his newspaper, *The Morning Freeman*, of Saint John.

In addition to the published debates of parliament, there are journals which provide an easily available reference for the business of the house, as well as the numerous papers presented to parliament which were frequently printed in the sessional papers. Thus, papers referring to such significant issues as the 'better terms' are available, but many other documents relating to Nova Scotia were not considered important enough to warrant publication and they have since disappeared.

Nova Scotia was more interested than was the Province of Canada in preserving some records of debates because it began to publish a résumé in the mid-1850s. This record can sometimes be supplemented by the accounts which appeared in various newspapers, which in turn are the principal source for debates of the Legislative Council. Although the debates of the upper house were published, the total run for each year was small and the Public Archives of Nova Scotia has only a handful of the debates for the nineteenth century. The journals of both houses, with accompanying appendices, are relatively accessible.

Virtually as important a source as the government records were newspapers, of which during the 1860s and early 1870s approximately thirty-four were being published at any given time. This large number was regarded as a guarantee of a well-informed electorate and a blow against rule by an oligarchy. As a tangible means of support, newspapers in Nova Scotia were carried free through the mails, until Confederation, when the federal parliament applied a postage rate. Even before Confederation, however, the mortality rate, particularly of county newspapers, was high and the files of several of them have disappeared. In other cases, existing files, even of papers with long runs, have serious gaps. The most ambitious listing of the existing Nova Scotian newspapers is G.E.N. Tratt, 'The Newspapers of Nova Scotia, with Special Reference to the Period Before Confederation' (unpublished MA thesis, Mt Allison University, 1960). This list may now be supplemented by *An Historical Directory of Nova Scotia Newspapers and Journals Before Confederation*, comp. T.B. Vincent, Occasional Papers of the Department of English, Royal Military College (Kingston 1977). Every researcher also owes a considerable debt to the Canadian Library Association for its efforts to microfilm the leading newspapers of the Confederation period.

About two-thirds of the newspapers published in Nova Scotia were county newspapers which appeared weekly. Although most of the files of these papers have virtually disappeared, the two newspapers published in Yarmouth, the *Eastern Chronicle* of New Glasgow and the *Sun* of Truro, provided an interesting glimpse into county politics. In addition, the *Eastern Chronicle* emerges in 1868 and 1869 as the main exponent in the province of annexation sentiment. The most independent and invigorating of the county papers was the Pictou *Colonial Standard*, which consistently commented at length on provincial and federal affairs. Falling into a different category were those papers such as the *Presbyterian Witness* and the *Burning Bush* which were supported by various Protestant bodies. These papers provide a useful insight into intellectual and social affairs although they rarely commented on political disputes. It is interesting that the Roman Catholics were only represented by lay papers, the *Antigonish Casket* and the *Evening Express* of Halifax. This may have been an attempt by the church to avoid public exposure which would have attracted undue criticism, or may have been caused by the division of the Roman Catholics into Scotch, French, and Irish factions.

The chief source of comment on political affairs was provided by the Halifax newspapers, which usually supplied the editorial leadership for the county newspapers. In the early 1860s the leading papers were published three times a week but there was a marked tendency throughout the decade for them to become dailies, which resulted in a strain on their financial resources. All newspapers were dependent on political patronage, and the need to establish political support was probably the reason they became the spokesmen for different groups of politicians. Circulation figures for most of the newspapers are unavailable but in January 1868 the *Morning Chronicle* claimed to have the largest circulation in the Maritimes. A more precise figure was provided by the *Evening Express* in March 1870 when it boasted of a circulation of 3350. A somewhat higher figure of 4000 had been claimed by the *Citizen* in April 1868 for its combined tri-weekly and weekly editions. This figure fell to 3100 by April 1871 but after a change in ownership, and the introduction of a daily, it rose, by April 1873, to over 6300. Despite this circulation figure, one of the owners in 1877 claimed that the paper had never made a yearly profit. The total circulation of the newspapers would appear to have been extensive, particularly since the population of the province in 1871 was 350,000. Readership of the newspapers was further limited by the illiteracy of one-fifth of the adult population, so it would seem that many people regularly supported more than one paper.

The search for information on the development of Nova Scotia often leads to the many local and county histories, as well as to publications issued by business firms and societies. This material is rarely found in any of the traditional bibliographies and is usually difficult to locate. Such material should not be ignored even if the contents are frequently disorganized, the quality uneven, and the books without any form of index. Those interested in finding additional works relating to county history should consult William F.E. Morley, *The Atlantic Provinces: Newfoundland, Nova Scotia, New Brunswick, Prince Edward Island*, Canadian Local Histories to 1950: A Bibliography (Toronto 1967).

Index

Abbott, J.J.C. 107
Acadian Iron Charcoal Company 151
Acadian Recorder (Halifax) 10, 86, 126
Allan, Sir Hugh 107, 150, 151, 152, 155, 158
Allison, Charles 44
Allison, William 166
Almon, Dr W.J. 143, 169
Annand, Charles 11, 62, 77
Annand, William 11; negotiations with confederates 22–4, 26, 34; 1867 election 51, 57; formation of ministry 62; repeal 67, 70, 72–3, 74, 76–8; 'better terms' 85, 86, 88; seeks settlement with Ottawa 103–4; mission to Washington on coal tariff 108–9; and federal–provincial relations 117; and new provincial building 119–20; 1871 cabinet changes and rivalries 126, 131; and 1872 federal election 143; resents Howe's appointment as lieutenant-governor 152–3; policy to Mackenzie administration 161–2, 166, 176; political position 178, 182; railway policy 185, 186; nears retirement 187

Annapolis County: by-election 9; railway 43, 152
Annexation 30–1, 70–1, 77–8, 85, 86, 89, 95, 103; Annexation Society 106–7, 108, 110–11, 115
Anti-confederate party 49–50; internal divisions 59; post-electoral policies 61–3; caucus 70–3; role of federal members 76–9; identification with federal Liberal party 141–2, 144
Antigonish County 176–7
Archibald, A.G. 9, 17, 23; Pictou Railway 26; consolidates political position 27, 29, 32; London Conference 34, 38; formation of federal ministry 43, 44; 1867 election 55, 57–8; Colchester by-election 102–3; appointed lieutenant-governor of Manitoba 114; and of Nova Scotia 153

Banner of Union (Halifax) 51
'better terms': conciliation policy 73; Macdonald selects Howe as conciliator 75–6, 78; Portland Conference 80–3; reaction of local

ministry 84–5; acceptance of by House of Commons 98–101; proposed revision 104–5; opposition by Blake 113; unanticipated political results 129, 148; 1873 revision 171, 191. See also British North America Act
Bill, Caleb 43
Binney, Bishop 10
Blackadar, Hugh 86
Blake, Edward 100, 113, 135
Blanchard, Hiram 44, 57; provincial ministry 61, 62; and anti-confederate riot 65; unseated 74; Inverness by-election 75–6; 1871 election 130–1; role in legislature 137–8, 140, 175; Maritime union 177; attacked by *Evening Express* 179
Bluenose (Digby) 70–1
Bourinot, John 43
Bright, John 35, 67–8
British Colonist (Halifax) 135
British North America Act: London Conference 36–9; objectives 41–2; financial terms 42–3; legality 47–8; revision 94–6; compact theory 99–100; disallowance 109. See also 'better terms' and Quebec Conference
Brown, George 22–3, 45, 61, 63, 67
Brown, Stayley 187
Brydges, C.J. 184, 185
Burpee, E.R. 185
Buckingham and Chandos, Duke of 67–8

Cabinet x; powers 6; 1867 federal election 44–5; representation 149; and parliament 157–9; selection 160–1, 164–5; authority 174–6;
Nova Scotian representation on federal cabinet 1874 178; federal-provincial relations 192–3. See also federal members
Cameron, H.J. 140
Cameron, R.D. 101–2
Campbell, Charles 44
Campbell, Colin 188
Campbell, Stewart 41, 42
Canadian Pacific Railway Company 153
Cape Breton: county 70; island railway 139–40, 152, 185–6
Cardwell, Edward 17, 20, 21, 25, 28, 31, 32, 33, 34
Carmichael, James 143, 144, 148, 173
Carnarvon, Henry, Earl of 33, 34, 35, 39
Cartier, Sir George Etienne 20, 44, 67, 73, 144, 164
Chambers, Robert 95, 115, 121
Charlottetown Conference 4, 5
Chiniquy, Rev. Charles 176
Chipman, Samuel 136, 142, 165
Chipman, William 112
Church, Charles 150
Clements, N.K. 89, 93
Coal mining 106–9, 112–13, 124–5, 132–3, 139, 151, 175
Coffin Thomas 114, 134, 154, 160–1, 164, 167
Colchester County 57; 1869 by-election 102–3; 1870 by-election 114–16; Orange Association 187
Colonial Office 4, 8, 17–18, 19, 21, 24–5, 32, 67–8, 125
'compromisers': attitudes to confederates 101–2; nominal support of government 117, 129; 1872 fed-

Index   233

eral election 142; and political balance 147
Confederates: difficulties of 1867 campaigns 52–3, 55–8; lack of morale 66; attitude to 'better terms' 73, 75–6, 85–6; view of 'compromisers' 101–2; dissension 114–15; 1871 election 129–31; overview 190–2
Connolly, Archbishop T.L. 10, 13; seeks legal status for separate schools 37–8, 52–3; alarm at dissension 54, 56–8, 65; and annexation 71; role in 1869 by-elections 76, 87, 91; in 1871 provincial election 130; 1872 federal election 143
Conservative party 9; colonial union 23, 41; 1871 provincial election 130–1; as national policy party 141–2; 1872 general election 143; disunity 147; federal election 149; support for party unity 153–4; Pacific Railway scandal 155–9; view of cabinet 164–5; role of patronage 166–9; support for Robb 171; party dissension 172, 179; acceptance of provincialism 191–3
Corporations 158–9
County Courts 112, 176
Creelman, Samuel 44
Croke, W.J. 90
Crown lands 122
Cumberland County: 1867 elections 51, 57; position of Purdy 97; 1870 by-election 114; railway, coal mining 130, 140; 1872 federal election 143–4
Currency 69, 112

Daly, M.B. 120
Desbrisay, Thomas 122, 131

Dickey, R.B. 8
Dickie, Charles 120
Dickie, D.M. 75
Digby County 49, 71
Doyle, Sir Charles Hastings: appointed lieutenant-governor 61; opposes repeal policy 65, 66; view of Howe 68, 69; rebuffs Annand and Wilkins 72; confrontation with ministry 74, 75, 86; Yarmouth by-election 90; possibility of new ministry 94; reconciliation with Ottawa 103–4, 109, 110; dissension in assembly 111; leave 114; support of union 123, 139; term expires 150
Drummond, George 107
Dufferin, Frederick, Viscount Clandeboyle and Earl of 155
Duffus, James 132

Economic development: role of union 14, 41. See also National Policy
Eisenhauer, James 131
Elections: practices 50–1; 1867 federal–provincial 46, 49–59; 1871 provincial 126–32; 1872 federal 140–6; 1874 federal 163–4; 1874 provincial 182–7

Federal members (Nova Scotian): basis of representation 6–7; relationship with provincial members 62–3, 71, 78–9; attitude to Liberal party 99–100; 1873 caucus revolt 149; view of federal parties 150–1, 159, 160; relations with provincial assembly 175; caucus 178–9; relations with provincial ministry 185–6
Federal–provincial relations: federalism 5, 14–15; restrictions on provin-

cial role 78–9, 85; 'better terms' legislation 99, 100; probing limits of jurisdiction 103–4, 108–9, 110; political control in the province 139, 161–2; nature of provincial politics 173, 174–6, 180, 182–4, 185–6, 191

Fenians 24, 35

Fergusson, John 107

Fielding, W.S. 146

Fish, Hamilton 124–5

Fisheries 24–5; licences 31–2, 38, 41–2, 54; provincial committee 109–10; Treaty of Washington 123–5, 127–8, 133, 181

Fleming, Sandford 26

Flynn, E.P. 111, 126

Forbes, Dr James F. 114, 134, 150, 154–5

Franchise: secret ballot 111–12, 121–2; qualifications 138–9

Galt, A.T. 15, 20

Garvie, William 34, 117, 126, 146

Gladstone, William 77, 84

Gordon, Sir Arthur Hamilton 18, 23–4

Goudge, Monson H. 87–8, 153

Grant, Alpin 169

Griffin, Martin J. 156, 186

Gun-Boat (Halifax) 51

Haliburton, R.G. 108, 113, 132, 137

Halifax British Colonist 169, 184

Halifax Citizen 34, 48, 62; financial vulnerability 86; criticisms of England 107; opposes power of disallowance 109; change of ownership 126; Treaty of Washington 132; supports party divisions 145; criticizes British government 157

Halifax Evening Express: position on Pacific Railway scandal 156–7, 164; dissatisfaction with Conservatives 169, 171, 179–80; returns to party 186

Halifax Evening Reporter 87; 1873 Halifax provincial by-election 147; Pacific Railway scandal 158; 1874 Halifax federal election 168–9, 170, 171; school issue 177, 179, 180; role of provincial ministry 183, 185, 188

Halifax (city and county) 55–7; 1870 provincial by-election 116–17; 1872 federal election 143; 1872 provincial by-election 146–7; 1874 federal election 168–71; 1874 provincial election 186–7

Halifax School Association 177, 179

Hants County: 1869 by-election 85, 87–8, 91–3

Hants Gazette 88

Henry, W.A.: supports union 11–12, 20, 34, 39; opposes agreement with Howe 91, 93; considered for ministry 182

Hill, P.C.: provincial ministry 44, 55, 56; resigns 61; 1870 Halifax by-election 117, 120; 1871 legislative session 124; refuses to be a candidate 143; leaves Conservative party 167–8, 179; enters Liberal ministry 182, 187, 188

Hincks, Sir Francis 144, 164

Holmes, Simon 175

Howe, Joseph: position on union 11–12; call for election 16; returns from Washington 26; reaction to union resolution 28–31; delegate to London 32, 34, 39–40; policy on

union 47–9, 50; election campaigning 51, 54; considers repeal 58, 61; view on provincial wing 61–2; restrains repeal policy 63, 65–6; delegate to England 67–8, 70, 71; negotiations with Macdonald 73, 74–5, 76–9, 80–3; enters cabinet 84; by-election 87–8, 91–3, 94; compact theory 100; rebuffs Vail 105; non-interference in by-election 117; recommended by provincial ministry for fishery negotiations 124; role in provincial campaign 128–9; policy on Treaty of Washington 133–6, 137; 1872 election 142; caucus revolt 149–50; appointment as governor 152–3; contrasted with Mackenzie's ministry 164; relationship with imperial government 175; rejected by Henry 182; Treaty of Washington 189; 'better terms' 191; view on cabinet 193
Hunt, Rev. A. 111
Huntington, Lucius 150, 151, 152
Hyde, Hiram 51, 102

Imperial relations ix; military defence 13–14; imperial federation 34–5, 40; criticism of British control 107–8; Treaty of Washington 124, 128, 133–4; Pacific Railway scandal 157–8; responsible government 175; imperial relations 189–90
Intercolonial Railway 8; attempted construction 1864 10; guarantees sought for construction 20, 36; appointment of A.W. McLelan 102; extension in Cumberland 130; branch lines 139, 151. See also Railways

Inverness County: 1868 by-election 75–6

James, Alexander 107–8
Johnson, George: accompanies Howe in by-election 87–8; supports Motton 146–7; arranges candidacy of Robb 168–9, 171. See also *Halifax Evening Reporter*
Johnston, J.W.: premier 4; support of colonial union 5; resignation 9; nominates Hunt 111; named lieutenant-governor 153; attitude to executive 175
Jones, A.G.: 'better terms' 76–7, 84, 88; opposes visit of governor general 103; does not attend parliamentary session of 1870 113; supports federal Liberal party 116; opposes Treaty of Washington 136; 1872 federal election 143, 144, 145; defeat hinders Mackenzie 148; opposition to Tobin 159; absence from cabinet 160, 168, 169–70, 171; aids transformation of anti-confederate party 173

Kaulback, H.A.N. 86
Kennely, D.V. 185
Kenny, Sir Edward: appointed to cabinet 44–5; forecasts confederate defeat 55; involved with conciliation policy 73, 91; administrator of Nova Scotia 114; Liberal Conservative Association 180
Kidston, William: opposes ministry 94–5, 97, 111; proposes abolition of council 121–2; annexation 124; 1871 provincial election 129, 130; seeks to join Liberals 166

Killam, Frank: Yarmouth by-election 89, 93; seeks additional 'better terms' 99; Treaty of Washington 134, 137; railway to Yarmouth 152, 171–2
Killam, Thomas 29, 31, 50, 88
King, James W. 50, 101–2

Langevin, Sir Hector Louis 38, 130
League of the Maritimes Provinces 29–30, 108
Legislature (provincial): Quebec Resolutions 6; ideology 15; council 28; reduced in size 42; council enlarged 62; qualifications for assembly 120; proposed abolition of council 121–2; role of opposition 138; role in federal system 174–6; government powers 182–3, 192–3. See also Provincial ministry
LeVesconte, Isaac 91, 93, 99, 165
Liberal Conservative Association 179–80, 186
Liberal Party (federal): Howe's opinion 61, 63; attacks 'better terms' 98, 100–1; appeals to anticonfederates 113, 116; supports additional concessions 119–20; fails to attract Nova Scotian members 142; strength in new parliament 148, 154–5. See also Mackenzie
Liberal Party (Nova Scotia): partial support of colonial union 9, 23; coalesces with Conservative opponents of union 41, 49–50, 59; movement towards federal Liberals 135; 1872 federal election 141–6; reaction to Pacific Railway scandal 157–8; 1873 by-election 166–7, 172; supports party system 183–4, 191–3

Lisgar, Lord (Sir John Young) 103
Locke, John 43
Lunenburg County: 1865 by-election 23; 1867 federal election 48, 86
Lynch, Archbishop John 38

McConnell, Robert 106–7
McCully, Jonathan: supports union 9; replaced as editor of *Morning Chronicle* 11; view of Howe 12; accepts Quebec Resolutions 28; foresees Annexation movement 30–1; delegate to London 34; patronage 43; reaction to 1867 election 57–8; urges moderation on tariffs 64; fears agitation 65; opposes conciliation policy 73, 75–6, 78, 87
Macdonald, Rev. Alexander 76
McDonald, E.M.: proposes union be modified 48; becomes queen's printer 62; role in 'better terms' 76, 84, 100; imperial relations 107; attacked by Garvie 117; negotiates to form new ministry 131
McDonald, Hugh (of Antigonish): delegate to England 34; supports Treaty of Washington 134; re-elected 142; cabinet position 153, 154, 160
McDonald, Hugh (of Inverness) 76
McDonald, James 26, 29, 130–1, 143, 180
Macdonald, Sir, John A.: Quebec Conference 5; Intercolonial Railway 10; refuses to modify Quebec Resolutions 16; urged to settle union issue 32; London Conference 39; forms federal cabinet 44–5; fishery policy 54; electoral success 55; policy to Nova

Scotia 60; tariff policy 63-4; adopts conciliation policy 67-70, 71-2, 76-9, 80, 84, 85, 89, 90, 96; introduces 'better terms' 98-100; supports Howe 102, 104, 105; rebuffs province 109-10, 119-20; Treaty of Washington 123-5, 126, 135-6; Pacific Railway scandal 150, 152, 154-5, 156-8; collapse of ministry 160; precedent of cabinet 165; defeat of supporters 172; Nova Scotian railway policy 185; view of cabinet 191

McDonald, W. 172

MacDonnell, Sir Richard Graves 4, 5, 8, 15, 16, 17, 21-2

MacDonnell, Samuel 26, 154

McFarlane, Alexander 34, 114

McGee, D'Arcy 5, 44-5

McHeffey, Richard 61-2, 77

McKay, M.L. 159-60

McKeagney, James 70

Mackenzie, Alexander: suspects fund-raising for Howe's by-election 91-2; seeks Nova Scotian support 113, 116, 119-20; Pacific scandal 148, 154, 155; forms ministry 160, 161, 163, 164, 165; 1873 revision of financial terms 174; problems with the cabinet 178-9; Nova Scotian railway policy 184-6

McKinnon, Bishop C.F. 27, 70

McKinnon, John 44

McLelan, A.W.: seeks party unity 72, 77, 78, 79; Portland negotiations 83, 84; 1869 Colchester by-election 102-3; supports Vail 105; 1870 Colchester by-election 115

McNab, James 44, 120

McNab, Peter 120, 121

Maritime union x, 3, 5; revived 1865 17; proposed 1874 177-8, 183

Marshall, John J. 62

Militia: Halifax 24; Pictou 65; bill 75

Miller, William: opposition to union wavers 22-3; proposes union in principle 26; invited to London Conference 34; appointed to the Senate 44; dissatisfaction with party 90-1

Mitchell, Peter 73

Monck, Viscount, governor general of Canada: Charlottetown Conference 4; suggests revisions of Quebec Resolutions 16; fisheries 25, 31-2; delays London Conference 33

Morning Chronicle (Halifax): editor 9; changes policy on union 11; opposition wavers 22, 23; attacks confederation 45; influence of Charles Annand 62; initiates break with Howe 77; criticizes tie with England 103, 108; position on union 115, 116, 126; view of Treaty of Washington 127, 128, 135; Pacific Railway scandal 145, 146, 157

Morrison, Thomas: opposes Howe 88; supports Pearson 115; threatens to break with ministry 130-1; attempts to revive anti-federal agitation 139; attacks Tupper 140

Moses, Nathan 89

Motton, George 146-7, 168, 170

Murray, Dr George: advocates repeal 65, 95, 110; attacks ministry 111, 121, 122; 1872 provincial election 129, 130; 1872 Pictou by-election 146

National Policy 113, 127, 190-1, 192. See also economic development

New Brunswick 3, 4, 16, 17, 22, 24, 177
New Glasgow Eastern Chronicle 106–7
New provincial building 82, 99, 109, 110, 119–20, 131–2, 139
Northup, Jeremiah 85, 87–8, 95, 97, 116
Novascotian (Halifax) 11
Nova Scotian Association for the Encouragement of Industrial Interests 181
Nova Scotian Coal Owners Association 108, 113, 132

Oakes, E.R. 167
Orange Association (Colchester County) 187

Pacific Railway 148, 150; Huntingdon's motion 150–2; newspaper discussion of issues 154–9; change of governments 159–60; 1874 election 163–4, 165, 172
Parker, Dr D. 120
Patronage: offsets economic power 51–2; use 92, 93; awarded to federal members 101, 129; demands of provincial ministry 161–2, 166–7; enhances role of ministry 172, 175
Pearson, F.M. 102–3, 115, 150
Pictou Colonial Standard 10
Pictou County: railway 26–7, 52, 139–40, 176, 185–6; 1867 elections 48, 49, 58; militia 65; annexation 106–7; 1872 provincial by-election 146; Presbyterian Synod 176–7; religious dispute 187
Pineo, H.G., Jr 57
Portland Conference 1869 80–3

Power, Patrick: 1867 federal election 56; distrust of federal Liberals 116–17; supports Treaty of Washington 136, 137, 143; 1872 federal election 168, 170, 171
Presbyterians 57, 176–7, 187
Prince Edward Island 3, 4
Provincial ministry: role in conciliation policy 78–9; moves away from repeal 104–6, 109–10; reorganization 178–9, 182–3, 187–8. See also Legislature
Provincial rights 98, 109–10, 116–17, 173
Public works: funding 105–6
Purdy, Amos 95, 97

Quebec Resolutions: conference 5–8; reception 10; method of approval 16–17, 27–8; basis for London Conference 36. See also British North America Act

Railways: Pictou 26–7, 52; Windsor-Annapolis 43, 152; Cape Breton 139–40; Yarmouth 140; Spring Hill 140, 143–4; Gut of Canso 176, 184–6. See also Intercolonial Railway
Rand, Theodore 11, 130
Reciprocity Treaty x, 20; 1865 colonial conference 21; abrogated 24–5; 1871 Washington negotiations 123–5; 1874 proposals 180–1. See also Treaty of Washington
Reform League 166
Religious dissension 176–8, 179, 186–7
Repeal: role of ministry 62–3; agitation 64–6; delegation to Lon-

don 67–8; used against House 85; difficulties with ministry 94–6, 104–6, 110; policy repudiated 126
Repeal League 85, 92, 93, 103, 106, 132, 166
Richmond County: 1869 by-election 90–1, 93; religious education controversy 111
Ritchie, J.W. 34, 36
Robb, Donald 168–9, 170–1, 177, 179, 181
Robertson, Robert 62, 94, 126
Roman Catholics 52–3; role in 1867 elections 56–7; 1869 by-elections 87, 91; growing dissension 111, 117, 122, 130; Antigonish riots 176–7; Halifax school issue 186–7
Rose, Sir John 80–3, 91, 133
Ross, John 129
Ross, William: opposes Howe's intervention in provincial politics 129; concern over Huntingdon's railway charges 150; selected for Mackenzie's cabinet 160–1; party opposition 164, 167; removed from office 178–9
Ryerson, J.K. 96

Savary, A.W. 49, 71, 142, 167
Schools: school act 9, 36, 37–8, 52–3; temporary concessions to Roman Catholics 91; dismissal of Rand 111; 'de facto' separate schools 122; Halifax 177, 179, 186–7
Schreiber, C. 90, 185
Sectionalism 15, 164–5, 173, 174, 177–8, 191–3
Secret service fund: provincial 75; federal 91

Senate: representation 6–7, 36; appointments 43–4
Shanley, Walter 10
Shipbuilding 181, 190
Smith, Albert 24
Smith, Henry 121, 126, 182
Smith, H.W. 67–8
Smith, Vernon 171–2
Stairs, W.J. 40, 61

Tariffs 14; increased 63–4; reduced 69; duties on coal 108–9, 112–13; protective tariff 170; opposition to tariffs on shipbuilding materials 175; Conservatives support high tariffs 180–1; search for sectional balance 191
Taylor, Captain John 146–7
Tilley, S.L.: electoral defeat 17; leaves for Great Britain 33; mediator between Howe and Macdonald 70; cautions Howe 92; refuses to attack Mackenzie for sectionalism 174
Tobin, John 56, 87
Tobin, Samuel 143, 159
Townsend, W.H. 44, 50, 54, 55, 90
Treaty of Washington: negotiations in Washington 123–5; impact on provincial election 127–9; attacked by Howe 132–6; supported by Power 143; benefits of treaty 181, 190; provincial interests 191, 193
Troop, J.C. 67, 70, 138
Tupper, Sir Charles, Bart.: colonial union conferences 3, 5, 6; meets opposition to union 8, 9, 10; view of Howe 11, 16; revives Maritime union 16, 17, 19; delegate to England 1865 20, 21; fisheries 25, 31–2, 64; union in principle 26, 27; dele-

gate to England 1866-7 33, 35, 36, 37, 38; 1867 legislative session 41; Senate appointments 43-4; declines cabinet seat 44-5; 1867 election 51, 54, 55, 57; Legislative Council 62; delegate to England 1868 67-8; isolation from negotiations with Howe 70, 72, 75-6, 81-2, 84, 86, 87, 88, 92, 94, 97, 101-2; suspicions of Annand's motives 104; National Policy 113, 181, 192; enters cabinet 114; accepts Pearson 115; McNab affair 121; 1871 provincial election 129-30; Spring Hill Mining Company 140; 1872 federal election 142, 143, 144; caucus revolt 149, 150; view of coalition 153; Pacific Railway scandal 159, 161; 1874 federal election 168, 172; appeals to sectionalism 173, 174; prepares to unseat Ross 178

Unionist (Halifax) 87
United States: military threat x, 13, 24; tariff on coal 109; 1874 trade agreement 180-1; economic ties 190. See also Reciprocity Treaty, Treaty of Washington

Vale Coal and Iron Company 151
Vail, W.B.: contests Digby 49; enters ministry 62, 76; supports repeal policy 79, 84, 89; 1869 legislative session 94, 95, 96; seeks agreement with Ottawa 105, 108, 109, 110; sensitivity on Catholic issue 111; concern with Colchester by-election 115; franchise 121; crown lands 122; fisheries 124; role as house leader 138, 139, 140; 1872 federal election 142, 145; relations with Mackenzie's ministry 161, 167, 174; cabinet system 175; school issue 177; dissension with Annand 178; enters federal cabinet 178-9

White, Alonzo 130-1
Wickwire, Dr William 169
Wilkins, Martin I.: opposition to union 48; Pictou election campaign 49; opposition to Howe 59; advocates repeal 62, 65-6, 73, 74-5, 86; intervenes in Yarmouth by-election 90; tacit acceptance of union 94, 95-6, 110-11; county courts 112; franchise federal employees 120; supports council 121; crown lands 122; attacks Washington negotiations 124; appointed prothonotary 126
Williams, Sir William Fenwick: appointed lieutenant-governor 22; approaches Annand 23, 24; fisheries 25; collapse of opposition to union 27, 28, 29; suspects Howe's loyalty 31; leaves office 61
Working men: political role 147, 168-9, 170-1

Yarmouth County 30; 1867 elections 48, 50, 58; repeal 70; *Yarmouth Tribune* 88-9; 1868 by-election 88-90, 93; annexation 107; railway 140; 1874 election 171-2
Young, John 47